BEING FORM'D

BEING FORM'D
Thinking Through Blake's *Milton*

Mark Bracher

Clinamen Studies
STATION HILL PRESS

for Donald Ault

First edition.

Published by Clinamen Studies, a division of Station Hill Press,
Barrytown, New York 12507.

Produced by the Open Studio Typography and Design Project, with
support in part from the National Endowment for the Arts.

Library of Congress Cataloging in Publication Data

Bracher, Mark, 1950–
    Being form'd—thinking through Blake's Milton.

    1. Blake, William, 1757–1827. Milton. 2. Blake, William,
1757–1827—Philosophy. I. Title.
PR4144.M63B73 1984   821'.7   84-24072
ISBN 0-88268-013-7
ISBN 0-88268-012-9 (pbk.)

CONTENTS

PART TWO
Toward a Metaphysics of Mediated Presence: Milton's Embrace of Eternal Death and the Re-Formation of Identity

CHAPTER IV

Eternal Death, Immortality, and the Nature of Individual Being

CHAPTER V

Beyond Presence: Metaphysical Ramifications of Milton's Embrace of Eternal Death

CHAPTER VI

Negativity, Eternity, and the Metaphysics of Presence

PART THREE
Mediated Presence and Individual Identity: Los and the Process of Actualization

CHAPTER VII
Negativity, Mediation, and Actualization

CHAPTER VIII
The Sons of Los: Identity and the Intrinsic Interrelatedness of Individuals

CHAPTER IX
Being Form'd: The Creation of Unique, Determinate Individuals

vii

PART FOUR
Desire and Presence: The Descent of Ololon and the Reconciliation with Finitude

CHAPTER X

Presence and Process: Beulah, Eternity, and Ecstasis

CHAPTER XI

States and Individuals: The Actuality versus the Being of Individuality

CHAPTER XII

The Discovery of Ecstatic Finitude in the Search for Immediate Infinity

PART FIVE
Beyond Presence: Ololon, Milton, and the Reconciliation of Desire with Finitude

CHAPTER XIII

Overcoming Satan, the Reductive Destruction of Individuals

CHAPTER XIV

Milton and Ololon United: Desire for Infinity Embraces Finitude

CHAPTER XV

Infinity Within the Finite Individual: An Alternative Vision of Being

Publisher's Note

The Illuminated page from *Milton* reproduced on the cover of this book is in several ways appropriate for a ground-breaking study. It shows the Visionary Form of a resurrected Milton as he strides forth to pull down rigidified projections of Selfhood, those stone tablets of the Law now barely supportable in Urizen's lifeless hands. Further ahead, the contrasting joyful figures suggest less grimly finite possibilities outside the skull-like cavernous space. On the previous page Milton's "falling star" has entered the tarsus of Blake's left foot, and here we see the poet filled with revolutionary energy and prophetic inspiration. Now he is *doubly* able "To Annihilate the Self-hood of Deceit & False Forgiveness"—once for himself (Blake) and once for his poetic counterpart (Milton). And a further, parallel double: a self-annihilation on one hand directed within his own being and on the other hand extending outward into history, culture, and humanity at large. This psychological and cosmological equivalence exists by virtue of a very particular created reality, the powerfully transformative medium of Illuminated poetic prophecy—the invention, on the scale implied here, of William Blake.

Virtually every verbal and visual moment within this complexly articulate medium gives some special instruction in how to see, hear, and read. The end of the Golden Thread is omnipresent, yet, like the Philosopher's Stone that is everywhere visible and nowhere seen, it becomes accessible only where faculties are roused to act. Given Blake's commitment to altering the capacity of those faculties in his readers, this picture of Mental Fight is a kind of primer of Imaginative reading, where the poet breaking through language seems almost ready to break out of the frame of the page. The star-struck foot of Blake becomes the word-splitting foot of Milton, a model of the mental (con)fusion that joins the two poets in a single transformative task—and beyond that, joins their visionary travail with that of any alert reading mind. Paradoxically the process of healing self-division involves further divisive rending, a conscious severing of true "Self" from illusionary "hood." This mysterious process, in which living and dead appear ready and willing to dialogue and be mutually transformed, is registered in the private/public medium of language. Here Blake gives us the poetic equivalent of the alchemist-engraver's "infernal method, by corrosives..., melting apparent surfaces away, and displaying the infinite which was hid." The infinite which was hid is a special kind of image, a Visionary Form Dramatic, which the transformed reader learns how to see with the faculty of Imagination; and in its most vivid manifestation it talks *with* the reading mind, and itself knows how to listen. So the poet *sculpts* language and copper alike (to play further on the engraver's convention of signing with Latin "sculpsit," combining writing and shaping); indeed, he carves out the new self, cutting through the old syntax and gestalt of determinate identity. The proverbial ten thousand words that any good picture is worth here become so many thought-creating fires.

Being Form'd takes seriously the setting of fires in the realm of thought, and it labors hard to read the whole poem in terms of transformative cosmology, inherently new metaphysics, and thinkable process. In the spirit of our striving poet, reborn out of the creative gaps he makes in language, thinking *through* a work means taking it apart down to and including its minute particulars, word by word, line by line. More problematic, it also means letting the mind "come apart" in its intellectual self-hood. The mind must fundamentally challenge discourse, the categories of thought, the stuff of identity which Blake sought so fervently to recontextualize.

"Thinking through Blake's *Milton*" is something we have needed to learn to do, and Mark Bracher's innovative approach is a giant, striving step in the right direction. The application of contemporary philosophical terms and methods offers a definite foothold—the Blakean kind, allowing understanding but no rest. Thinking "through" the poem, like seeing through (not with) the eyes, is above all a way of traveling in the text that takes seriously Blake's revolutionary cosmology. Keeping in mind that certain "travelers' advisories have been posted," we can get somewhere new without reifying our own conceptual objects. Happily the author does not lose track of how radically open Blake's thinking is, how entering the work anew we take apart our own thinking and identity, like the poet pushing apart syllables of his name on Plate 1.

Being Form'd is a book that argues that Blake is translatable into metaphysical thought, just as he might usefully be translated into French, and that a translator is not necessarily a traitor. Granting translation a creative role we see that Blake too is translating Milton, and that both poets dialoguing in "mediated presence" might well say with Peter Quince, "Bless thee! thou art translated!"

George Quasha
Barrytown, New York

Preface

Despite the attention which *Milton*, like the rest of Blake's poetry, has received in the past decade or two,[1] we lack a grasp of the poem commensurate with our understanding of, say, *Paradise Lost* or *Prometheus Unbound*. As Hazard Adams recently observed, "[Although] things have improved somewhat since the sort of amateurism that identified, here, the occult references to such and such, or, there, certain political allusions, . . . we still do not have the kind of reading that capitalizes on detailed knowledge and manages to set it in a context without the sort of distortion that has made Blake everything from a Platonist to a prophet of Blavatsky. . . . Many of the efforts at readings that we do have are unsensitive to the process of the work, or without sufficient attention to detail or gesture."[2] Morris Eaves makes a similar observation, remarking upon "the discrepancy between the ghostly explanations that Blake scholars stir up and the works that I try to explain to myself when I open my Blake."[3] In light of this situation, Adams concludes that "we must have readings, heuristic efforts of *communication* and simplicity, available to reasonably informed readers."[4] It is my hope that the present study provides such a reading of *Milton*.

In attempting to provide a coherent and comprehensive reading of the poem, avoiding the selectivity to which discussions of Blake's prophecies seem so easily to succumb,[5] I found that the metaphysical aspects of Blake's myth assumed a greater significance than they are normally accorded in Blake criticism, which tends to give priority to the psychological dimensions of the myth. This psychological bias is clearly evident in the commentary on *Milton*, where even those critics who warn against reducing the poem to autobiographical elements and who acknowledge the ideological and metaphysical dimensions of the poem's message take the primary level of meaning to be psychological.[6] The bias is most apparent in the interpretation of Blake's characters, which, when not reduced to historical persons, are usually identified as various psychological faculties or affects.[7] The present study questions this priority which has been accorded to the psychological dimension, and attempts to demonstrate that while a psychological interpretation is not invalid, it is incomplete—more so than most recent critics have acknowledged. Thus while Los, for example, is indeed a psychological power (the imagination or the poetic spirit), as most critics assume, he is also—and, I would argue, primarily—a cosmological power or metaphysical principle. As Murry observed some fifty years ago, Los and Enitharmon "are, on the one hand, an embodiment of the creative powers of the Universe . . . [and, on the other hand] those creative powers [as they are] manifest in the individual being of Blake and his wife . . . ; [and the activity of Los and

Enitharmon] is at one and the same time a cosmic evolution and an individual
autobiography."[8] Los is indeed the imagination, but the imagination, as
Murry implies, far from being merely a psychological faculty in the normal
sense, is a fundamental dimension of reality itself.[9]

In pursuing the metaphysical aspects of Blake's poetry, I have been aided
significantly by the thought of Hegel, Heidegger, Whitehead, and Derrida.
But while I want to acknowledge that these philosophers have informed my
thinking, I also want to make it clear that I do not find Blake's vision identifi-
able with or reducible to the systems (or non-systems) of any of these thinkers. For this reason it is crucial that readers avoid assuming a complete
equivalence between certain terms that I employ and similar or identical
terms found, for example, in Hegel or Derrida. The most important caveat
concerns my use of the phrase "metaphysics of presence," which gained
currency through Derrida's earlier works. While for Derrida every
metaphysics is ultimately a metaphysics of presence, my usage of the phrase
is more restricted: I employ it to refer to any metaphysical system or perspective that equates Being with immediate presence, which in most cases means
assuming that a thing's being is coterminous with its actual existence in and
for itself. My use of the word "being" (or "Being") also needs some clarification. While most Heideggerian echoes would not be a distortion of my
meaning, I use the term simply to denote what is ultimate—in reference
either to individuals, or to the cosmos as a whole. (Capitalization is employed
when the gerund might mistakenly be read as a participle, but it is omitted in
all other instances in order to avoid substantializing the gerund.) Thus "the
being of the individual" refers to that aspect of the individual that determines
the individual's value or significance in the ultimate scheme of things. Similarly, "Being itself" signifies the ultimate aspect (or principle, or meaning) of
the cosmos as a whole, without making any assumption about the nature of
the individual's relation to "Being." By "individual," I mean to include both
"person" and "thing" wherever the context allows, following Blake's notion
that things, too, have inalienable value ("every thing is Human, mighty!
sublime!" *Jerusalem* 34:48). Two other terms, "immediate" and "mediated,"
deserve brief comment. By "immediate" I mean occurring in and of an
individual or event itself, apart from any temporal displacement or any intervention or assistance by another individual or event. By "mediated" I mean
occurring only by virtue of temporal displacement or the intervention or
assistance of another individual or event.

Other philosophical concepts which I employ are, I believe, defined
adequately by their context in this study, or by traditional usage. No degree

of clarification, however, can keep these terms from limiting and distorting the possibilities of signification inherent in Blake's text. Thus, in addition to insisting that Blake's vision not be reduced to the concepts or systems of other thinkers, I must also warn against reducing the poem to the (more or less conceptual and systematic) reading I am offering here. That Blake's prophecies are "allegory addressed to the intellectual powers" makes it hard to speak of them without having recourse to conceptual language; but it also demands that we remain aware of the fundamental non-equivalence between Blake's allegory and our accounts of it, and that we acknowledge, in principle, the ultimate undecidability of the "meaning" of Blake's characters and terms. Speaking in traditional terms, we might say that we must avoid taking the map for the landscape itself. But such a statement would be misleading, for Blake's poetry is not a fixed and definite topography that is susceptible to mapping. We can never establish a set of coordinates that will clearly locate the significance of any character, event, or detail in relation either to other elements in the poem or to our own perspectives; for the only means we have of orienting ourselves is by relating Blake's elusive and polysemous words to other words, whose significance is itself anything but fixed and definite. Thus making sense of Blake's poetry is not like mapping a definite topography through a sort of triangulation, but rather like sailing the high seas with shifting winds and changing currents, trying to locate drifting islands while taking our bearing from stars that move according to no known laws. My reading of *Milton* should therefore be read more like a captain's diary than a navigation chart: its purpose is not so much to establish precise coordinates for all ports of call as to describe, with some rigor and attention to detail, the enchanted isles and infinite vistas of Blake's strange seas of thought. Like all readings, the present one has had to pass over many features without comment—most notably the illuminations, the analysis of which was precluded by considerations of space. I have also eschewed discussion of textual issues, accepting tacitly the text, including the ordering of plates, established by David Erdman. My intention has been not to offer a substitute for Blake's poem, or to respond to all issues concerning its interpretation, but rather to call attention to important features of the poem which have been suppressed to a significant degree by most other explorations.

I hope that the reading offered here will aid others in the same way that previous investigations of Blake have helped me: not by providing a prefabricated understanding of the poem, but by suggesting new dimensions of significance for it. Of greatest benefit to me in this regard has been the work of Donald Ault, whose *Visionary Physics* alerted me to realms uncharted by other explorations, and whose *Narrative Unbound: Re-Visioning Blake's Four Zoas* (Station Hill Press, 1985) encouraged me by its example to depart, if only slightly, from the established routes of Blake criticism and steer my own course. Others to whom I owe debts of gratitude, for reading all or part of the manuscript and offering important suggestions and encouragement, include David Erdman, Leslie Tannenbaum, Vereen Bell, Roy Gottfried, Charles Scott, Paul Elledge, and Marshall Alcorn. George Quasha, Charles Stein, and Michael Coffey of Station Hill Press provided valuable advice and assistance, and my wife Nancy sustained me throughout the project with her love and patience.

Special thanks to Daniel L. Griffen, Jr., of the Iowa State University Research Foundation, which provided generous financial support for the publication of this book.

INTRODUCTION

The Argument of *Milton*

The Purpose of Milton

No one has understood better than Blake the extent to which metaphysical perspective creates the human condition. As early as the fourth memorable fancy of *The Marriage of Heaven and Hell*, Blake portrayed the fact that one's metaphysics creates one's world: where an angel, representing the perspective of orthodox Christianity, sees a void filled with horrors, Blake's persona perceives a pleasant scene of a peaceful moonlit river, and declares to the angel, "All that we saw was owing to your metaphysics."[1] As Blake demonstrates in this episode, the tacit, implicit, and usually unconscious assumptions that one has about the fundamental nature of existence will determine the form which one's existence actually takes: one's own being is formed on the basis of one's implicit formulation of the notion of Being itself. How one unconsciously answers the question, what does it mean to *be*, determines to a significant degree what one actually is. For one's implicit understanding of what Being means will determine the course one takes in attempting to achieve full being. This realization forms the center of the redemptive vision of *Milton*, a poem which is simultaneously a re-formulation of the notion of Being—or the presentation of a new vision of Being—and a re-formation of the being of the individual, of the very principle of individual identity. For in reformulating the notion of what it means to be—and to be fully, or fulfilled—*Milton* also re-forms the individual: in theory and also, through the effect on the reader, in actuality, by altering the ultimate goal (the goal of full or infinite being) which guides human actions and desires.

The most crucial aspect of this reformulation/re-formation concerns the significance of human finitude—i.e., the significance which the frustration, suffering, and death of individuals are accorded in the ultimate scheme of things. To be in any way redemptive, a vision of human existence must justify this apparently absurd and scandalous finitude. Thus it is that a central purpose of *Milton*, attested to by its motto, is "To Justify the Ways of God to Men" (plate i). This reprise of Milton's project of *Paradise Lost* demonstrates

1

not only Blake's view of the importance of such a justification, but also his conviction of the inadequacy of the justification which Milton provided (an inadequacy which Blake dramatizes, at the beginning of the poem, by Milton's unhappiness in heaven). Milton, in Blake's view, was right to try to reconcile humans with the ground of their being (God), which is responsible for their finitude, but he was wrong in attempting to do so by presenting this ground as an omnipotent tyrant who simply must be obeyed. Such a portrait justifies nothing, and persuades only the cowardly. In Blake's poem, Milton's attempt achieves a more satisfactory form. To the question, why must humans suffer and die, Milton had apparently answered: because "of man's first disobedience"—i.e., because of a choice humans have made or a mode of existence they have adopted, which is not a necessary part of their being. Blake, in contrast, answers: because suffering and perishing are part of the very structure of Being itself. Only through suffering and perishing can the multiplicity and individuality of existence occur at all; and only through suffering and ultimately through perishing can an individual achieve its authentic essential identity. In fact, it is this very destruction, paradoxically, which forms the basis of the irreducible and eternal value of each individual, for as Blake put it in *Jerusalem*, "The Infinite alone resides in Definite and Determinate Identity" (55:64).

Blake's justification of human finitude involves a reformulation of the very notion of individual identity, a reformulation which functions to liberate individuals from the fear that their being is ultimately nought, and thus allows individuals to lead lives of greater fulfillment. Indeed, the ultimate goal of *Milton*, as with all of Blake's poetry, is to bring about a state of affairs in which all beings are completely fulfilled—i.e., a state in which their essential being, their inmost possibilities, are actualized. Blake expresses this goal in the lyrical preface to *Milton*:

> I will not cease from Mental Fight,
> Nor shall my Sword sleep in my hand:
> Till we have built Jerusalem,
> In Englands green & pleasant Land.

(13-16)

In order to build Jersualem, the state of total fulfillment, it is necessary to engage in "Mental Fight," re-forming the understanding of what Being means and what the being of individuals consists in. This is the task of *Milton*: to provide a more liberating vision of Being, which in turn will allow greater fulfillment for individual beings.

The Bard's Song:
Formlessness and Satanic Metaphysics

In order to re-formulate our notion of Being, it is first necessary to understand the inadequacies of the habitual, traditional notion—to give form to error that it might be cast off. Blake thus begins by identifying false vision and explaining its origin. Book I, as Thomas Herzig observes, "examines the Fall, its causes and effects; it treats the opposition between a false sense of the infinite and true infinity; it presents a conflict between the world view which insists that the only reality is that which can be immediately and directly perceived and the poetic understanding that the world is not totally sensate, immediate, and one-dimensional."[2] After a recapitulation of the origin and ground of existence and its vain attempts to overcome its finite form (a reprise of *The Book of Urizen*[3]), Blake introduces in the Bard's song Rintrah, Palamabron, and Satan, three sons of Los and Enitharmon—i.e., three principles which are implicit in Los, who as Time and Imagination is the form-giving power or process of actualization itself. Rintrah is the principle of wrath, the legitimate violence and destruction of otherness that is necessary for the individual to maintain its own form or identity. Palamabron is the principle of pity, the legitimate relaxation of the individual's boundaries to allow relatedness and union with otherness. Satan, in his authentic form as the Miller of Eternity, is the homogenizing power that "Refus[es] Form" (3:41)—i.e., reduces the unique forms of individuals to a common substance so that the process of transformation of one actuality into another can occur.

The Bard's Song focuses on Satan's usurpation of Palamabron's function: true to its nature, the principle of homogenization (Satan) ignores the distinction between his own function of homogenization (the achievement of immediate union, or non-differentiation) and Palamabron, the similar but absolutely distinct function of accommodation (mediated unity, unity-in-difference), or pity. The homogenizing power (Satan), which produces *immediate* unity or identity among individuals, obliterates the distinction between itself and *mediated* unity (Palamabron)—i.e., that unity in which the individuality of identity is maintained. This action of Satan constitutes the establishment of the false vision, an ontology of presence which equates Being with immediate presence, and which thus prevents individuals from realizing (in both senses of the word) the infinity that lies within their finitude. This failure of vision, in turn, stymies Los, the very principle of actualization.

Throughout the poem Blake presents numerous instances of the way in which the tacit assumption of an ontology of presence leads to suffering and destruction by viewing Being as extrinsic to the individual, and as a homogeneous substance dispensed through a feudalistic, *quid pro quo* system. If one assumes, as is the tradition, that Being is identical with presence—i.e., that fully to be means to be permanently present, unchanged by existence— then Being must be separate from existence, which is continuously changing. And if Being is extrinsic to the existing individual, then the being of one individual is not necessarily unique or different from that of another, and individuals are ultimately interchangeable. Such a view—that Being is an extrinsic homogeneous substance and that individuals are interchangeable— leads to two further consequences. First, if Being is extrinsic and homogeneous, then it seems logical to derive it from a single central source: the ontology of presence thus leads to a feudalistic metaphysics in which individuals are alloted being on consignment by the supreme being and are required to repay this loan with interest by sacrificing other entities to the supreme being. Second, the vision of Being as extrinsic and homogeneous leads to a *quid pro quo* system of existence, in which a gain in being by one individual occurs only by virtue of an equivalent loss by another element in the system. Such an assumption that, as Bacon put it, "whatsoever is somewhere gotten is somewhere lost,"[4] leads inevitably to self-aggrandizing behavior in all its modes, with each individual competing with all other individuals for a limited quantity of being. Blake flatly rejected this assumption, remarking in his annotations to Bacon, "Man is not Improved by the hurt of another.... Bacon has no notion of anything but Mammon."[5]

Beyond Presence: Blake's Vision of Being

To overcome the mutual oppression and obstruction of individuals and help them realize infinity within finitude, it is thus necessary to overcome the metaphysics of presence and form a new vision of Being. Blake embodies this overcoming in the action of Milton, who, in going to Eternal Death— i.e., in deliberately annihilating his actual being and renouncing any immediate actuality for himself in the future—affirms that his unique individual being does not consist merely of its immediate presence and that this individuality will continue to *be* even when it no longer actually exists. It is this particular vision, rather than simply the overcoming of rationality (as John Howard assumes), which underlies the transformation of the individual which Howard describes so well: "As [a person's] non-self-centered urges begin to expand the domain of the self to include all, then the selfhood's rigid

holds and its exclusively prudent attitude toward others, that attitude which
lies behind all government, law, and extremes of justice, will begin to relax.
Anxiety about personal security or esteem (which is an extension of security)
will be reduced and the grip that represses and divides the whole man will be
erased...."[6]

Blake's most important tenet regarding the individual existent is the
uniqueness, intrinsicness, and indestructibility of its being—i.e., the ultimacy of its unique form, or "Definite and Determinate Identity." At the same
time, however, as he maintains the absolute integrity of the individual, Blake
also insists that individual entities are intrinsically and essentially constituted
by relationship to one another, asserting, as Daniel Stempel notes, the
"unlimited intersubjectivity, the sharing of the experience of the Other without violating the individuality of either Self or Other...."[7] This simultaneous
differentiation and unity of the individual in relation to others is effected
through what we might call mediated presence, the fact that in every
influence or effect which one individual has on another, part of the unique
intrinsic being of the first individual becomes indirectly actualized in the
second. This notion, which has affinities with Whitehead's concept of objective immortality, as Donald Ault has noted,[8] and with Hegel's notion of
Aufhebung, forms the cornerstone of *Milton* and is Blake's way of explaining
how a finite individual can achieve infinity. "The Ruins of Time," Blake
declared, "builds Mansions in Eternity." He explained, "I know that our
deceased friends are apparent to our mortal part. Thirteen years ago I lost a
brother & with his spirit I converse daily & hourly in the Spirit & See him in
my remembrance in the regions of my Imagination. I hear his advice & even
now write from his Dictate."[9] Blake earlier found this same vision of
mediated presence expressed in Lavater's comment: "Whatever is visible is
the vessel or veil of the invisible past, present, future—as man penetrates to
this more, or perceives it less, he raises or depresses his dignity of being."[10]
Such mediated presence, in addition to constituting the infinity of the individual, is also the basis for what Murry called "the unity of the cosmic and the
individual happening" in Blake's poetry.[11] For Blake, as for Whitehead, all
novelty both originates and is preserved by the activity of the unique individual; history is constituted less by universal powers than by the action of
individual entities.

The notion of mediated presence also explains Milton's going to Eternal
Death: since the individual's real being is preserved and even enhanced by the
being of others after the individual perishes, the individual's death is actually
a boon to the true being of the individual. This view is of course contrary to

our normal notion of identity, and as a result, Milton's embrace of death is opposed by Urizen, the very principle of identity, which is re-formed by Milton's new vision and action. Milton's re-formation of the principle of identity also constitutes his awakening of Albion, the authentic form of society as a mediated unity of all individuals—a unity in which distinctions are maintained.

Mediated Presence and the Forming Process

After developing these various dimensions of the affirmation of mediated presence, Blake concentrates, in the final eight plates of Book the First, on Los, the actualizing or form-giving principle itself, which underlies and makes possible all occurrences, including the mediated action of Milton in Blake's writing of this poem. As the power of actualization which moves all things to develop beyond their present state, Los is the principle of organic growth and evolution—the alchemical Vulcan, who, according to Paracelsus, works in the unfinished being of all things in order to bring them to more satisfactory forms. As this principle of growth and evolution which is present in all things, Los is also the human imagination, the power by which humans grow and evolve beyond their present states and assume new forms of action and being. "Thus," as Howard observes, "the artistic creative process and the biological procreative process are manifestations of the same spiritual cause."[12] Blake's account of Los's activity thus presents a profound analysis of the destructive/productive, forming/re-forming ground of existence, a portrayal which constitutes the focal point of Blake's reformulation of the notion of Being.

Re-Forming Desire

After analyzing the process of becoming and thus demonstrating the primacy of process and mediation, Blake focuses in Book the Second on the way in which desire, which motivates and guides the process of becoming, can also be re-formed, reoriented from immediate presence to mediated presence, from finite to infinite. Susan Fox has observed that while "the basic mode of Book I is...visionary[,] the basic mode of Book II is the lyricism of Beulah, with its variant, a very intimate kind of prophecy which is a translation into personal, temporal terms of the grand impersonal vision of Golgonooza."[13] This change in style which Fox notes in Book II testifies to the fact that this book places greater emphasis on the affective and emotional aspect of overcoming the metaphysics of presence.

Blake presents this transformation as the descent of Ololon, the principle of lamentation, from the immediate infinity of Eternity to the mediated infinity of finite existence. As the principle of lamentation to the gods,[14] Ololon is the constant implicit or subliminal awareness of finitude and the urge to overcome it—i.e., the urge to be fulfilled, or achieve infinity. Ololon is thus the fundamental disposition which gives rise to particular desires—the ground of desire, which, when relocated, will necessarily result in a freeing of desire itself from its fixation on immediate presence. The point of concern is not simply to transform desire but rather to relocate the very ground of desire—i.e., to reorient the urge to infinity from the realm of *immediate* presence or infinity to the region of *mediated* presence, or infinity-in-the-finite. This relocation of Ololon occurs as a result of Milton's affirmation of the ultimacy of mediated presence, which allows Ololon to find infinity within the finite, and it constitutes the union of Ololon and Milton—the reconciliation of the (instinctual, affective) urge to infinity (Ololon) with the (rational) urge to accept finitude (the reality principle: Milton, the justifier of the ways of God to men).

Re-Forming through Poetic Form: Blake's Technique

The Disjunctive Style

This regrounding of lamentation occurs, then, as the result of Ololon/lamentation's gradual (affective and instinctual) recognition of the differential and mediatory nature of Being. But Ololon, the principle of radical lamentation, occurs only as the attitudes of individual beings. The union of Milton (vision) and Ololon (affect) thus occurs at the end of the poem only insofar as the reader's own Ololon/lamentation, as well as the reader's vision, has been reoriented toward finite existence. Overcoming the Satanic, *quid pro quo* metaphysics of presence, that is, is not simply a matter of intellectual assent to a group of abstract propositions: it is a matter of the total transformation of one's manner of existing—a re-forming of Urizen, that "Creator of Men" (*Visions*, 5:3) who is the very principle of individual identity. As David E. James notes, "*Milton* ... manifestly attempts, through its poetic form, to change the reader's consciousness."[15] As such, it involves the transformation of the way in which we immediately, pre-reflectively, and affectively apprehend things and discover meaning and value in them.

As we have seen, while the Satanic metaphysics of presence locates meaning in the immediate actuality of a thing, Blake's vision of Being has shown
that meaning is relational and differential. Long before the advent of structuralist and post-structuralist thought, Blake realized that the unique, indestructible identity of a particular individual or sign is dependent upon its
differentiation from and relation to all other individuals or signs.[16] Normally,
however, we are only subliminally aware of the mediated presence of the
non-present individuals, and it is this dulled awareness which allows us to
sink into a metaphysics of presence. Blake opposes this tendency by forcing
us to confront, at virtually every moment of reading, the implicit, mediated
presence of events or agents which are not immediately present in the text.
He does this in several ways. His most general manner is simply to confront
the reader, through abrupt transitions and changes of perspective, with elements that are mutually implicit. At times he will adumbrate an event or
introduce a character that will receive elaboration only considerably later in
the text, thus forcing the reader, with a radical prolepsis, to remain in an
extreme degree of negative capability, or deferral of judgment with regard to
the character or event. At other times Blake will allude to an obscure character or event that has received cursory but significant treatment much earlier in
the text, forcing the reader to cultivate the posthumous presence of this item.
In still other instances, Blake will juxtapose elements which make sense
together only in light of an element which is never connected immediately
with any of them, thus making the reader search for the mediated presence of
an unmanifest reality—a metaphysical principle—which is never
immediately present at all. Unfortunately for the impatient reader, Blake
does not always juxtapose events which have the same type of relation to each
other. At times, as we shall see, he presents an account of a metaphysical
principle (e.g., Los) and then moves to some phenomenon—physical,
psychological, or political—which embodies this principle. At other times
he will merely name the principle (e.g., Satan) and then proceed to list
various manifestations of it (e.g., the Twelve Gods of Ulro). And in still
other instances Blake will, as James notes,[17] simply present several
phenomena or events and force the reader to induce the principle which
relates them. Blake thus coerces the reader to move continually from a
metaphysical principle to phenomena (and vice versa), from one aspect of
phenomena to another, or from a metaphysical principle to the perversion or
distorted understanding of that principle. The effect of these disjunctions is
to engage the reader with the fundamental, metaphysical dimensions of
Being itself in all the variegated multifariousness of its actualization. The

technique has the additional effect of never allowing the reader to engage for long in abstract metaphysical thinking without being forced to confront the minute particulars of specific phenomena, including, at times, the phenomenon which this thinking itself *is*. The reader thus comes to see the various metaphysical principles not as mere abstractions, but as real powers that are constantly encountered everywhere.[18]

The Mythical Mode

Through these tactics, Blake lures, goads, and shocks the reader out of that form of being—that mode of seeing, of finding meaning, and, indeed, of desiring—which *is* the metaphysics of presence, with the conviction that by thus rousing our faculties to act, he will help us arise from the finitude of our identity and enter into its infinity.[19] This is also the function of Blake's use of the mythical mode rather than the mode of abstract philosophical analysis. The use of characters such as Urizen and Los, instead of abstract principles such as differentiation and entelechy, supports this effect in several ways. First, it frees Blake from the forms of thought imposed by the philosophical tradition. Second, characters portray aspects or principles of Being not in terms of an abstract schema of external relationships but rather from the perspective of the inner purposes or functions of these principles, thus revealing Being as a plurality of definite powers, each with its intrinsic function or dynamism, and each intrinsically interrelated with the others. The use of characters thus helps the reader realize these principles as what they really are: powers operating throughout the phenomenal world, the world of our experience. The use of anthropomorphic characters—or principles that at times assume an anthropomorphic form—unites the experiential category with the metaphysical principle in a single image. This is the reason for the distinctly psychological dimension of many of Blake's characters: Blake is attempting to give us the fullest, most intense experience possible of these ultimate, invisible realities, and he realizes that the best access to this dimension of Being is through the presence of those realities in ourselves. Blake is simply putting into practice the insight which Schopenhauer later expressed when he said that the best way to understand the cosmic Will is in our own acts of willing.

Blake's use of characters is thus a direct result of his metaphysics itself. For one of his purposes is to show the immanence of the transcendent in the phenomenal—to overcome the idea of a God beyond the skies or of Being beyond individual beings and establish infinity within the finite identity.

This tenet is also embodied in the fact that Blake's mythological characters interact with individual historical human beings.[20] When Milton wrestles with Urizen, or when Blake is united with Los or confronted by Ololon, these encounters manifest the intrinsic and fundamental connexity of ultimate principles with individual beings and demonstrate, moreover, the astonishing proposition that the ultimate principles of Being are not immutable: they can be affected—even re-formed—by the actions of individuals. Blake's re-formations thus take the Reformation of Luther one step further, beyond Luther's direct relation between the individual and the Absolute to a denial of any ultimate separation between them at all.

Poetry and the Being of the Individual

On the basis of these observations, it begins to appear that the most efficacious re-forming occurs in the writing of poetry, a *poiesis* of language which is also a *poiesis* of Being. Like Heidegger, Blake believes that poetry has the power both to deform and to re-form both individuals and transcendental powers. The impetus for poetry, he observes, comes from the "Daughters of Beulah! Muses who inspire the Poets Song" (2:1), and who inhabit "Realms / Of terror & mild moony lustre" (2:2-3) and "delight the wanderer and repose / His burning thirst & freezing hunger!" (2:4-5). Poetry offers delight and repose, providing a respite from the deficiencies of actual existence, and as such it has a negative side, as the word "terror" implies: poetry can be destructive, by creating a haven from the rigors of actuality—a realm of "mild moony lustre" which casts a pleasant homogeneous glow over everything and thus distorts reality and blurs (deforms) identities. This same power also constitutes the False Tongue:

> Tell also of the False Tongue! vegetated
> Beneath your land of shadows: of its sacrifices. and
> Its offerings; even till Jesus, the image of the Invisible God
> Became its prey; a curse, an offering. and an atonement,
> For Death Eternal in the heavens of Albion, & before the Gates
> Of Jerusalem his Emanation, in the heavens beneath Beulah.
>
> (2:10-15)

The danger of poetry, we are shown here, is the danger of language in general: the inherent falseness of all speaking, due to the fact that language is composed of universals while the things it speaks of are individuals. All speaking ultimately violates or devours individual entities by obscuring their individual form with the homogeneity of its universal categories. Language

thus sacrifices individuals, offering them up on the altars of its generalizations. It is in this way that the False Tongue reduces "Jesus, the image of the
Invisible God" —i.e., the manifestation or embodiment of Being itself—to "a
curse, an offering. and an atonement": a magical saying, or a piece of currency that can be exchanged for something else. The False Tongue is the great
leveller, reducing individual entities to instances of universals, and transcendent realities to hypostatized beings. It is thus, as Blake showed in *The
Marriage of Heaven and Hell* (plate 11), that poetry can initiate a process of
abstraction and generalization which subordinates individuals to a higher,
abstract and universal being.

Blake, then, is very much aware of the dangers of poetic utterance and has
taken pains to make the reader share this awareness. Yet if there were no
benefits resulting from poetry, the writing of this very poem would be
unjustifiable. Hence Blake also takes note of the positive results of poetry,
asking the Daughters of Beulah,

> Come into my hand
> By your mild power; descending down the Nerves of my right arm
> From out the Portals of my Brain, where by your ministry
> The Eternal Great Humanity Divine. planted his Paradise,
> And in it caus'd the Spectres of the Dead to take sweet forms
> In likeness of himself.
>
> (2:5-10)

The physiological description of the poetic act completely confounds the
reader's —and even Blake's —normal view of poetry as a sublime and elevated
endeavor. Yet beneath the apparent irony and mockery is the affirmation that
poetry is the means whereby being is re-formed "in likeness of" the infinite
and Absolute—"The Eternal Great Humanity Divine." This re-formative
power of poetry is reemphasized by the question, "What cause at length
mov'd Milton to this unexampled deed?" The answer, "A Bard's prophetic
song!" (2:21-2), indicates that the central, re-formative action of *Milton* is
precipitated by a poem: Milton is moved, by hearing a poem, "to go into the
deep [his Sixfold Emanation] to redeem & himself perish" (2:20). This point
is crucial, for the power of a poem is unquestionable if it can cause someone to
perish voluntarily, and the Bard's Song does just that. The inescapable con-
clusion is that when we hear Blake's prophetic song, it might move us,
through its reformulation of the notion of Being and its consequent re-
formation of the very structure of our identity, to accept our finitude and
annihilation as the preservation and fulfillment of our being.

PART ONE

"Narrow Doleful Form": The Origins of The Fallen Human Condition

CHAPTER I

Destruction and the Finite
Form of Individuality

The Nature of Human Finitude

The Bard's Song, as we have noted, presents a vision of the Fall—a vision of why humans are frustrated and unfulfilled. The answer which the Bard provides is twofold: human frustration derives largely from a distorted vision of the nature of human existence, but this distorted vision is itself due to human nature. Humans view the reductive destruction of Satan's mills as ultimate and insurmountable, and as a result of this view, reductive destruction actually becomes more powerful. This view and the vicious circle that it involves are reinforced by the particular embodied form which human individuals have been given. Blake adumbrates this twofold origin of the fallen, finite human form in the Bard's opening words, which identify envy both as a primary cause of human limitation and as the means of overcoming that limitation. The Bard tells us:

> Three Classes are Created by the Hammer of Los, & Woven
> By Enitharmons Looms when Albion was slain upon his
>   Mountains
> And in his Tent, thro envy of Living Form, even of the Divine
>   Vision
> And of the sports of Wisdom in the Human Imagination
> Which is the Divine Body of the Lord Jesus. blessed for ever.
> Mark well my words. they are of your eternal salvation!
> (2:26-3:5)

"Envy of living form," we are told, is the cause of the destruction of Albion, the unity of individuals.[1] But who is envying what: is "Living Form" the subject or the object of the envy? The ambiguity suggests that it is both—that Living Form envies Living Form. The form of life is such that each living entity covets the being of other entities. In order to survive, each living thing must expropriate and devour the being of other forms of life: as *The Book of*

Urizen put it, "life liv[es] upon death" (VIII.5). This situation reaches to all living things, and even the "Divine Vision"—the manifestation of Being itself—is implicated in this universal envy. Envy, the coveting of one individual's being by another individual, is thus a fundamental reality which is intrinsic to the finite form of individual existence. Envy is found everywhere, including "the sports of Wisdom": even the most sublime endeavors of the human spirit are constituted fundamentally by this envy, for the search for wisdom is at bottom an appropriation of being that is other than oneself—an appropriation motivated by a deficiency in one's immediate individual actuality.

But the fact that the "three classes" are said to be created suggests that the particular forms which individuals have assumed are not inevitable, since whatever has been created can be destroyed. And the fact that these "sports of Wisdom" are grounded "in the Human Imagination / Which is the Divine Body of the Lord Jesus" suggests that envy, in addition to being a manifestation of deficiency or finitude, provides the means for transcending the limits of individuality and attaining "eternal salvation." Imagination, as the act of giving form to possibilities and thus re-forming actuality, is inherently a response to a deficiency of actuality, and as such, it is a type of envy, envy being the fundamental urge to make actual and immediate that which one immediately is not or does not have. The "Human Imagination" is thus a movement beyond one's immediate, actual existence into being that is other, a movement which sacrifices one's present self to the self which one desires to be. And since this movement of self-sacrifice constitutes Jesus' ultimate nature (i.e., "is the Divine Body of the Lord Jesus"), it follows that imagination and the envy in which it originates are the way to fulfillment—a fact which is emphasized by the Bard's immediate repetition of the refrain, "Mark well my words. they are of your eternal salvation" (3:5). Envy, then, is not only a manifestation of human finitude but also a way of attaining a less limiting form of being. That existence in all its modes and forms is a process of attempting to overcome the limitations of individual form is also indicated by the fact that the three classes which envy and the consequent slaying of Albion occasion "are created by the Hammer of Los." For Los, as the cosmic blacksmith, is the alchemical Vulcan, or the principle of entelechy—the power which, as Paracelsus said of Vulcan, moves things to surpass their present deficient state. "Nothing is finished," Paracelsus declared, "but Vulcan must bring all things to their completion . . . Nothing has been created as *ultima materia*—in its final state. Everything is at first created in its *prima materia*, its original stuff; whereupon Vulcan comes and by the art of alchemy develops it into its final substance."[2]

Organic Development: Strategies for Overcoming Finitude

Existence, then, is inescapably formed—finite—and thus envious. But the particular forms which existence takes are not absolutely unalterable, although the alteration cannot be accomplished quickly or easily. Since individual existence is formed, it can also be re-formed. In fact, human existence is actually a continuous process of re-formation, both ontogenetically and phylogenetically. This fact can be observed at its most basic level in the development of the human body, which Blake presents as a creation of Los, the Eternal Prophet, or entelechic power, which is continually trying to re-form the most fundamental forms of human existence in order to open existence to Eternity, or infinity. Blake's presentation of the development of the human body at this point thus manifests the fundamental strategies by which existence attempts to overcome its finitude, and if we consider the order of the various states presented here, it becomes evident that organic development simultaneously embodies two strategies which are ultimately mutually contradictory. The one strategy is that of assimilation, by which an individual entity attempts to survive and to overcome its finite form by itself remaining unaltered and devouring all otherness which it encounters, reducing it to part of itself. The other, opposite strategy is that of accommodation, by which the individual attempts to overcome its finitude through changing its form to accommodate or accord with the otherness which it encounters.

The "first Age," which is constituted by a roofing or protecting of "the Abstract Horror," signifies the originary differentiation (extraction or abstraction) of a separate, individual entity from the inchoate ground of mere possibility, which is intrinsically resistant to the limitation constituted by "Definite Form": "Refusing all Definite Form, the Abstract Horror roofd. stony hard / And a first Age passed over & a State of dismal woe" (3:9-10). This establishment of a separate identity (which, however, is still largely amorphous—"refusing all Definite Form") makes possible the second moment, that of further differentiation and growth, the entity's putting forth part of itself into the abyss of otherness surrounding it: "Down sunk with fright a red round Globe hot burning. deep / Deep down into the Abyss. panting: conglobing: trembling" (3:11-12). This amoebic act, which is given further elucidation at the end of the seventh age, is the prototype of all growth, of all desiring, venturesome attempts to overcome limitation and *be* in the fullest sense. While the first age involves separation and withdrawal (abstraction), the second age entails a venturing forth.

In the third age, the development of perception, these two movements are combined, in the ability of an entity to take account of what lies beyond the boundaries of its immediate, nuclear identity: "Rolling round into two little Orbs & closed in two little Caves / The Eyes beheld the Abyss: lest bones of solidness freeze over all" (3:14-15). Perception—taking account of otherness at a distance—is the ground of both assimilation and accommodation; it both enlarges the perimeter of an entity's being (by allowing it to join with and participate in distant events) and encloses the entity ever more securely in its own unique region of existence by objectifying otherness and keeping it at a distance. Perception is thus the factor which allows an entity a certain amount of flexibility ("lest bones of solidness freeze over all"), freeing it from the determinism of its immediate surroundings, while also preserving the entity's integrity.

The emergence of the ears in the fourth Age signifies a continuation both of the entity's participation in otherness and its avoidance of otherness: "From beneath his Orbs of Vision, Two Ears in close volutions / Shot spiring out in the deep darkness & petrified as they grew" (3:17-18). On the one hand, the ears, which "shot spiring out in the deep darkness," allow an entity to encounter those obscure—invisible or intangible—events or dimensions of reality. As such, the ears signify an entity's intuitive or even vatic ability to grasp and bring into reality even the most distant and obscure possibilities. But in providing the entity with such extreme attunement to otherness, the ears also constitute an increasing vulnerability to otherness, as well as an increasing radial contraction or petrification with regard to alternative possibilities—i.e., possibilities which lie outside the trajectory of the entity's own unique actuality.

These simultaneous movements toward greater participation with otherness, on the one hand, and on the other hand greater separation from otherness, attain their respective culminations in the fifth and sixth ages—culminations which, however, turn out to be self-contradictory and counterproductive. The appearance of the nostrils in the fifth Age signifies the most intense attunement to otherness which is possible: "Hanging upon the wind, Two Nostrils bent down into the Deep" (3:20). Since the nostrils are attuned to what is "in the wind," as well as to the invisible essence of things, they constitute a virtually absolute attunement and total accommodation to otherness—even the most distant and intangible otherness. As such, the nostrils constitute the entity's loss of definiteness and its return to the amorphous flux of mere possibility—a return suggested by the fact that the "Nostrils bent down into the Deep." The nostrils, then, embody the culmination of the organic strategy of accommodation, in which an entity attempts to survive and to overcome its finitude by changing its form to accommodate the conditions which confront it. We see here, however, that total accommodation—and accommodation must be total if it is to be a totally successful strategy for overcoming finitude—is tantamount to total loss of identity.

The nostrils, however, also embody the assimilative strategy—both in the fact that smelling, as Empedocles had observed, devours tiny particles of other beings, and in the fact that smelling is a primary means of locating prey. The nostrils, like the ears, thus function as ancillaries to the tongue of hunger and thirst, whose appearance in the sixth age embodies the culmination of the strategy of assimilation, in which an entity simply devours the otherness which it encounters, reducing that otherness to part of the entity's own being: "In ghastly torment sick, a Tongue of hunger & thirst flamed out" (3:22). The problem with assimilation—and assimilation must also be total if it is to be totally successful—is that like accommodation, it ultimately leads right back to the inchoate state of non-differentiation which is by definition inimical to individuality. For under the assimilative strategy all individuals will ultimately be devoured by other entities.

We are thus shown how living form envies living form, and how such envy constitutes an impasse in the attempt by existence to overcome finitude. The impasse reached by these strategies of Los/entelechy is signalled by his stifled and enraged condition at this point, together with his terror and dismay:

> Enraged & stifled without & within in terror & woe, he threw his
> Right Arm to the north, his left Arm to the south, & his Feet
> Stampd the nether Abyss in trembling & howling & dismay
> And a seventh Age passed over & a State of dismal woe.
>
> (3:24-7)

Here, in the seventh age—the final age of creation, and the state in which existence is now arrested—entelechy finds itself stymied ("enraged and stifled") both practically or existentially and logically or ontologically (i.e., both "without and within"). There is no way to avoid this impasse in the attempt to overcome the limitations of individual identity, for all attempts ultimately result in perpetuation of that very finitude which they were designed to overcome.

With neither assimilation (the strategy of permanence) nor accommodation (the strategy of change) providing a viable solution to the problem of individual finitude, Los can carry on only through a synthesis of, or alternation between, these two strategies. This synthesis of the strategies of permanence and change, or assimilation and accommodation, is portrayed in the subsequent passage, where the process of development is recapitulated. First we are told that Los "became what he beheld" (3:29), indicating that entelechy is the act of becoming the possibility which it beholds—i.e., the act of turning against oneself as actuality and giving oneself over to the otherness which one is to become. This self-othering or becoming-other which constitutes the essence of entelechy occurs in two steps. First there is the activity of positing—imagining, or putting forth out of one's bowels, as it were—that which one is to become. This act, which corresponds to the strategy of accommodation, manifests itself as the emergence of a desire or the recognition of a goal and constitutes identity's giving birth to a new form, another identity:

> ...a red
> Round Globe sunk down from his Bosom into the Deep in pangs
> He hoverd over it trembling & weeping. suspended it shook
> The nether Abyss in tremblings. he wept over it, he cherish'd it
> In deadly sickening pain....
>
> (3:29-33)

The second step is constituted by the process of actualizing this imaged and desired possibility—grasping or embracing it, identifying with this new identity and assimilating it. This duality of entelechy is presented in the image of Los's separation into a desiring male and the desired female—i.e., the spectre and Enitharmon:

> ...till separated into a Female pale
> As the cloud that brings the snow: all the while from his Back
> A blue fluid exuded in Sinews hardening in the Abyss
> Till it separated into a Male Form howling in Jealousy.
>
> (3:33-6)

Entelechy thus manifests itself as the activity of desiring its counterpart which it has posited, projected, or emanated.

This relationship between Los and Enitharmon is developed at some length in *The Book of Urizen*, with desire itself being portrayed by the figure of Orc. Here in *Milton*, however, Los and Enitharmon are seen as engaging in a synthetic, constructive activity, which subdues the insubstantial (spectrous) desiring aspect of Los, and in doing so, presents Los as an actualizing power that is more general than mere individual entelechy:

> Within labouring. beholding Without: from Particulars to
>   Generals
> Subduing his Spectre, they Builded the Looms of Generation
> They Builded Great Golgonooza Times on Times Ages on Ages.
> (3:37-9)

The relationship between Los and Enitharmon—i.e., between the actualizing principle and the product (whether as merely posited *qua* possibility, or as actualized) of that power—is a productive one. And the products of this relationship are themselves means of further products: "the Looms of Generation" and "Great Golgonooza," the latter being the locus, as we shall see, of all productive activity. This production occurs by virtue of an internal transformation ("within labouring") of individuals, whereby they apprehend otherness ("beholding without") not as particular alien beings but rather as members of the same general order as themselves. This transformation of perception "from Particulars to Generals" constitutes the construction of the Looms of Generation, for this apprehension of otherness as being in some way the same as oneself is the basis of that interweaving (uniting) of different beings which constitutes organic growth and transformation. This synthetic, constructive activity is not simply the appropriating, assimilating activity of desire; in fact, it opposes jealous desire, since it subdues Los's spectre. For the real activity of Los is a synthesis of assimilation and accommodation, not assimilation or expropriation by itself.

Destruction as the Condition
of the Possibility of Process

Even Los's synthesis of accommodation and assimilation, however, cannot overcome destruction. In fact, it presupposes destruction, which is implicit in the very notion of change: assimilation, as we have seen, involves the destruction of the assimilated being, while accomodation entails a certain destruction of the accommodating entity. Destruction of the body—and thus a radical finitude—is intrinsic to the form of individual existence. This is the aspect of the Fall which is insurmountable: we cannot overcome the fact that "life liv[es] upon death," i.e., that our bodies must destroy other bodies in order to survive, and must themselves be destroyed for other bodies to survive. But if destruction is inevitable, the type of destruction, and its significance, are not. And it is in distinguishing (or failing to distinguish) types of destruction that humans perpetuate and exacerbate their own fallen, finite form. Blake thus elucidates the various types of destruction, embodying them in the qualities and actions of Los's three sons, Satan, Rintrah, and Palamabron, who are all essential dimensions of the process of actualization:

> They builded great Golgonooza Times on Times Ages on Ages
> First Orc was Born then the Shadowy Female: then All Los's
>   Family
> At last Enitharmon brought forth Satan Refusing Form, in vain
> The Miller of Eternity made subservient to the Great Harvest
> That he may go to his own Place Prince of the Starry Wheels
> Beneath the Plow of Rintrah & the Harrow of the Almighty
> In the hands of Palamabron.
>
> (3:39-4:2)

The fact that Orc is the first-born indicates that the first function produced by the process of actualization is eros, the movement to appropriate an otherness which is regarded as a necessary part of one's own being. But this movement, as well as the process of actualization itself, also presupposes various types of destruction: defensive destruction, which cultivates and protects the organic growth from alien actuality (the Plow of Rintrah); preparatory or productive destruction of the host ("the Harrow of the almighty in the hands of Palamabron"), which supports the seed and fosters new, germinating actuality; and reductive destruction (Satan's mills), which transforms the ripened fruit (actuality) into nourishment for other beings.[3]

Reductive Destruction:
The Homogenizing Function of Satan

Satan's title, "the Miller of Eternity," although somewhat ambiguous (does he grind Eternity, or for Eternity, or just eternally?), indicates that his activity has a fundamental function in the universal scheme of things. And when we consider more closely exactly what a miller does, we must conclude that Satan's function is to provide food by grinding the grain from the Great Harvest, which is the universal destruction of individual beings (a point which becomes clearer later in the poem). Satan is the principle which destroys the unique identities of individuals, grinding them down (into uniform, elementary forms) so that their being can be devoured and assimilated as nourishment by other individuals. Satan is thus the principle which makes it possible for life to live on death, and for growth and progress to take place, for if individuals were not interchangeable or the same at some level—i.e., if they did not have some commonality—one actuality could not pass into another, and all identities would be petrified.

Satan's reductive/destructive function is explained further by his association with the three classes of men, which we have tentatively identified as three modes of responding to one's finitude or inevitable destruction:

Where the Starry Mills of Satan
Are built beneath the earth & Waters of the Mundane Shell
Here the Three Classes of Men take their Sexual texture[.] Woven
The Sexual is Threefold: the Human is Fourfold.
(4:2-5)

It is in Satan's realm that all individuals, no matter what their class, take on their "sexual texture," their desiring and propagating aspect. This realm is that of the material and tangible—or perhaps more accurately, the realm of quantity, which lies "beneath the Earth & Waters of the Mundane Shell." It is in this quantitative realm—produced by Satan's reduction of individuals' qualitative uniqueness to quantities of a homogeneous substance—that the subject/object mode of relatedness (i.e., the "sexual texture" of desiring and desired individuals) is created. For in Satan's quantitative realm, all intercourse and commerce among individuals takes the form of a quasi-material exchange in which being changes hands from one positive, conglomerate entity to another. As the producer of such quantitative interaction and union among individuals, Satan is also the Weaver or textile Miller of Eternity. And just as Satan's destructive activity (the grain mills) produces homogeneity, so the constructive activity that occurs in his region (the textile mills) presupposes such homogeneity of individuals (the fibers).

Satan's reductive function is further elaborated in Los's address to him, in which Los tries to convince him of his unique nature and role:

If you account it Wisdom when you are angry to be silent, and
Not to shew it: I do not account that Wisdom but Folly.
Every Mans Wisdom is peculiar to his own Individuality
O Satan my youngest born, art thou not Prince of the Starry Hosts
And of the wheels of Heaven, to turn the Mills day & night?
Art thou not Newtons Pantocrator weaving the Woof of Locke[?]
To Mortals thy Mills seem every thing & the Harrow of Shaddai
A scheme of Human conduct invisible & incomprehensible[.]
Get to thy Labours at the Mills & leave me to my wrath.
(4:6-14)

Los's description of Satan as "Prince of the Starry Hosts / And of the Wheels of Heaven" and "Newtons Pantocrator weaving the Woof of Locke" reinforces Satan's identification with the mechanistic and material—i.e., quantitative—aspects of Being. Satan's "Starry Mills" are the cosmic forces that both grind everything down and weave things together in an endless atomistic cycle of coming to be and perishing. The reductive destruction which accompanies the inexorable march of time is thus Satan's work, as Los indicates when he tells Satan, "Thy work is Eternal Death" (4:17). This destruction is constantly confronting individuals, most intensely as their own mortality, and hence to them the force behind the destruction seems to be the ultimate power, since it affects everything. "To Mortals," Los tells Satan, "thy Mills seem every thing & the Harrow of Shaddai / A scheme of Human conduct invisible & incomprehensible."

Productive Destruction:
The Accommodating Function of Palamabron

But the reductive destruction of Satan is not ultimate, Los implies. For the Harrow of Shaddai, we can surmise, produces a positive, salutary destruction. Harrowing, like the grinding of a mill, reduces conglomerate identities to elemental particles; but it does so not in order to assimilate (i.e., devour) the grain-seed, but rather in order to accommodate the seed and sustain and enhance it. In this way the Harrowing of Palamabron, although virtually identical in appearance to the reductive destruction of Satan, is actually the contrary of Satanic destruction, for its ultimate purpose is the preservation of both the accommodating and the accommodated entities. As such, the Harrow of Shaddai is "a scheme of Human Conduct"; for as a violence and destruction which simultaneously preserves, it embodies that mode of being—i.e., that perspective—which, we shall see, is the truly human: the mode (perspective) in which all destruction involves indirect or mediated preservation of that which is destroyed. Such a scheme of things is not manifest or even comprehensible to Mortals, because they are aware only of what is immediate: the annihilation of that which is destroyed. Thus the atomistic systems of Newton and Locke seem an accurate description of the nature of things, and the Harrow of Shaddai seems "invisible & incomprehensible." We are given a hint of this scheme, however, when Los tells Satan, "Thou canst not have Eternal Life," in the same breath with which he forbids Satan to drive the Harrow, thus implying that driving the Harrow "in pity's paths" (i.e., accommodating otherness) and having Eternal Life are identical, or at least causally related.

Homogeneity and Satanic
Quid Pro Quo Metaphysics

Having distinguished Palamabronic destruction from Satanic, Blake proceeds to show how Satanic, reductive destruction insidiously usurps, in human vision and praxis, the productive, redemptive destruction of Palamabron. Blake warns us of the insidiousness of the Satanic power when he writes: "Satan trembling obeyd weeping along the way" (4:19). The strong-willed heroic Satan which we might expect to encounter at this point (especially in a poem entitled *Milton*) is nowhere to be found: instead, we are presented with a cringing coward who seems incapable of harming anything. Yet, lest we dismiss this image as mere humor, Blake, in the voice of the Bard, immediately exhorts: "Mark well my words, they are of your eternal Salvation" (4:20), advising that it is of great importance that we note Satan's action here. This vignette of Satan slinking away in apparent obedience is designed to alert us to the fact that this Miller of Eternity grinds down our identities—i.e., destroys our being—not only through direct aggression and frontal assault on our will, but also through apparent obedience and support, i.e., through apparent attempts to enhance our being.

One such instance can be found in the phenomenon of sacrifice, in which the Satanic, reductive view of destruction is promoted because it appears to offer a way to overcome finitude—i.e., to serve the Divine humanity:

> Between South Moulton Street & Stratford Place: Calvarys foot
> Where the Victims were preparing for Sacrifice their Cherubim
> Around their loins pourd forth their arrows & their bosoms beam
> With all colours of precious stones, & their inmost palaces
> Resounded with preparation of animals wild & tame.
>
> (4:21-5)

The various types of sacrifice which this passage alludes to—judicial/political, religious, and alimentary—are all instances of that Eternal Death which is Satan's work. And more important, each instance of sacrifice absolutizes the Satanic perspective, assuming that all individuals are composed solely of a homogeneous substance and that therefore one individual can be substituted for another in the ultimate scheme of things. Sacrifice furthermore presupposes a corollary to this principle: that since the being of individuals is ultimately identical, each individual competes for this homogeneous being with all other individuals, and one individual can come into being and grow and develop only through the destruction or diminution of other individuals. The truth of this *quid pro quo* view is obvious in regard to physical subsistence, and can be seen in the "preparation of animals wild & tame" for food: corporeal life, as we have seen, lives upon corporeal death of other life. This existential fact, however, has been universalized into an ontological principle by those who engage in religious sacrifice, because "to Mortals [Satan's] Mills seem every thing." Sacrifice, that is, presupposes that not only physical existence but Being itself obeys this crude economics of reciprocity: humans sacrifice other beings (including other humans) to gods (the dispensers of this homogeneous being) in order that they, the humans, may retain and perhaps increase their own being. This practice, together with the *quid pro quo* metaphysics on which it is based, has extended itself even to Christianity, where it manifests itself at "Calvarys foot," in the crucifixion of Jesus and the doctrine of Atonement.[4] As we shall see, Blake regards this *quid pro quo* metaphysics as the most pernicious doctrine imaginable, for it is this doctrine—often only tacitly or even unconsciously assumed—which founds and motivates the various types of reductive destruction to which the unique and ultimate being of individuals is subjected. The Bard thus warns against the extrapolation from the physical to the metaphysical or spiritual which gives rise to this metaphysical perspective: "Mark well my words! (Corporeal Friends are Spiritual Enemies)" (4:26).

Blake criticizes this deadly perspective by contrasting it with Palamabron's activity, in which destruction preserves and enhances that which it destroys (as well as that *for which* it destroys):

> Mocking Druidical Mathematical Proportion of Length Bredth
>   Highth
> Displaying Naked Beauty! with Flute & Harp & Song
> Palamabron with the fiery Harrow in morning returning
> From breathing fields.
>
> (4:27–5:2)

The *quid pro quo* metaphysics of Satan is based upon the principle of "Druidical Mathematical Proportion," seeing individuals and the relations between them in purely quantitative (i.e., "mathematical") terms (as Druidic sacrifice implies), and assuming that the being of one individual can be added to, subtracted from, or substituted for that of another, like quantities in a mathematical equation. This negating reduction performed by Satan contrasts with the redemptive, productive reduction effected by Palamabron, whose harrow produces life—"breathing fields"—by reducing the hard ground to its elemental constituent entities: the Harrow, by opening up the ground to become host to what is other, not only nourishes the seed, but also gives the ground life (turns it into "breathing fields") through the life which the ground fosters. Here, however, there is only the slightest hint of such happenings, the ultimate manifestation of which is embodied in Milton's going to Eternal Death; at this point the purpose is simply to present an alternative vision to the reductive *quid pro quo* metaphysics in which "Christ took on Sin in the Virgin's Womb, & put it off on the Cross [and] / All pitied the piteous & was wrath with the wrathful" (5:2-4) — i.e., the state in which all give an eye for an eye and a tooth for a tooth, in a system of brutal reciprocity.

Destruction as the Origin of Quid Pro Quo Metaphysics

This *quid pro quo* approach to existence, however, although false and pernicious, is in a sense a valid response to finitude, as Blake now demonstrates through the figures of the Daughters of Albion, who prepare the victims for sacrifice and thus determine the type or class of identity for each individual:

> And this is the manner of the Daughters of Albion in their beauty
> Every one is threefold in Head & Heart & Reins, & every one
> Has three Gates into the Three Heavens of Beulah which shine
> Translucent in their Foreheads & their Bosoms & their Loins
> Surrounded with fires unapproachable: but whom they please
> They take up into their Heavens in intoxicating delight.
>
> (5:5-10)

The rationale which the Daughters offer for their destructive activity of sacrifice explains how the *quid pro quo* metaphysics arises: sacrifice, the Daughters imply, is necessary to overcome the finitude of existence. The Daughters and the males that assist them look at the narrow, restrictive forms of individuals and lament:

> Ah weak & wide astray! Ah shut in narrow doleful form
> Creeping in reptile flesh upon the bosom of the ground
> The Eye of Man a little narrow orb closd up & dark
> Scarcely beholding the great light conversing with the Void.
>
> (5:19-22)

These restrictions, they imply, keep existence from achieving its full realization: "Can such an Eye judge of the stars?" they ask. "Can such closed Nostrils feel joy?... / Alas! folded within themselves / They touch not ought" (5:28, 32, 36-7). In this urge to rid existence of the separation and isolation which constitute the finitude of individuals, the Daughters reveal themselves to be offspring of Albion, the unity of individuals: their actions are attempts to overcome finitude by unifying individuals in one of three ways—intellectually, emotionally, or sexually—which correspond to "the Three Heavens of Beulah which shine / Translucent in their Foreheads & their Bosoms & their Loins." In order to effect this union, the restrictive forms of existence must be destroyed, to make room for the truer, more authentic forms. It is to this end that the three classes or types of identity are created: "Thus [the Daughters] sing," we are told, "Creating the Three Classes among Druid Rocks" (5:38). These three classes constitute a sort of eugenics, in which certain types (or aspects) of beings are judged truer than others and thus worthy of preservation: "whom they please [the Daughters] take up into their Heavens in intoxicating delight." According to the *quid pro quo* metaphysics, however—symbolized by the "Druid Rocks" where humans were sacrificed—one being continues to exist only through the destruction of another being: "the Elect cannot be Redeemd, but Created continually / By Offering & Atonement" of other beings (5:11-12). It is this fact that necessitates the selection and categorization of individuals according to the type and degree of their preservation and destruction: "Hence the three Classes of Men take their fix'd destinations" (5:13).

For this metaphysics, then, in order for true existence to be enhanced, false forms of existence must be destroyed. This is the assumption of all revolutions, as Blake indicates through an allusion to the British Revolution, which is presented as contemporary—and perhaps even identical—with the sacrifice of the Daughters of Albion:

> Thus they sing Creating the Three Classes among Druid Rocks
> Charles calls on Milton for Atonement. Cromwell is ready
> James calls for fires in Golgonooza. for heaps of smoking ruins
> In the night of prosperity and wantonness which he himself
>   Created
> Among the Daughters of Albion among the Rocks of the Druids.
>
> (5:38-42)

Satanic metaphysics thus has a certain validity, for although such sacrifice is evil, it also seems to be redemptive at times. On the one hand of course, in addition to destroying individuals, wanton sacrifice tends to inaugurate a cycle of vengeance and retribution and thus perpetuate that very baseness and finitude of existence which it is designed to overcome. On the other hand, however, real historical amelioration often does occur as a result of destruction, as Blake indicates by the fact that this destruction is contemporary with the moment "when Satan fainted beneath the arrows of Elynittria/ And Mathematic Proportion was subdued by Living Proportion" (5:43-4).

Moreover, the sacrifice which occurs in revolution is only a special instance of the continuous, universal process of striving for full actualization of being, as is indicated by the juxtaposition of the allusion to revolution with a description of the universal process. The universality of this process—the building of "Golgonooza the Spiritual Fourfold London eternal" (6:1)—is indicated by the fact that it is said to take place

> Thro Albions four Forests which overspread all the Earth,
> From London Stone to Blackheath east: to Hounslow west:
> To Findley north: to Norwood south: and the weights
> Of Enitharmons Loom play lulling cadences on the winds of
> Albion
> From Caithness in the north, to Lizard-point & Dover in the
> south.   (6:4-7)

The fact that Los's process of actualization centers around London Stone, the place of Druid sacrifice, indicates that sacrificial destruction of individuals is central to the process of actualization itself, which, moreover, is said to occur "in immense labours & sorrows, ever building ever falling" (6:2). Instead of being merely negative, this destruction is productive and fulfilling: it is a harvest more than a sacrifice. In this vision, which resembles but is also fundamentally different from that of druidism, the entire countryside is seen as the workshop in which Los "forge[s] the instruments / Of Harvest: the Plow & Harrow to pass over the Nations" (6:12-13). The natural and political events of the world are manifestations of the attempt of Los, the productive, forming, actualizing power, to transcend present actuality by harvesting those individuals which have developed to the limits of their finitude and using their being to help actualize new, less restricted forms of existence.

It is in its apprehension of the universality of destruction and sacrifice, and in its attempt to achieve fulfillment in embracing this destruction rather than in avoiding it or denying it, that the Satanic Druidic religion has its validity. This validity is portrayed as an agreement between the Satanic view and Blake's vision—an agreement which is expressed as an identity of origins for the two visions in "Lambeth's vale":

> The Surrey hills glow like the clinkers of the furnace: Lambeths
> Vale
> Where Jerusalems foundations began; where they were laid in
> ruins

Where they were laid in ruins from every Nation & Oak Groves
   rooted
Dark gleams before the Furnace-mouth a heap of burning ashes.
When shall Jerusalem return & overspread all the Nations
Return: return to Lambeths Vale O building of human souls
Thence stony Druid Temples overspread the Island white
And thence from Jerusalems ruins. from her walls of salvation
And praise: thro the whole Earth were reard from Ireland
To Mexico & Peru west, & east to China & Japan.

(6:14-23)

The inference to be drawn from this identity of origins is that Druidic religion and imperialistic politics are both attempts, like the building of
Jerusalem, to actualize Being more fully. The Druidic, Satanic effort, however, has a fatal flaw, indicated by the fact that "Jerusalems foundations," the
incipient fulfillment or total actualization of Being offered by the Edenic
Lambeth's Vale, were destroyed by "every Nation and [by] Oak Groves
rooted." Fulfillment (Jerusalem) was destroyed, that is, by the usurpation of
individual being in the consolidation and centralization of political power
(the formation of nations) and the analogous centralization of ontological
power or being in hierarchic religious systems, epitomized by the sacred Oak
Groves of the Druids. This attempt to centralize Being precluded the full
actualization of Being, because it suppressed actualization of the uniqueness
of individuals, which constitute the only actuality there is.

   This attempted circumvention of individuals is due to the attempt to reach
(actualize) Being in a single leap—to make Being fully present here and now.
And this desire for full presence—indeed, the assumption that such presence
or immediacy is even possible—constitutes a fundamental misapprehension
of the nature of Being. We will have occasion to discuss these ramifications
more fully later on; here the point is that such regal or feudalistic attempts to
expropriate being are self-defeating, resulting in more destruction than
actualization of being. This fate is epitomized in the image of "Babel / The
Spectre of Albion frown[ing] over the Nations in glory & war" (6:24). The
centralization of political power (the Nations), that is, is presided over by
Babel, the attempt to gather all individuals into a single unity. Such total,
immediate, positive unity is illusory or spectrous; it is based on the reductive
Satanic view of individual being as a homogeneous substance, a view which
produces a false appearance or "spectre" of the true unity of individuals
which is Albion, the unity of individuals that leaves difference and even
opposition intact. Because it is based on a misapprehension of the nature of

Being itself, the enterprise of Babel—the attempt to bring all individuals together as a means to overcome the finitude of individuality and ascend directly to Being, i.e., to actualize Being in full presence—always issues ultimately in fragmentation and lack of actualization.

The sacrificial activity of the Daughters of Albion, then, is a perverted form of that redemptive reductive (sacrificial) destruction which is an aspect of the actualizing process itself. This point is made in the description of Los's activity which Blake now gives:

> Loud sounds the Hammer of Los, loud turn the Wheels of
> Enitharmon
> Her Looms vibrate with soft affections, weaving the Web of Life
> Out from the ashes of the Dead; Los lifts his iron Ladles
> With molten ore: he heaves the iron cliffs in his rattling chains
> From Hyde Park to the Alms-houses of Mile-end & old Bow
> Here the Three Classes of Mortal Men take their fixd destinations.
> (6:27-32)

The final line here, which is virtually identical with the description of the activities of the Daughters of Albion, locates the Daughters' activities within the actualizing process of Los, and thus reinforces the sacrificial and destructive aspects of Los's activity.

Three Aspects of Destruction and Three Modes of Identity

The actualizing process, then, is necessarily destructive, and this destruction affects individuals in three different modes or classes:

> Here the Three Classes of Mortal Men take their fixd destinations
> And hence they overspread the Nations of the whole Earth & hence
> The Web of Life is woven: & the tender sinews of life created
> And the Three Classes of Men regulated by Los's Hammer.
> The first, The Elect from before the foundation of the World:
> The second, The Redeem'd. The Third, The Reprobate & form'd
> To destruction from the mother's womb. . . .
> (6:32-7:3)

In relation to Calvinist doctrine, the Elect would be those individuals who are predestined to salvation, the Redeemed those who can become transformed, and the Reprobate those who are doomed to damnation.[5] In Blake's hands, however, the classes come to signify three aspects and thus also three types or views of individual identity, each with a different ontological status.

The Elect are individuals (and that aspect of each individual) whose being is unchanging and unchangeable. Their identities are seen to be rigid and inflexible: "the Elect cannot be Redeemd" (5:11), i.e., transformed in any way. For this type of identity, an individual's true being is not a process or the result of a process, but is seen instead as a substance—i.e., as originating "from before the foundation of the World." The actual existence of these individuals has no real bearing on their being. Furthermore, since their being derives from beyond the actual events of their existence, their being is not really unique and intrinsic to their identity, but is rather infused from an external, transcendent source, by which they are "created continually" (5:11). And since their being derives from a general reservoir of Being, as it were, their being can be maintained only "by Offering & Atonement in the crue[l]ties of Moral Law" (5:12)—i.e., only through the destruction of other individuals by a system that subordinates all individuals to a single universal standard. This view of identity both derives from and leads to the *quid pro quo* metaphysics, in which an increase in one place involves a decrease somewhere else, since all individuals are constituted by a common substance that is distributed among them by a central distribution system. This principle of identity, as we have seen, is the atomistic, Satanic principle of quantitative diversity based upon qualitative homogeneity.

The Redeemed are individuals whose essential being is a product of development; they embody a view of identity as the result of a process, an achievement. Their being is thus bound up with their actual existence, and the events of their existence *qualitatively* alter their being. This type of identity implies an ontology that involves process, where Being itself is a matter of development and growth, rather than substance or presence.

The Reprobate are "form'd / To destruction from the mothers womb" (7:2-3), and thus have no permanent, positive being. They come into being and eventually perish and have no real being beyond their short-lived existence. For them, existence is everything; their identity consists in the process itself, and is thus continuously becoming and continuously perishing.

Each type of identity reflects an aspect of all individuals, and all three types are thus present in varying degrees in all individuals. The regulation of the three classes by Los's hammer, then, refers to the proportion of each aspect of identity given to each individual.[6] Some individuals are essentially Elect: their being and fulfillment are given to them without any effort on their part. The Elect is the aspect of one's identity which remains the same by means of its opposition and resistance to—and even destruction of—other beings. Other individuals are primarily Reprobate, and the accretions produced by their existing constitute the entirety of their being, which is always inadequate and which is lost forever when their existence ends. The Reprobate is that aspect of identity which destroys and is destroyed and thereby effects the emergence of otherness; the Reprobate has no essence or permanent identity to actualize. The Redeemed, on the contrary, has a true being that is achieved only through existing, and the Redeemed's identity is the product of living. The Redeemed is that aspect of identity which is cumulative and is altered incrementally in the process of existence. Like the Elect, it retains its previous identity, but like the Reprobate, it also undergoes essential alteration.

The three classes of men are thus three aspects of every individual's being and also, derivatively, three types of actual existence and three metaphysical perspectives on identity—perspectives that we might call the essentialist, the organicist, and the existentialist. Each aspect has its own validity and necessity: permanence, transformation, and destruction are all necessary and inescapable aspects of individual identity. The exact status and proportion of each aspect, however, is a question which can be resolved in different ways, giving rise to various fundamentally opposed formulations of Being (metaphysical systems) and forms of existence (strategies of fulfillment). *Milton* is an attempt to examine critically several of these differing perspectives and to achieve a more adequate vision of the status of each class. Accordingly, the poem revolves around three primary questions: What is the nature and significance of the destruction of individual beings? What is the ontological significance of the transformation of individuals? And in what way is individual identity permanent? And implicit in these questions is the single question: what, exactly, does an individual's *being* consist in?

CHAPTER II

Satanic Destruction and
The Consequences of its Misprision

Satan's Usurpation of Redemptive Destruction

Having demonstrated the inevitability of destruction, and the significance of one's vision of destruction, Blake goes on to portray the struggle among the various aspects of, or perspectives on, destruction. We are shown that Rintrah, Palamabron, and Satan—as the three aspects or principles of destruction—are engaged in strife, with one principle, the Satanic power, tending by its very nature to achieve ascendancy and thus destroy the equilibrium which constitutes the destructive/productive process of becoming. This usurping movement of the Satanic principle, Blake demonstrates—which occurs in the realms of both theory and praxis—has fundamental consequences in all realms of being, including the natural, the political, the psychological, and even the metaphysical realm.

From the perspective of Satan, the Miller of Eternity whose work is Eternal Death, individuals are mere grist for the mills of destruction, which ignore the uniqueness of each individual as they grind it down. For this view and dimension of being, individuals are created through the destruction of other individuals, which, having no intrinsic being, thus have no aspect which is preserved in the destroying. The Satanic view of identity, then, is that of the Elect, and since this view has no respect for—and, indeed, no real perception of—individuals' uniqueness, it denies significance to the other aspects, attempting tyrannically to assume their "stations":

> Of the first class [the Elect] was Satan: with incomparable
> mildness;
> His primitive tyrannical attempts on Los: with most endearing
> love
> He soft intreated Los to give to him Palamabrons station;
> For Palamabron returnd with labour wearied every evening

35

> Palamabron oft refus'd; and as often Satan offer'd
> His service till by repeated offers and repeated intreaties
> Los gave to him the Harrow of the Almighty....
>
> (7:4-10)

As the principle of reductive destruction, Satan is inherently tyrannical in expropriating individuals' being. But Satan's tyranny also assumes another, more sinister form: the reductiveness of Satan's destroying tends to usurp— metaphysically, in our minds—the redemptive aspect of destruction, i.e., destruction as providing the ground for actualization of new possibilities. Los's giving Satan the Harrow of the Almighty thus signifies the displacement of the productive, redemptive aspect of destruction and the assumption of greater importance by the reductive aspect in the entelechic process by which individuals acquire more fulfilling forms.

Just as significant as the fact of this usurpation is the manner in which it occurs. The way in which Satan pursues "his primitive tyrannical attempts on Los" indicates that the type of destruction which he embodies does not occur primarily as overtly violent aggression. The Satanic, reductive principle, that is, does not homogenize individuals by frontally assaulting their unique being, but rather by ontologically undermining that uniqueness, using "incomparable mildness," "endearing love," and soft "intreaties" to get the individual to desert its own being. Satan also works through accusation, destroying the authentic being of an individual by falsely attributing negative qualities to the individual:

> alas blamable
> Palamabron: fear'd to be angry lest Satan should accuse him of
> Ingratitude, & Los believe the accusation thro Satans extreme
> Mildness.
>
> (7:10-13)

The consequences of this usurpation demonstrate that Satanic, homogenizing destruction is by itself incapable of producing the developmental process: Satan returns from the labor "terrified overlabourd & astonished" (7:14), indicating that mere reductive destruction alone cannot prepare the ground for new being. The extent of Satan's inadequacy is further revealed when Palamabron rises the next morning and discovers that "...the horses of the Harrow / Were maddend with tormenting fury..." (7:17-18). Palamabron's reaction to the situation provides clarification:

> You know Satans mildness and his self-imposition,
> Seeming a brother, being a tyrant, even thinking himself a brother

> While he is murdering the just; prophetic I behold
> His future course thro' darkness and despair to eternal death
> But we must not be tyrants also! he hath assum'd my place
> For one whole day, under pretence of pity and love to me:
> My horses hath he maddend! and my fellow servants injur'd.
>
> (7:21-7)

Palamabron's statement reveals that beneath the facade of mildness and kindness, Satan is really a murderous, tyrannical usurper—yet without knowing himself to be such, since his very nature is to be unaware of the unique being which his ignorance of essential difference is destroying. Palamabron now realizes that he should have opposed Satan, since the very principle of the uniqueness of individuals precludes the possibility of Satan's being able to perform the functions of Palamabron: "How should he[,] he[,] know the duties of another?" Palamabron asks. "O foolish forbearance / Would I had told Los, all my heart!" (7:28-9). In his very failure to oppose Satan, Palamabron was already handing over the harrow—yielding to the Satanic perspective, which fails to take account of individual uniqueness and difference. Satanic destruction ignores individual difference and uniqueness, while Palamabronic destruction depends upon them and preserves them. The blindness of the Satanic perspective to individual uniqueness is manifested by the fact that Satan accuses Palamabron "of crimes / Himself had wrought" (7:34-5) and believes "that he had nor oppres'd the horses of the Harrow, nor the servants" (7:40). Satan is unaware that he is guilty of oppressing other beings and aspects of beings, because the oppression is not his conscious goal but is rather the unconscious by-product of his nature—his ignorance of individual uniqueness.

Irreducible uniqueness or difference is thus seen to be an absolutely necessary aspect of existence, and this important point is reinforced by the fact that Los rectifies the chaos by enforcing the differentiation of the elements. "Henceforth Palamabron," he says, "let each his own station / Keep: nor in pity false, nor in officious brotherhood, where none needs, be active" (7:41-3). The total breakdown in the process of becoming reveals that the process is the result of several distinct types or aspects of destruction, each of which must be active if becoming is to occur. The process of becoming requires that each principle remain within the boundaries of its own identity and perform its unique and necessary function.

Los's declaration reveals another point, which we have already identified as central to Blake's vision of Being and of fundamental importance to the action of *Milton*: the fundamental principles that constitute becoming can be altered. As indicated by the intransigence of Satan and the unresponsiveness of the horses—the motive forces or efficient causes of the harrowing process—such alteration is effected by the strife of the entelechic power with aspects of itself (the strife of Los with his sons and of the sons with each other). Satan's usurpation itself, in fact, implies the same thing: that these principles and their various subordinate forces (e.g., the horses and gnomes) can affect each other—that, in fact, while they are intrinsically unique, they are also related to each other, in an intrinsically unique way that can nonetheless always be transformed. The ways in which these principles affect each other are, moreover, of ultimate concern: in the Bard's words, they are "of [our] eternal salvation." For if the Satanic principle of individual obliteration is allowed to assert itself in the wrong way, there can be no eternal salvation for individuals. In order for individual identity to be ultimate, it must in some way continue to *be* even after it perishes. Destruction must occur, but it must not be identical to annihilation; therefore Satan must be held in check.

But Satanic reduction is nonetheless necessary, for without ignoring in some way the uniqueness of individuals, no union or assimilation of different entities—in fact, no change whatsoever—could occur, and the process of becoming could not go forward. Thus the confusion which *Palamabron* causes in Satan's mills is equally unacceptable to Los:

> Los beheld
> The servants of the Mills drunken with wine and dancing wild
> With shouts and Palamabrons songs, rending the forests green
> With ecchoing confusion, tho' the Sun was risen on high.
>
> (8:7-10)

Under Palamabron's rule the reductive aspect of destruction does not take place. Palamabron, with his pity—i.e., his sensitivity and receptivity to individual uniqueness—is incapable of marshalling the servants of the mills to perform the necessary work of reduction and homogenization. We are thus shown that the complete lack of uniformity and reductiveness is just as unproductive as complete homogenization.

Both aspects of destruction, then, are necessary for the process of Being: both Satan—the reduction of beings to a common denominator by destroying their unique identities—and Palamabron, the receptivity and preservation of the destroyed beings in different form. Without both aspects of destruction—i.e., without both reduction of otherness (assimilation) and receptivity to otherness (accommodation, which entails suppression and destruction of one's own uniqueness)—Los's creation cannot take place, for the process of becoming entails the simultaneous supersession and preservation of the present actuality in the actualization of new beings; hence it is that "this mournful day / Must be a blank in Nature" (8:20-21), i.e., a time when the process of becoming ceased.

Los thus realizes that each of the two functions must be kept intact and therefore distinct, and he signifies this realization by "[taking] off his left sandal [and] placing it on his head, / Signal of solemn mourning" (8:11-12). Just as a sandal cannot serve the head as a hat, so Satan cannot serve the Harrow nor Palamabron the Mills. Los blames the disruption on his having forgotten this fact: "Mine is the fault!" he says. "I should have remember'd that pity divides the soul / And man unmans" (8:19-20). Los realizes that Satan has used Palamabron's pity to draw Palamabron out of his unique identity and thus usurp Palamabron's function. By evoking Palamabron's pity, Satan has in a sense emasculated ("unman[ned]") him, for in pitying, one's vital force—one's attention, concern, and energy—is cut off from one's being and invested in the being that is pitied. And as a result, one's essence, or inmost, most private parts, are effectively lost.

Thus, in order to counter the unifying principles of seduction (Satan) and pity (Palamabron), there is required another power which can maintain the uniqueness and separation of individual beings. This is the principle of the Plow of Rintrah, which cultivates and preserves an entity by destroying the otherness which encroaches upon it. The Plow, as the implement of "Rintrah who is of the Reprobate: of those form'd to destruction" (8:34), is the instrument of destruction or uprooting pure and simple—the absolute destruction of one being to make room for another, in contrast to reductive, predatory destruction (Satan) and productive, preservative destruction (Palamabron).

Metamorphosis and Dissimulation of the Satanic Principle

Satanic destructiveness is rendered even more insidious by virtue of the fact that it can be present in actions which seem to protect the integrity of the individual—for instance, in the act of mourning, which seems to be an acknowledgement of the individual's uniqueness and irreducibility. Mourning, while ostensibly affirming the irreducibility of the individual, implicitly affirms the opposite, Satanic perspective, for in lamenting that one is deprived of the irreplaceable beloved, one assumes that the beloved's being is annihilated, reduced to the uniform, elementary particles ("earth to earth") of which it was constituted. This subversive effect of mourning is portrayed in the events which accompany it:

> Wildly they follow'd Los and Rintrah, & the Mills were silent
> They mourn'd all day, this mournful day of Satan & Palamabron:
> And all the Elect & all the Redeem'd mourn'd one toward another
> Upon the mountains of Albion among the cliffs of the Dead.
> They Plow'd in tears! incessant pourd Jehovahs rain, & Molechs
> Thick fires contending with the rain, thunder'd above rolling
> Terrible over their heads; Satan wept over Palamabron
> Theotormon & Bromion contended on the side of Satan
> Pitying his youth and beauty; trembling at eternal death:
> Michael contended aganst Satan in the rolling thunder
> Thulloh the friend of Satan also reprovd him: faint their reproof.
>
> (8:23-33)

Here it is revealed that mourning is of the same order as the rain of Jehovah and the fires of Molech, for all are instances of the denial of absoluteness to the individual. Just as Jehovah's rain destroys by covering over all individuals in a flood of homogeneous substance, and the fires of Molech (whose worship required the sacrifice of children in furnaces) destroy by consuming individuals, so mourning destroys individuals by implicitly denying the absoluteness and eternal integrity of that which is mourned. The Satanic perspective here triumphs once again by disguising itself and infiltrating the very heart of the opposing perspective.

Satanic reduction is also present, we are shown, in the theocentric perspective and the Bacchanalian attitude, represented by Theotormon and Bromion, respectively.[1] Their alliance with Satan lies in the fact that like Satan they deny the intrinsic being of the individual. For theocentrism is the theoretical aspect of Satan's feudalistic metaphysics, while natural Bacchanalian religion, with its sacrifices, is the practical embodiment of this metaphysics. Both Theotormon and Bromion, moreover, are attempts to overcome "eternal death," the absolute annihilation which they regard as the ultimate ontological fact concerning individual being; and in thus taking eternal death as merely reductive annihilation with no preservation of the identity which is destroyed, Theotormon and Bromion are tacitly assuming and supporting the position of Satan. Against such powerful support for Satan, all opposition to ontological reduction of individuals is rendered ineffective: neither Michael, the Providential minister of justice—and, as such, the preserver of individuals' rights and integrity—nor Thulloh, symbol of opposition to tyranny in the political sphere,[2] can overcome the Satanic denial of individual being.

Blake clearly indicates the Satanic aspect of other apparently friendly, supportive acts. As Rintrah

> Flam'd above all the plowed furrows, angry red and furious,
> Till Michael sat down in the furrow weary dissolv'd in tears[,]
> Satan who drave the team beside him, stood angry & red
> He smote Thulloh & slew him, & he stood terrible over Michael
> Urging him to arise....
>
> (8:36-40)

The redness of Satan portrays the murderous rage which had been covertly present all along in Satan's mildness but which now explodes in a fit of overt lethal aggression. The aggressive aspect of Satan's mildness is further manifested in the fact that after slaying Thulloh, Satan stands threateningly over Michael and weeps—indicating that weeping is itself an act of aggression, by calling forth pity. For it is Satan's weeping which causes Michael to "[sit] down in the furrow weary dissolv'd in tears" (8:37)—Michael's power of enforcing justice, i.e., of safeguarding individual integrity, being dissolved by the pity elicited by the tears of Satan.[3]

The efficacy of Satan's dissimulated destructiveness is thus made clear, and it must be opposed. The most effective way to do so is to expose the dissimulation, which is what Palamabron attempts to do,

> ...call[ing] down a Great Solemn Assembly,
> That he who will not defend Truth, may be compelled to
> Defend a Lie, that he may be snared & caught & taken.
>
> (8:46-8)

Having realized the devastating effectiveness of Satan's technique of destruction by infiltration and seduction, Palamabron hopes to get Satan to manifest himself in his true form—i.e., as mild, soft-spoken, and cowardly—and thereby show that mildness or friendliness can be murderous, since it is now public knowledge that Satan has slain Thulloh. By showing a mild, friendly murderer, Palamabron hopes to prove the (potential, if not inevitable) turpitude of mildness and friendliness and thus muster opposition to such insidious "friendly" destructiveness. "O god, protect me from my friends," Palamabron prays, "that they have not power over me / Thou hast giv'n me power to protect myself from my bitterest enemies" (9:5-6). Blake emphasizes the crucial importance of this insight with the refrain, "Mark well my words, they are of your eternal salvation" (9:7), for it is vital that the destructive and sinister effects of apparently friendly modes of being like unmitigated and indiscriminate pity and love be recognized so that these modes of being can be opposed and their destructiveness avoided.

But the unexpected occurs: the murderer Satan enacts yet another metamorphosis and appears to the Assembly not in his mildness and friendliness, but in Rintrah's rage, with which he opposes Palamabron. And as a consequence of this new disguise, the Assembly blames the murder on rage and remains oblivious to the culpability of mildness and "friendship":

> . . . Palamabron appeal'd to all Eden, and recievd
> Judgment: and Lo! it fell on Rintrah and his rage:
> Which now flam'd high & furious in Satan against Palamabron
> Till it became a proverb in Eden. Satan is among the Reprobate.
> (9:9-12)

Eden recognizes and condemns the destruction, but assumes the agent of the destruction to be the Reprobate Rintrah, the most obviously destructive power. The Satanic destructiveness of mildness thus goes undectected, and Eden accounts it as an unquestionable certainty that "Satan is among the Reprobate"—that destruction of individual uniqueness is the product of rage and aggression rather than of (often mild and naive) oblivion to the intrinsic worth of individuals (the perspective of the Elect), which is embodied in such apparently harmless acts as mourning and weeping.

Repercussions of the Metaphysical Misprision of Satanic Destructiveness

The Great Solemn Assembly, which comprises "all Eden," seems to be a congregation of Powers that decides or controls the fundamental form or direction which Becoming takes in a particular epoch; and an epoch, conversely, is constituted by the particular constellation or dispensation of these forces. Such, at least, are the implications of the effect of the Assembly's judgment, for the effect is nothing less than a transvaluation of values:

> Los in his wrath curs'd heaven & earth, he rent up Nations,
> Standing on Albions rocks among high-reard Druid temples
> Which reach the stars of heaven & stretch from pole to pole.
> He displaced continents, the oceans fled before his face
> He alter'd the poles of the world, east, west & north & south
> But he clos'd up Enitharmon from the sight of all these things.
> (9:13-18)

The judgment of the Assembly, and the dissemblance of Satan which occasioned the judgment, provoke the displacement of continents, the alteration of poles of the world, and other radical changes in the realm of existence. Even Los, the power of actualization itself, is altered: now under the influence of the Assembly's *quid pro quo* Druidic perspective (i.e., "standing . . . among high-reard Druid temples"), Los ignores the unique station of the various powers, principles, and values and interchanges them. That these changes are fundamental rather than merely epiphenomenal is indicated by the fact that they are not perceptible to Enitharmon, the immediate actuality emanated or actualized by the entelechic power Los. The point is that a fundamental change can occur in the dispensation of Being without the change being visible to one situated in the phenomenal world; the change becomes visible only in retrospect.

Yet despite her ignorance of these fundamental changes, it seems that Enitharmon has been instrumental in producing them, for it is her forming a space for Satan that immediately precedes Palamabron's calling of the Assembly: Enitharmon, or actuality, by giving Satan or reductive annihilation a certain legitimacy, has paved the way for Satan to take over the entire universe. That is, by according reality to annihilation in just one instance—i.e., by weaving it into her web of actuality—Enitharmon has falsely established ultimate, total Satanic reduction as *possible*, and has thus induced individuals to take action to avoid such annihilation.

The Ascendancy of Satan and the Ontological Decline of Individuals

This increased significance attributed to reductive Satanic destructiveness is portrayed in Satan's actions following the Assembly's judgment:

> He created Seven deadly Sins drawing out his infernal scroll,
> Of Moral laws and cruel punishments upon the clouds of Jehovah
> To pervert the Divine voice in its entrance to the earth.
>
> (9:21-3)

Here Satan, in his Yahwistic mode, establishes universal codes ("Seven deadly Sins"), which "pervert the Divine voice in its entrance to the earth"—i.e., cause misapprehension by those on earth of the nature of ultimate Being, which is now conceived as a powerful and capricious individual whose ability to annihilate actual individuals "with thunder of war & trumpets sound, with armies of disease / Punishments & deaths mustered & number'd" (9:24-5) is taken as evidence of the ontological nullity of individuals. More specifically,

Satan claims that he, as the principle that destroys individuality, is the ultimate being or power in the universe,

> Saying I am God alone
> There is no other! let all obey my principles of moral individuality
> I have brought them from the uppermost innermost recesses
> Of my Eternal Mind, transgressors I will rend off for ever,
> As now I rend this accursed Family from my covering.
>
> (9:25-9)

Once again Satan ignores individual uniqueness, demanding that all obey his "principles of moral individuality"—i.e., conduct themselves according to his monolithic rules rather than according to the dictates of their own unique being. This suppression of unique individual being is a rejection and obfuscation of Being itself, or divinity, for as Satan rages, "his bosom [grows] / Opake against the Divine Vision" (9:30-31). The only way Being itself occurs is in the being of unique individual entities—"God only Acts & is in existing beings or Men" (*Marriage*, 16)—and in rejecting individual being, Satan thus rejects the true God, or Being itself. This rejection of true being opens up a realm of nothingness instead of being: "And there a World of deeper Ulro was open'd in the midst / Of the Assembly. In Satans bosom a vast unfathomable Abyss" (9:34-5). Satan's lack of respect for individual uniqueness is further revealed by his "accusing loud / The Divine Mercy, for protecting Palamabron in his tent" (9:41-2): just as he is ignorant of the intrinsic value of individuals, so he sees no justification for the preservation of Palamabron's unique power, since he has no comprehension of its value — and especially since that power is pity, the acknowledgement and cultivation of others' unique being.

Rintrah, on the other hand, is aware of the value of individual uniqueness and the necessity of Palamabron for its preservation, for

> Rintrah rear'd up walls of rocks and pourd rivers & moats
> Of fire round the walls: columns of fire guard around
> Between Satan and Palamabron in the terrible darkness.
>
> (9:43-5)

Rintrah, as the power of wrath, is the principle which protects the integrity of individual entities and powers by opposing what threatens to usurp an individual's being. Wrath provides a counterbalance to pity, preventing pity from resulting in complete abdication of one's being. As such, wrath functions as a limit to pity and usurpation, forming, as it were, a barrier between them to keep the reductive destruction of Satan in its proper sphere and to allow pity—donation of self to otherness—to occur without succumbing completely to the Satanic homogenizing process.

But Satan does not respect this boundary: "not having the Science of Wrath"—i.e., having no apprehension of opposition and separation—"but only of pity" (homogenization, the merging or submersion of identity in otherness), Satan fails to temper pity with wrath or to mitigate wrath with pity, "and wrath was left to wrath, & pity to pity" (9:47). Pity, untempered by wrath, becomes total abdication of one's individual uniqueness through immersion in the concerns of another, and wrath, unmitigated by pity, becomes complete destruction of otherness—both of which are virtually identical to Satanic destructiveness. Ironically, the conjunction of the forces of wrath and pity is so crucial that without this equilibrium, Satan himself can no longer live. This point is portrayed by the fact that when wrath and pity are separated, "[Satan] sunk down a dreadful Death, unlike the slumbers of Beulah / The Separation was terrible" (9:48-9). Without the conjunction of wrath, the protector of one's own identity, and pity, the protector of the other's identity, there is no individuality left for Satan to consume, and thus, like a fire without fuel, he dies; the process of becoming grinds to a halt, and Being becomes static and unmoving.

Manifestations of the
Metaphysical Ascendancy of Satan

Satanic Ascendancy in History

The historical manifestation of the Satanic disjunction of wrath and pity, and of Satan's consequent self-destruction as a vital dimension of the process of becoming, is found in feudalistic and imperialistic systems of all types: the dead Miller of Eternity, we are told, "was repos'd on his Couch / Beneath the couch of Albion, on the seven mou[n]tains of Rome / In the whole place of the Covering Cherub, Rome Babylon & Tyre" (9:49-51). This place of repose is constituted by religious and political tyrannies which accorded all power and being (political and ontological) to a single central source, thus denying the intrinsic being of individuals. This imperialistic, feudalistic system is symbolized by the Covering Cherub, which, as the purported guardian of the Divine Presence in the Ark of the Covenant, is the supreme instance of the restriction of Being to a single locus extrinsic to individuals. Individual beings ultimately count for nothing in such a system, in which

Being is finally static and lifeless. It is in such systems that the "Spectre" of Satan (9:52) dwells—i.e., the autonomous, and thus inauthentic and perverted, form of reduction of individual being.

When Satan, the reductive principle, thus manifests itself in spectrous, inauthentic form in these religious and political institutions, "then Los & Enitharmon knew that Satan is Urizen / Drawn down by Orc & the Shadowy Female into Generation" (10:1-2). This statement is paradoxical, for Urizen, as the "Creator of Men" (*Visions*, 5:3), is the principle of identity or individuation, while Satan is the opposite principle—the force which obliterates individual identities. How, then, can Satan be Urizen? The paradox is resolved, however, when we consider that Satan is the principle of individuation as it manifests itself in "Generation"—i.e., in the process of actual existence, where life is generated out of death, and one generation is produced by the destruction of its predecessor. For the actual occurrence of individuation is a continual process of destroying the uniqueness of individuals—both one's own form of being, which is exceeded and superseded in the process of growth, and the being of other individuals, which is devoured and assimilated in order to nourish one's own process of individuation. The process of individuation (Urizen) thus occurs in actuality as the process of destroying other individuation, which process is the principle of Satan. This process of Generation also takes place through the agency of Orc (eros, the instinctive impetus toward fulfillment) and the Shadowy Female—the obscure reproductive principle of nature through which individuals attempt to perpetuate themselves beyond the end of their existence.

Satanic Ascendancy in Nature

This spectrous instantiation of the Satanic principle in the phenomenal world presupposes space, for as the medium of co-presence, space is the means by which individuals come into contact and devour each other. Space, we have seen, is at the disposal of Enitharmon, the immediate actuality or presence produced by the actualizing power Los. But when the spectrous form of Satan holds ascendancy in the phenomenal world—i.e., when annihilation of individuals is seen as total and final, rather than provisional and instrumental—then the immediate actuality (Enitharmon) produced by Los ceases to control space by disposing of it according to individual uniqueness. Instead, space becomes a universal category, a homogeneous container, as it were, that subjects immediate actuality to its universal laws. Thus when Enitharmon—the total immediate actuality of a moment—enters into this

Satanic space, she appears decrepit and impotent, i.e., completely inconsequential:

> Oft Enitharmon enterd weeping into the Space, there appearing
> An aged Woman raving along the Streets (the Space is named
> Canaan) then she returnd to Los weary frighted as from dreams.
> (10:3-5)

Generation, like Canaan, is supposedly the promised land where all desires can be fulfilled; in truth, however, it is a place of lethal suppression. This suppression is sensed by actuality (Enitharmon) only in a dim and indirect way, as in dreams, for as pure presence or immediate actuality, Enitharmon is oblivious to the non-actual dimensions of events, and it is only through attunement to these dimensions of being that she could become aware of suppression (since suppression involves by definition the difference between the actual state and the non-actual but desired or fulfilling state of an entity). Enitharmon's ignorance and vulnerability derive from the fact that, as immediate presence, she is always temporally at the verge of perishing (i.e., "aged"), and in the context of the total process of Generation, each single present moment which she is seems to count for nought.

The suppressive character of this generative (i.e., "female") space is immediately made explicit:

> The nature of Female Space is this: it shrinks the Organs
> Of Life till they become Finite & Itself seems Infinite
> And Satan vibrated in the immensity of the Space! Limited
> To those without but Infinite to those within: it fell down and
> Became Canaan: closing Los from Eternity in Albions Cliffs
> A mighty Fiend against the Divine Humanity mustring to War.
> (10:6-11)

Because of its boundless extension, generative space—or the world of existence, in which individuals come into being and then perish—seems to possess unlimited being; individual entities, in contrast, appear to have only a very restricted being, because of their limited extension. This equation of infinitude of being with quantitative limitlessness is Satanic: for it equates being with quantitatively homogeneous substance and thus denies all unique being to individuals. The ontological limits of spatial extension are apparent to those who realize that actual magnitude (quantity) is not the ultimate ontological principle, but to those whose vision is enclosed within the ontological principles of space—i.e., to those who assume that individuals are fundamentally homogeneous—space seems everything. For if the being of all individuals is ultimately the same, then the differentiation of individuals must, in the final analysis, be purely quantitative or spatial—a function of extension and density (or intensity) of whatever kind. This metaphysical system manifests itself most clearly as Canaan, the place where material abundance is equated with fulfillment and coexists with ontological degradation of individuals. In such a system, where material satisfaction is counted as the ultimate goal of existence, Los is closed from Eternity—i.e., the entelechic actualizing power is no longer actualizing the ultimate being of individuals, but is merely satisfying immediate, superficial desires. This Satanic female space is thus destructive of Being, hindering its actualization and diminishing individuals, in which Being occurs; the space is therefore "a mighty Fiend against the Divine Humanity mustring to War." But despite the prevalence in existence of this distorted image of Being and its restriction of the entelechic power, entelechy remains intrinsically oriented beyond the immediate presence of female space, toward Being: "Satan! Ah me! is gone to his own place, said Los! their God / I will not worship in their Churches, nor King in their Theatres" (10:12-13).

Satanic Ascendancy in Spirit

This Satanic view of individuality manifests itself in, and is also caused by, jealousy. In refusing to worship Satan, Los exclaims: "Elynittria! whence is this Jealousy running along the mountains / British Women were not Jealous when Greek & Roman were Jealous" (10:14-15). Jealousy occurs when individual being is not seen as intrinsic: for, the implicit reasoning goes, if individual being is not intrinsic and unique, then one individual's being could just as easily belong to another. On the basis of this assumption, individuals covet each other's being and strive to expropriate it for their own hoard. However, in a metaphysical system that does not equate being with immediate presence, and that values the former above the latter, jealousy does not occur, for the being of each individual is intrinsic and cannot be expropriated by another individual: in Los's words, "Every thing in Eternity shines by its own Internal light" (10:16). This internal light or intrinsic being is destroyed by Elynittria, the frigid, virginal—i.e., self-possessive—Diana-figure (as she is revealed to be in *Visions of the Daughters of Albion*) who, Los says, "darkenest every Internal light with the arrows of [her] quiver / Bound up in the horns of Jealousy to a deadly fading Moon" (10:17-18). The "arrows" are apparently arrows of desire (mentioned in the introductory lyric "Jerusalem"), for desire, the impetus deriving from the incompleteness of the individual, causes individuals to view other individuals as means of fulfillment or completion, and thus can lead to the assumption that individuals have no intrinsic being, but merely reflect being, just as the moon, having no light of its own, reflects the light of the sun. Jealousy, then, is based upon and contributes to the feudalistic metaphysics of Satan, in which individuals are merely reflections of true Being, which is located in a single, central source. Or, in the image Los uses, the Sun (Being) is bound "into a Jealous Globe / That everything is fixd Opake without Internal light" (10:19-20). This vision is the essence of Satan, and insofar as such a view prevails, Satan triumphs over Los's attempt to actualize Being in the only way possible: through the enhancement of the being of individuals.[4]

Satanic Metaphysics in Christianity

Blake concludes his account of the ascendancy of the Satanic principle by revealing the presence of the Satanic perspective at the heart of Christianity itself, in both the Old and New Testaments. He first reminds us of the precise nature of Satanic ascendancy:

> And the Mills of Satan were separated into a moony Space
> Among the rocks of Albions Temples, and Satans Druid sons
> Offer the Human Victims throughout all the Earth, and Albions
> Dread Tomb immortal on his Rock, overshadowd the whole
>   Earth:
> Where Satan making to himself Laws from his own identity.
> (11:6-10)

Satan's establishing of himself as the ultimate principle, the source of all "Laws," occurs at "Albion's / Dread Tomb": it is founded upon the destruction of Albion, the authentic unity of all individuals, as opposed to the spurious unity of mere non-differentiation (homogeneity) which Satan achieves through the obliteration of individual uniqueness. And as we have already seen, because Satan is able to destroy individual beings, he is seen as having control over them and thus as himself constituting ultimate Being, or God:

> . . . Satan making to himself Laws from his own identity.
> Compell'd others to serve him in moral gratitude & submission
> Being call'd God: setting himself above all that is called God.
> And all the Spectres of the Dead calling themselves Sons of God
> In his Synagogues worship Satan under the Unutterable Name.
> (11:10-14)

This description of God fits the God of the Decalogue, the Yaweh who told his followers, "I am a jealous God," and "Thou shalt have no other gods before me," whose name was unutterable, and whose followers, the Hebrews, worshipped him in synagogues and called themselves the chosen people, or Sons of God. These lines thus suggest that the God of the Old Testament is actually Satan, the destroyer and perverter of true being.

But if the God of the Old Testament is condemned as ultimately Satanic, the New Testament is revealed to be an even more scandalous perpetration of Satanic metaphysics. For the very heart of the new dispensation—the doctrine of atonement—is revealed to be based upon the feudalistic metaphysics of Satan. This foundation is made explicit in the answer which the Eternal gives to the question of "why... / The Innocent should be condemned for the guilty" (11:15-16). The Eternal declares:

> If the Guilty should be condemn'd, he must be an Eternal Death
> And one must die for another throughout all Eternity.
> Satan is fall'n from his station & never can be redeem'd
> But must be new Created continually moment by moment
> And therefore the Class of Satan shall be calld the Elect & those
> Of Rintrah. the Reprobate, & those of Palamabron the Redeem'd
> For he is redeem'd from Satans Law, the wrath falling on Rintrah,
> And therefore Palamabron dared not to call a solemn Assembly
> Till Satan had assum'd Rintrahs wrath in the day of mourning
> In a feminine delusion of false pride self-deciev'd.
>
>   (11:17-26)

The actual agent of destruction, the Eternal argues, cannot be condemned, because to do so would initiate a vicious cycle of vengeance and retribution in which "one must die for another throughout all Eternity"; that is, if the original destroyer were destroyed, then his destroyer would also have to be destroyed, and so on, *ad infinitum*. Condemning the innocent, on the other hand, does not initiate such a devasting principle. This preposterous rationalization—which closely resembles the Doctrine of Atonement—can be offered only on the assumption that individual uniqueness counts for nought, and that the purpose of justice and punishment is not to give individuals their due but is rather to maintain equilibrium in the entire system (either social or ontological). The Eternal is thus himself Satanic in ignoring the intrinsic being of individuals, and his Satanic nature is reiterated by his assertion that Satan "must be new Created continually moment by moment"—a declaration which makes sense only if one makes the Satanic

assumption that individual uniqueness *can* "be new Created," or redup-
licated. It thus becomes evident that the Assembly's misapprehension of
Satan's true guilty nature is itself an instance, in several ways, of the Satanic
obliteration of individual uniqueness. And it is this misapprehension of Satan, occasioned by a misprision of the nature of Being itself, which constitutes the new dispensation of Christianity. For Christianity's power comes
from the dominance of the Satanic assumption that total annihilation of an
individual's being is possible: the life after death promised by Christianity
would not be a marketable commodity if individuals did not fear that their
death constituted their utter annihilation. The ascendance of the Satanic
perspective is thus even more powerful and insidious, and the question concerning its means of ascendance becomes pressing. That question is now
pursued further with the descent of Leutha to the Assembly.

CHAPTER III

The Vicissitudes of Satanic Vision and Satanic Affect in Biblical History

Leutha and the Metaphysics of Homogeneity

The Satanic expropriation of the being of others is not simply a matter of vision or optics; affective and instinctual forces are also involved in such usurpation, as Blake proceeds to demonstrate. The reductive, homogenizing principle, that is, manifests itself not only as a certain metaphysical perspective (Satan), but also as a particular affect, which Blake names Leutha. Leutha is the affective dimension of the Satanic principle: she is the expropriative self-aggrandizement of cupidity,[1] and in her relationship with Satan, Blake portrays the way in which the Satanic *quid pro quo* metaphysics of homogeneity (Satanic vision) and self-aggrandizing cupidity (Satanic affect) support and transform each other. Cupidity, Blake shows, perverts those affective, instinctual powers which carry forward the redemptive, productive destruction, and through this perversion disrupts the process itself.

Leutha's nature and actions make it clear that she is thoroughly Satanic. This fact is evident first of all in her offer of atonement ("offering herself a Ransom for Satan," 11:30), for the idea of atonement is based, as we have seen, on the Satanic view that Being is homogeneous. The act of atonement, which supposedly embodies great love and valuation of the ransomed individual, is thus actually a denigration of individual uniqueness, for it assumes that the other's being is qualitatively and essentially no different from one's own, or from anyone else's, since in atonement it can be exchanged for another being. The doctrine of atonement is thus a Satanic doctrine, and always serves ultimately to preserve not the individual atoned for, but rather Satan, the principle of homogeneity and destruction of individual uniqueness.

That Leutha and her offer of atonement are offspring of Satan and the *quid pro quo* feudalistic metaphysics is soon made explicit, when she declares herself to be "the Author of this Sin" and identifies Satan as "My Parent power" (11:35-6). Leutha, then, is a product or result of the Satanic principle (her "Parent power"), but is also the ambiguous agent ("Author") of a specific action of Satan: the attempted usurpation of Palamabron's function (i.e., the usurpation of pity, or redemptive, productive destruction). Her designation as "Author" suggests that she is both the creator of Satan's usurpation and the creature of it—i.e., the passive recipient and re-presenter of Satanic vision. This ambiguity is reinforced by Leutha's subsequent account of how she caused Satan's transgression, which reveals that she is the affective or emotive embodiment of the Satanic metaphysics of homogeneity—a power which both results from and reproduces or reinforces the purely optical, or theoretical aspect of Satanic metaphysics.

The origin of Satan's transgression, Leutha implies, is to be found in the fact that "I loved Palamabron & I sought to approach his Tent / But beautiful Elynittria with her silver arrows repelled me" (11:37-38). The Satanic metaphysical denial of the independence and uniqueness of redemptive, productive destruction is here seen to be grounded in and motivated by a prior denial by Leutha of the uniqueness and non-interchangeability of herself and Elynittria, the respective emanations or products of Satan and Palamabron, reductive and productive destruction. Leutha assumes, that is, that the accommodative destructiveness of Palamabron ultimately produces the same result (or emanation) as the reductive, assimilative destructiveness of Satan: namely, the annihilation of one individual and the transfer of its being to another individual.

Leutha's urge to substitute for Elynittria as Palamabron's result or telos indicates a certain similarity between Elynittria and Leutha. For since pity, like Satanic reduction, assumes a union and sameness of the pitier and the pitied, actual results of the two principles can be confused and Leutha can seem to be identical with Elynittria. But there is also an essential difference between the two principles, indicated by the fact that when Leutha moves toward the domain of pity (the tent of Palamabron), she is repelled by Elynittria. For true pity, unlike cupidity, is a discriminating and respectful union with otherness, an embracing of a particular other which jealously guards that other's unique individual being and preserves it from usurpation.[2]

Elynittria is thus the principle of support and preservation of the unique intrinsic being of individuals—a uniqueness and intrinsicness which from the Satanic perspective are not even seen to exist. This contrast between the two perspectives is portrayed ironically as Leutha's apprehension of Elynittria's internal light, which is terrible to Leutha, because she feels it is brighter than her own: "her light is terrible to me," Leutha laments. "I fade before her immortal beauty" (12:1). Actually, Elynittria's light is different but probably not brighter, for we have just been told that "Leutha stood glowing with varying colours immortal, heart-piercing / And lovely" (11:32-3). Leutha recognizes the uniqueness of Elynittria, but in true Satanic fashion she ignores the qualitative distinction on which it is based and sees the difference purely in terms of quantity. Elynittria, that is, is seen from the Satanic perspective as having being that is essentially no different from Leutha's but merely greater in quantity—i.e., brighter. Leutha's torment, like that of all jealousy, is due to a failure to realize the inherent qualitative uniqueness of individual being; if this uniqueness were realized, there would be no common ground—i.e., no identical quallity of being—that could serve as the basis for the comparison that gives rise to jealousy. Her belief that her own being fades in the light of Elynittria's being thus indicates that for Leutha, being is simply a quantifiable, homogeneous commodity which all individuals possess in various degrees, and that the wealth of one individual thus necessarily entails the poverty of another.

Feudalistic Metaphysics and Expropriative Self-Aggrandizement

Leutha is thus revealed to be an embodiment of the Satanic perspective in which the individual has no irreducibly unique and intrinsic being. More specifically, as we have said, Leutha is the affective counterpart of the Satanic vision, which both derives from and reinforces the Satanic vision. The expropriative, self-aggrandizing nature of Leutha is clearly manifested by the fact that "a Dragon-form forth issue[d] from [Leutha's] limbs / To seize [Elynittria's] new born son" (12:2-3)—i.e., to expropriate Elynittria's offspring or actualization. The fact that this impulse is involuntary (Leutha apparently does not even know why the dragon-form appears) indicates its intimate, primal connection with Leutha's essence, which seemingly automatically manifests itself as a devouring monster. This inherence is further revealed by the fact that the Dragon-form issues from her limbs; for limbs are, it seems, Leutha's essence, her name being homophonous with *leothe*, the Anglo-Saxon word meaning limbs. Limbs, as the grasping, expropriating organs, constitute Leutha's very being, and as such, Leutha is the most powerful actualization of Satanic reduction: she is the urge of expropriative self-aggrandizement, or cupidity. As such, she is the natural offspring of Satan, the Miller of Eternity who grinds all individual uniqueness down to a homogeneous substance: for as we noted in discussing jealousy in the previous chapter, if all individuals are of the same substance, then they are inherently in competition for the same being, which can be transferred from one individual to another. Satanic vision thus naturally gives birth to the Satanic affect and action of cupidity.

The most obvious course for this self-aggrandizing Satanic action is frontal assault on other beings. But such a tactic produces a counterattack by the individual being assaulted—as we see from Elynittria's response—and can thus actually lead to a diminution of the attacker's being (if the defendant is more powerful than the attacker). Another tactic for expropriation is thus called for, and that tactic allows Leutha to gain access to Palamabron's tent and usurp Elynittria's place in his bed—all with the assistance of Elynittria herself. This more subtle tactic of self-aggrandizement involves the use by Leutha of Satan himself: Leutha, the cupidous desire produced by the Satanic perspective, effects a subsequent transformation of her producer. Leutha reveals:

> ...entering the doors of Satans brain night after night
> Like sweet perfumes I stupified the masculine perceptions
> And kept only the feminine awake.

> (12:4-6)

Leutha/cupidity neutralizes the overt modes of destruction and activates the covert modes embodied in seduction and infiltration: "hence rose [Satan's] soft / Delusory love to Palamabron: admiration join'd with envy / Cupidity unconquerable!" (12:6-8). Instead of overtly opposing individuals and pillaging their being, Leutha/cupidity here usurps that being by forming a union with the individuals and thus getting them to abdicate their own identity. This is the Satan who begs to help Palamabron; it is the "feminine" mode of destroying individual uniqueness, expropriation by seduction rather than by overt aggression.

Leutha/Cupidity, Satanic Ascendance, and the Biblical Dispensations

Cupidity and the Instincts

Having portrayed the nature and *modus operandi* of Leutha/cupidity, Blake proceeds to elucidate the manner in which this principle of expropriative self-aggrandizement accompanies and partially enables the ascendance of the Satanic principle of reductive destruction. The role of cupidity in this event is indicated first by Leutha's admission that it was she who maddened the Horses of Palamabron, by trying to "unloose the flaming steeds / As Elynittria used to do" (12:11-12). This apparently simple event is crucial for our understanding of the way cupidity functions to pervert the process of becoming. The first point to note is that cupidity acts on the horses, "those living creatures" (12:12) which, as the motive forces of productive destruction, are the instinctive life forces by means of which this productive/destructive process of becoming moves forward. In attempting to influence the horses, then, Leutha/cupidity is acting upon the primal, instinctive dimension of living beings.

The manner of Leutha's attempt and her timing are also significant. The fact that she tries to influence the horses "when . . . / [They] call'd for rest and pleasant death" (12:8-9) suggests that cupidity becomes active at the moment when the instincts yearn to cease striving (and thus in effect cease existing). This moment (continuously present) is the yearning for fulfillment, for the full presence of the "noon of day" (12:8), when striving has born fruit and can give way to enjoyment. This passive enjoyment, as opposed to active striving, is precisely what is offered by Leutha, who as "a Daughter of Beulah" (11:28), inhabits the ideal realm of pure presence and immediate gratification. (This point will become clearer in our discussion of Beulah at the beginning of Book II.) Leutha, that is, attempts to influence the horses by "over the Harrow beaming / In all [her] beauty . . . / As Elynittria use'd to do" (12:10-12) — i.e., by substituting herself for Elynittria as the result or telos which entices the horses (forces of life) onward. Leutha/cupidity, that is, offers immediate fulfillment, passive enjoyment — self-aggrandizement — as the goal and purpose of productive destruction, in place of the true purpose, which is the fostering of growth through the accommodation of otherness, a process embodied in the discriminating desire of Elynittria.

The instinctive life forces, however, are not so easily manipulatable: "Those living creatures," Leutha discovers, "knew that I was not Elynittria" (12:12-13). The instinctive forces are not merely raw, homogeneous units of power which can be used as means to just any end; they, too, have their own unique, irreducible being, in the form of an intrinsic telos or purpose. While these forces do need external guidance to achieve their purpose (as we shall see clearly in a moment), they are not so completely without internal direction that they can be diverted to any end whatsoever. But although cupidity cannot by itself guide the instincts to the Satanic path, it is able to arouse and pervert the instinctual energies—to break them loose from all restraint ("they brake the traces," 12:13)—and thus create in them a turmoil and confusion ("terribly rag'd the horses," 12:15), which provides Satan himself, or the Satanic vision, with an opportunity to divert the instincts to its path.

Satan, Gnomes, and Instinct: The Mosaic Dispensation

It is noteworthy that Satan's perversion of the instincts after their arousal and confusion is effected by his control over the servants of the Harrow. These servants of the Harrow, as the gnomes who drive the horses (12:17), are the external forces which guide and direct the instincts. More specifically, in addition to being those folkloric beings who inhabit the interior of the earth and thus control the ground on which the instincts run their course, the gnomes are also those aphoristic judgments which guide human behavior by embodying the common wisdom and morals of a people. A gnome in this sense is "a saying pertaining to the manners and common practices of men, which declareth, by an apte brevity, what in this our life ought to be done or not done."[3] As Blake's use of them in *The Marriage of Heaven and Hell* indicates, such gnomes or proverbs embody implicitly an entire metaphysical system, together with its concomitant ethics and epistemology, which one unconsciously embraces when one is guided by the gnome. Just a few plates earlier in *Milton*, in fact, Blake implied much the same thing when Satan's dissimulation as a Reprobate was said to be completed and validated when it became "a proverb in Eden"(9:12).

Such maxims, moreover, are particularly effective with those who are not guided by a more comprehensive vision of themselves and their place in the ultimate scheme of things—i.e., those whose instincts are confused and in need of direction. It is in such a situation that the Satanic power becomes dominant, particularly through the activity of proscribing certain paths for the instincts:

> Satan astonish'd, and with power above his own controll,
> Compell'd the gnomes to curb the horses, & to throw banks of sand
> Around the fiery flaming Harrow in labyrinthine forms.
> And brooks to intersect the meadows in their course.
>
> (12:16-19)

The curbing, restricting action of the gnomes portrays the effect of aphorisms of the "thou shalt not" variety—such as those found during the Mosaic dispensation in the Decalogue and also among the Proverbs in the Old Testament. Such gnomes are in service to Satan not only because they homogenize individuals by prescribing universal laws, but also because, as Blake argues in many of his earlier works, in denying the sovereignty of individual desire, they deny the absoluteness and ultimacy of the individual's unique being.[4] They also set a confusing and often self-contradictory ("labyrinthine") course for instinctual energy, as Blake argued in the *Marriage* when he had the devil declare that "no virtue can exist without breaking these ten commandments" (plate 23).

The gnomes' complicity with a particular metaphysical or religious system is made explicit when we are told:

> The Harrow cast thick flames: Jehovah thunderd above:
> Chaos & ancient night fled from beneath the fiery Harrow:
> The Harrow cast thick flames & orb'd us round in concave fires
> A Hell of our own making. see, its flames still gird me round[.]
> (12:20-23)

It is here made quite plain that the perversion of the instincts from the path of accommodative, productive destruction occurs during the ascendancy of Jehovah, the perpetrator of a tyrannical, feudalistic metaphysics which Blake had criticized earlier, in *The Song of Los*. For in the Yahwist dispensation, destruction has the function of establishing the absolute sovereignty of Yahweh by annihilating whatever is contrary to his order, as is indicated by the Harrow's routing of "Chaos & ancient night" and also by its creation of the fires of Hell, which here are seen (humorously and ironically) to be produced by those very powers they are supposedly designed to torment: Satan and Leutha/cupidity.

The alliance between the Satanic principle and the Yahwist cosmology is given further emphasis as we are told that

> Satan in pride of heart
> Drove the fierce Harrow among the constellations of Jehovah
> Drawing a third part in the fires as stubble north & south.
> To devour Albion and Jerusalem the Emanation of Albion.
> (12:24-7)

Satan's driving the Harrow among the constellations of Jehovah indicates that the Satanic perversion of productive destruction to the paths of reductive

destruction forms an integral part of the Yahwist order. And his driving the
Harrow in pity's paths expresses the fact that he makes his reductive destructiveness seem to be beneficent, just as Jehovah's thundering wrath was
asserted to be a manifestation of love for his people. That this view is merely a
Satanic ploy that passes off the sickness as the cure is made explicit
immediately, as Leutha acknowledges that

> ...'twas then, with our dark fires
> Which now gird round us (O eternal torment) I form'd the Serpent
> Of precious stones & gold turn'd poisons on the sultry wastes.
> (12:28-30)

The formation of this serpent, which alludes to the erection of the brazen
serpent in the wilderness to cure the snake-bitten Israelites when they looked
upon it, reinforces the connection between Satanic metaphysics and the
Yahwist dispensation and also reveals the insidious power of Leutha/
cupidity, which is able to pass off the poison, expropriative self-
aggrandizement, as the cure—by making it appear beautiful and valuable,
i.e., covering it with precious stones and gold, and hence masking the serpent
form itself—and thus promote the predatory attitude, through which productive, accommodative destruction is displaced by reductive, assimilative
destruction. Leutha, that is, promises that self-aggrandizement will cure all
ills and bring fulfillment, when actually it will only exacerbate and intensify
the mutual destruction and plunder of individuals.

Metamorphosis of Satan:
The Prophetic Dispensation

The gnomes, however, eventually recognize that cupidous self-
aggrandizement does not produce the fulfillment it promises:

> The gnomes in all that day spar'd not; they curs'd Satan bitterly.
> To do unkind things in kindness! with power armd, to say
> The most irritating things in the midst of tears and love
> These are the stings of the Serpent! thus did we by them; till thus
> They in return retaliated, and the Living Creatures maddend.
> (12:31-5)

When, after having displaced the principle of productive destruction, the
principle of reductive, expropriating destruction thus assumes the position
of the premier force in the cosmos, Satan's self-contradiction also becomes
manifest: like Urizen, he on the one hand proclaims fulfillment—"laws of

peace, of love, of unity" (*Urizen*.II.8)—but on the other hand presides over a
universe in which the reductive, expropriative destruction of one being by
another is the most fundamental principle. When this expropriative self-
aggrandizement ("the stings of the Serpent") is now seen to characterize even
"kindness" and "tears and love," the gnomic wisdom that previously supported Satan now turns against him: "They in return retaliated, and the
Living Creatures maddend." Gnomic wisdom now also rejects cupidous love
and brands it as a sin, recognizing the difference (which it had earlier failed to
take account of) between cupidous, expropriating love (Leutha) and pitying,
accommodating love (Elynittria):

> I weeping hid in Satans inmost brain;
> But when the Gnomes refus'd to labour more, with blandishments
> I came forth from the head of Satan! back the Gnomes recoil'd.
> And call'd me Sin, and for a sign portentous held me.
>
> (12:36-9)

As a result of this recognition of the destructive nature of Satan and Leutha,
and their subsequent rejection by gnomic wisdom, the day of dominance by
cosmic reduction and rapacious self-aggrandizement draws to a close, and
the principle of pitying, accommodating destruction returns to its rightful
place: "Soon / Day sunk and Palamabron return'd" (12:40). Under this new
dispensation, cupidity is forced into covert activity once again: "trembling
[Leutha] hid [her]self / In Satans inmost Palace of his nervous fine wrought
Brain" (12:40-41). But the new gnomic awareness of hidden dimensions of
actions, and the consequent return of accommodating activity and true pity
(Palamabron and Elynittria), do not dispose of the perverted Satanic power.
Rather, the Satanic reductive power merely undergoes another metamorphosis, renouncing its cupidous aspect and continuing to assert itself in an
even more subtle, insidious form. Leutha describes Satan's transformation:

> For Elynittria met Satan with all her singing women.
> Terrific in their joy & pouring wine of wildest power
> They gave Satan their wine: indignant at the burning wrath.
> Wild with prophetic fury his former life became like a dream
> Cloth'd in the Serpents folds, in selfish holiness demanding purity
> Being most impure, self-condemn'd to eternal tears, he drove
> Me from his inmost Brain & the doors clos'd with thunders sound.
>
> (12:42-8)

Leutha is here describing the internal dynamics of the transformation which
we witnessed earlier, when Satan, in appearing before the Assembly,

exchanged his facade of Palamabronic meekness for a mask of Rintrahic wrath. This transformation, we see, is the result of Satan's seduction by Elynittria, the affect of pity, or accommodating love. The heady wine of this valorization of self-abnegation—supported now by the gnomic wisdom of the new dispensation—overcomes the cupidous and predatory urge and establishes the rule of inner purity and holiness. But as Leutha/cupidity observes, this demand for inner purity and holiness is itself selfish and thus impure. While Satan's former (Mosaic) activity had been a usurpation of individual being—either through overt aggression informed by covert cupidity, or through the overt enticement by an object of cupidous desire (which leads to abdication of self through yielding to the principle of quantitative self-aggrandizement)—his new embodiment seems not to destroy individual uniqueness. On the contrary, Satan's new embodiment, the prophetic, self-righteous upholding of one's own being, seems designed to preserve the individual's uniqueness by embodying the wrath of Rintrah. Self-defense, however, while legitimate and necessary in the form of Rintrah, is reductively destructive in its Satanic form. For the upholding of one's own being, as we have seen, entails the denigration of other beings, in two ways. First and most obviously, one must oppose and destroy otherness in order to survive; but logically prior to such overt opposition, one must implicitly reduce the ontological status of otherness—first, in order to assume that becoming other involves a diminution of one's own being, and second, in order to excuse destroying otherness.

Metamorphosis of Leutha/Cupidity:
Christian Humility contra Self-Righteousness

When Satanic destruction of individuality takes this route and turns against cupidity, cupidity reciprocates and opposes self-righteousness. But cupidity does not, for all this, cease to be Satanically destructive. It merely changes its form and continues to operate. Now, instead of being overtly self-aggrandizing, Leutha appears to renounce her greed and embrace inner purity: "O Divine Vision who didst create the Female: to repose / The Sleepers of Beulah: pity the repentant Leutha" (12:49-50). But in this very act of eschewing overt greed she manifests a covert cupidity. For her plea for pity is nothing other than an attempt to have others abdicate their being to her. Thus cupidity simply changes its locus of operation from the subject of desire to the object: instead of enticing the subject to expropriate the being of the object, cupidity now elicits pity from the object and thus causes the object to abdicate its being to the subject.[5]

This form of cupidity—apparent self-abnegation combined with self-pity—is opposed to Satanic wrathful self-defense and self-righteousness and thus appears to oppose Satanic destruction per se. In actuality, however, Leutha is opposed only to what seems to her to be a perverted and counter-Satanic form of Satan:

> My
> Sick Couch bears the dark shades of Eternal Death infolding
> The Spectre of Satan. he furious refuses to repose in sleep.
> I humbly bow in all my Sin before the Throne Divine.
> Not so the Sick-one; Alas what shall be done him to restore?
> Who calls the Individual Law, Holy: and despises the Saviour.
> Glorying to involve Albions Body in fires of Eternal War.
>   (12:50-13:6)

Leutha here, in the Christian dispensation, continues to serve the feudalistic system of centralized being, "humbly bow[ing] in all [her] Sin before the Throne Divine." Satan, however, is identified by this dispensation as the power that "calls the Individual Law, Holy: and despises the Saviour" who preached love and community. Such militant individualism creates opposition among individuals and thus "involve[s] Albion's Body [the form of unity of individuals] in fires of eternal War." Because this Satan is thus destroying Albion's Body, the unity of individuals, Leutha is right in condemning him. She is wrong, however, in her reasons for doing so: she is wrong because the destructiveness of Satan's action is due not to Rintrah's self-defense or to the Individual Law per se but rather to the perversion of those principles, with the result that they ultimately lead to the destruction of individual uniqueness by provoking Eternal War among individuals. And, of course, she is also wrong because she desires the unity of individuals only as a means to effect her end of self-aggrandizement. Leutha's moral opposition to Satan is thus that of the slave morality which condemns straightforward power only because it is itself overpowered. But this slave morality is a successful tactic of self-aggrandizement: "Now Leutha ceas'd: tears flow'd: but the Divine Pity supported her" (13:7). By appearing to be self-abnegating, she elicits the self-giving of others, which supports her.

    In her new and effective guise as penitent and suppliant, Leutha/cupidity continues to condemn her previous form and that of Satan, and in doing so she gives us further insight into these forms. "All is my fault!" she confesses. "We are the Spectre of Luvah the murderer / Of Albion..." (13:8-9). Although the Spectre of Luvah is a character which we know nothing about from this poem, "Luvah" is roughly homophonous with "love" or "lover," and if Luvah is indeed the principle of love ("the Prince of Love," as he is referred to in *The Four Zoas*), then the Spectre of Luvah would be an inauthentic or debased form of love, in which case the Spectre of Luvah would be identical with Leutha/cupidity, as she asserts. Cupidity, or possessive love, then—as well as Satanic individualism—kills Albion, the true form of unity of individual beings. Possessive desire has this effect, moreover, by destroying individual being through instituting the *quid pro quo* metaphysical system of mutual plunder in which the sanctity of unique individual being is destroyed and individuals are reduced to mere possessors of extrinsic, homogeneous being.

But this situation was not brought about by a gratuitous act, Leutha reveals."The Sin was begun in Eternity," she says, "and will not rest to Eternity / Till two Eternitys meet together, Ah! Lost! lost! lost! for ever!" (13:10-11). As we saw earlier, the very form of individual existence entails the opposition and mutual destruction of individuals. Reduction of individual uniqueness and destruction of individual being are necessary consequences of the a priori conditions of existence—i.e., of the simultaneous individuation and connexity of individuals—and according to Leutha, the inherent lack in individual being, together with possessive desire and its destructiveness, will not cease "till two Eternitys meet together": i.e., till existence fully actualizes Eternity and thereby eliminates that lack which plagues individual existence and manifests itself as possessive desire. In Leutha's view, only when infinite desire meets infinite satisfaction will the mutual plunder of individuals cease.

But, in fact, only by an overthrow of the Satanic metaphysical system of which Leutha is a part can individuals be saved from mutual plunder and achieve true fulfillment. This, we shall see, is precisely Milton's function in the poem: to overthrow the feudalistic metaphysics of presence and destroy the vicious circle of destruction—constituted by finitude and the rapacious desire for infinity.

Satanic Aggressiveness in Old Testament Deities

The embodiment of Satan as wrathful and self-righteous rather than mild and seductive is the form in which the destructiveness of individual being has manifested itself in religions from the beginning of history, and the form has been entrusted to a number of avatars through the course of time.[6] First was Lucifer: the Assembly "...sent Lucifer for [the space's] Guard. / But Lucifer refus'd to die & in pride he forsook his charge..." (13:17-18). The prideful Lucifer, the name of Satan before his fall, was the first manifestation (or conceptualization) of the aggressive Satan. The next manifestation of the aggressive Satanic destructiveness was Molech, the Semitic deity who further diminished individual being with a feudalistic metaphysics that demanded sacrifice of human children in order to sustain the system. When humans thus imagined that their being was not their own and that it must be returned, in part, to its rightful possessor through brutal sacrifice, the intrinsic value and being of the individual threatened to vanish entirely. Molech's impatience—the insatiable impulse of Being (like Kronos) to devour its offspring the instant they appear—had to be restricted. Hence, "...when Molech was impatient / The Divine hand found the Two Limits: first of Opacity, then of Contraction / Opacity was named Satan, Contraction was named Adam" (13:18-20). This concept of limits describes that structure of Being whereby absolute destruction of individuality cannot occur; the limits denote the point beyond which the reduction of individual being cannot proceed. Opacity, named Satan, denotes total lack of internal light or intrinsic being and thus constitutes complete negation of individual being. Contraction, or Adam, is the ultimate reduction of individual actuality to a mere point in space—the homonymic "atom"—a state of mere existence, immersion in mere immediacy with no movement beyond one's immediacy through preservation of the past or actualization of new potential.

Through this providential establishment of a minimal ontological integrity for individual being—corresponding to the original dispensation of the Old Testament, in which Adam and Satan first appeared—human sacrifice is overcome and the simple existence of individual being is thus preserved. But Satanic destructiveness continues to rule, only in more subtle forms: "Triple Elohim came: Elohim wearied fainted: they elected Shaddai. / Shaddai angry, Pahad descended: Pahad terrified, they sent Jehovah..." (13:22-3). Elohim, the name the Hebrews from Adam to Abraham used for their God, was a remote and shadowy god whose name—meaning "*the* god," "the divine being," or "the Possessor of Heaven and earth"[7]—identifies him as a purveyor of feudalistic metaphysics. "Shaddai," used by the Hebrews from Abraham to Moses, is often translated as "God Almighty" and may mean something like "to act violently;"[8] it is thus also an embodiment of feudalistic metaphysics. "Pahad," the god worshipped by Isaac, means "fear,"[9] and thus embodies the same metaphysics, but expressed as the response it evokes from the individual. "Jehovah," or "Yahweh," which originated in God's revelation of himself to Moses, means "I am that I am." It is with Jehovah that the Hebrew God first achieved universal significance, being recognized as the ultimate source and being of everything: with Jehovah, "nothing could be independent of the power and purpose of the everlasting God—'the Eternal.'"[10]

Satanic Reduction in Christianity

With the emergence of Jehovah, then, the diminution of individual being reaches a culmination:

> And Jehovah was leprous; loud he call'd, stretching his hand to
>   Eternity
> For then the Body of Death was perfected in hypocritic holiness,
> Around the Lamb, a Female Tabernacle woven in Cathedrons
>   Looms
> He died as a Reprobate. he was Punish'd as a Transgressor!
> Glory! Glory! Glory! to the Holy Lamb of God
> I touch the heavens as an instrument to glorify the Lord!
>
> (13:25-9)

In Jehovah's ascendancy, the Body of Death is perfected—i.e., the body as dead matter, with all power and glory and being residing in the central source, Jehovah. This view of the body, which constitutes the actual being of individuals, culminated in the doctrine that grew up around the crucifixion ("the Lamb" of God), where the individual body was sloughed off as inessential and inconsequential. In the Christian vision that emerged from this event, the body was seen as "a Female Tabernacle woven in Cathedrons Looms"—i.e., as a mere receptacle for being, which it received from Jehovah. The individual body itself has no real being; it is an artificial existence, a fabrication of Cathedron's Looms and—like the heavens themselves—a mere "instrument to glorify the Lord," in whom all being is seen to reside. This attitude, although not quite the same as worshipping Molech, is nonetheless based on the same view of individual being: the being of individuals is held to be extrinsic, belonging to a central external source rather than to individuals themselves.

This centralization of being, which the crucifixion reinforces, will ultimately result in an ideological or religious conflict between two fundamentally opposed metaphysical systems:

> The Elect shall meet the Redeem'd. on Albions rocks they shall
>   meet
> Astonish'd at the Transgressor, in him beholding the Saviour.
> And the Elect shall say to the Redeemd. We behold it is of Divine
> Mercy alone! of Free Gift and Election that we live.
> Our Virtues & Cruel Goodnesses, have deserv'd Eternal Death.
> Thus they weep upon the fatal Brook of Albions River.
>
> (13:30-35)

The Elect assert the nullity of unique, intrinsic individual being. As their name implies, they see individual identity as a lifeless, static entity that owes its existence to an ultimate source of being and thus has no claim to intrinsic being. In thus abdicating their intrinsic being and worshiping an extrinsic lord of their being, the Elect are seeking fulfillment ("beholding the Saviour") in Satan, "the Transgressor" who is actually, in their very act of worship, surreptitiously depriving them of any possibility of ultimate fulfillment. The Redeemed, as we have seen, view identity as a process of fulfillment which is self-motivated and auto-telic. Their response is yet to be made, and requires one of Milton's stature to make it.

The Christian dispensation, as well as institutionalizing the Satanic usurpation of individual being, also constitutes the triumph of cupidity:

> ... Elynittria met Leutha in the place where she was hidden.
> And threw aside her arrows, and laid down her sounding Bow;
> She sooth'd her with soft words & brought her to Palamabrons bed
> In moments new created for delusion, interwoven round about,
> In dreams she bore the shadowy Spectre of Sleep, & namd him
> Death.
> In dreams she bore Rahab the mother of Tirzah & her sisters
> In Lambeths vales; in Cambridge & in Oxford, places of Thought
> Intricate labyrinths of Times and Spaces unknown, that Leutha
> Lived
> In Palamabrons Tent, and Oothoon was her charming guard.
>
> (13:36-44)

Under the Christian dispensation, Elynittria, or authentic pity, gives way to Leutha, the self-serving, inauthentic pity of cupidity, a transformation indicated by the fact that it is in repentance and self-abnegation, "the place where [Leutha has now] hidden," that Elynittria, the true actualization of pity or self-othering, meets Leutha: in the phenomena of repentance and self-abnegation, that is, the true actuality of pity approaches the masked cupidity of the slave morality, in which apparent self-giving or pity (accommodation) is merely a ruse for self-aggrandizement (assimilation). When authentic accommodation of otherness thus gives way to cupidous self-abasement, the latter brings forth monstrous and destructive offspring from Palamabron, the principle of fulfillment through destruction, or accommodation. That is, when the principle of accommodation (Palamabron) is actualized as the perverse form of inauthentic, cupidous self-abasement (Leutha), the delusory notions of both destruction (Death as the Spectre of Sleep) and fulfillment

(Rahab) are produced. The Spectre of Sleep, called Death, is born "in dreams"—i.e., it is a delusory vision of death in which the dead are seen not as destroyed but as merely in a temporary state of inactivity, like sleep. This view of death is a delusory offspring of Leutha, because possessive desire coerces one into refusing to believe that one's willing, desiring consciousness can cease to be. For when one equates self-aggrandizement with fulfillment, the cessation of this self-aggrandizing cupidity seems to be the end of one's being. Thus real death, as the permanent annihilation of one's immediate, conscious self-presence, must be denied, and death must be viewed as a temporary state of inactivity. This fear and consequent denial of death must be overthrown if Satanic metaphysics and praxis are to be overcome. This, we shall see, is precisely the function of Milton in the poem.

"Rahab the mother of Tirzah & her sisters" is also born in dreams—i.e., in delusion. As a whore, Rahab (who helped Joshua's spies to escape from Jericho) represents delusory or superficial fulfillment, the gratification of immediate, cupidous desire rather than the enhancement of one's true being. Such gratification manifests itself in several forms, the most prominent of which is pleasure, or "Tirzah" (which means "pleasure" in Hebrew). And if we take Rahab to be either Egypt or the mythical monster, and Tirzah to be Zelophehad's greedy daughter who tried to benefit materially from her father's death, we have instances of another kind of false fulfillment, in the form of expropriative, quantitative self-aggrandizement rather than true self-enhancement.[11]

The fact that the delusory destruction and false fulfillment are produced by Leutha/cupidity "in Cambridge & Oxford, places of Thought" implicates learning in general and philosophical thought—"intricate labyrinths of Times and Spaces unknown"—in particular in the perversion of human praxis. Such speculation has resulted in the elevation of general categories, particularly the abstract category of Being, to positions of ontological supremacy, depriving individuals of significance. Cambridge and Oxford, as the home of this speculation, are the dreams or delusions which provide the context and the possibility for the emergence of false destruction (Death as the Spectre of Sleep) and delusory fulfillment (Rahab and Tirzah). Yet the false destruction of Death and the delusory fulfillment of Rahab are not merely the products of philosophical speculation. For these phenomena have an internal dynamism of their own, deriving from the captivating quality which Leutha/cupidity herself possesses by virtue of the fact that she appears to be a way to triumph over (or to mitigate) one's finitude and destruction. The charm or magic spell which renders Leutha/cupidity invulnerable is constituted by Oothoon, whom Blake portrayed in *Visions of the Daughters of Albion* as that aspect of existence which demands the fulfillment of individual desire. This demand for fulfillment is seen here to constitute Leutha's charming guard because it is precisely this demand which allows cupidous self-aggrandizement to occur. Thus in order for Leutha/cupidity to be overcome, fulfillment must be envisioned as it truly is—as mediated and even posthumous presence (as we shall see), rather than as immediate, actual self-presence.

Here the Bard's Song ends, with Satan and Leutha/cupidity in ascendancy and individuality totally negated by the fact of death, individuals believing that they have no intrinsic being and that what being they are entrusted with would be taken away if they were ever to suffer true death (i.e., annihilation). Fulfillment of individual being is thus sought through worship of a monotheisic deity, on the one hand—in an attempt to graft one's existence onto what is perceived as the only true being—and in hedonistic pleasure, on the other hand, confusing Being with immediate actualization, and individual being with immediate gratification in superficial delights. With this debasement of individuals, Being itself is stymied and perverted, for it is deprived of the only actuality it has: individual beings.

The Bard's Song has articulated a metaphysical problem to which the rest of the poem must find a solution: what fulfillment is possible for individuals in a world in which life lives on death and in which one individual attains completion or fulfillment of its being only through the expropriation of another individual's being? This dilemma of existence, while arising from the structure of existence itself, is seen as aggravated and compounded by distorted vision of the elements of being—elements which, while transcendental, are nonetheless affected by views of individuals. These transcendental factors, in fact—the actions of Los's offspring and their emanations—are affected and even produced by misguided attempts to escape or mitigate the finitude of existents: the feudalistic systems, together with the hedonistic, cupidous modes of conduct, are at once causes of finitude and attempts (as we saw earlier) to mitigate finitude. As such, they constitute a vicious circle which has trapped individuals. It will be the function of the remainder of the poem to show a way out of this circle by proposing a radically different view of the essence of individual being, especially regarding its fulfillment and its destruction. Through Milton's actions and pronouncements, Blake will propose a vision of Being which denies the fundamental assumptions of the *quid pro quo* metaphysics of homogeneity, and, in doing so, points the way to ultimate fulfillment for the individual.

PART TWO

Toward a Metaphysics
of Mediated Presence:
Milton's Embrace of Eternal Death
and the Re-Formation of Identity

CHAPTER IV

Eternal Death, Immortality, and the Nature of Individual Being

Blake, the Bard, and Milton: Identity, Past Identity, and Otherness

The significance of the Bard's revelations concerning the vicious circle of destruction, feudalistic metaphysics, and the fear of death is not widely apprehended. In fact, many who hear the Bard ignore this dimension of his vision entirely and focus only on his demystification of love and pity. Some are indignant, refusing to believe that pity or love could be an instance of Satanic destruction: "many condemn'd the high ton'd Song / Saying Pity and Love are too venerable for the imputation / Of guilt (13:47-9). Others who hear are willing to entertain the Song's assertions regarding pity and love, but demand some sort of external, historical evidence to demonstrate the truth of the vision, saying: "If it is true! if the acts have been perform'd / Let the Bard himself witness. Where hadst thou this terrible Song" (13:49-50). They are unable to see that the vision is its own proof; they look for proof among "acts [that] have been perform'd"—among actual events in the world of experience rather than in the principles governing those events. Confronted with this positivist attitude, for which only the actual and tangible has being (an attitude which is often, ironically, held by the same people who in a religious context accord all being to a transcendent and invisible deity) the poet is powerless, for he cannot point out his characters and their acts in the world of immediate experience, since they inhabit a transcendental realm. The only response he can give is to say:

> I am Inspired! I know it is Truth! for I Sing
> According to the inspiration of the Poetic Genius
> Who is the eternal all-protecting Divine Humanity
> To whom be Glory & Power & Dominion Evermore Amen.
> (13:51-14:3)

But to those who are not already aware of the truth of poetic vision, this assertion is unconvincing, and seems no more than the formulaic recitation of pious cliches which it is on the surface.

The Bard's response, however, carries weight with those who move "in the Heavens of Albion," i.e., those who are at home with transcendental principles that lie beyond the actual and visible world. Here the Bard's vision strikes home:

> Then there was great murmuring in the Heavens of Albion
> Concerning Generation & the Vegetative power & concerning
> The Lamb the Saviour: Albion trembled to Italy Greece & Egypt
> To Tartary & Hindostan & China & to Great America
> Shaking the roots & fast foundations of the Earth in doubtfulness.
>
> (14:4-8)

The Bard's revelations identifying the doctrine of atonement ("The Lamb the Saviour") and the popular view of physical existence ("Generation & the Vegetative power") with the *quid pro quo* metaphysics of Satanic destructiveness challenges the received opinion regarding the nature of individuality and of reality itself, "shaking the roots & fast foundations of the Earth in doubtfulness."

When the Bard sees the tremendous ramifications of his vision and realizes his inability to convince skeptics of its truth, "the loud voic'd Bard terrify'd took refuge in Miltons bosom" (14:9), hoping to find guidance in Milton's example. This action, and Milton's response to it, provide the key to understanding what this poem reveals about poetry, tradition, individuality, death, immortality, time, and eternity. The rest of *Milton* consists in a clarification and elaboration of the relation between the Bard (Blake before he wrote *Milton*), Milton, and Blake (as he writes *Milton*).

The refuge which the Bard finds in Milton's bosom consists of the guidance and encouragement which Milton's posthumous presence provides. By reading Milton and studying his vision, by observing how he conducted himself politically, and by apprehending Milton's unrealized potential, the Bard/Blake acquires a stronger realization of his own situation and the possibilities open to him. But the more important point to be made here is that this action of the Bard also affects Milton, even though he has been dead for over a hundred years. For by contemplating Milton's vision, the Bard in a sense—a very real sense, as we shall see—revives Milton and helps him grow and develop even though he is dead: "The loud voic'd Bard terrify'd took refuge in Miltons bosom / *Then* Milton rose up from the heavens of Albion ardorous!" (14:9-10, emphasis added). All the actions which Milton takes in Blake's poem are made possible by the Bard's resurrection of Milton, which he effects by taking refuge in Milton's bosom—i.e., by contemplating and dwelling (consciously and unconsciously) with Milton's works and actions. Milton's actions in the poem, however, should not be seen as the mere product of Blake's fantasy, for it is Milton himself, in his unique essential individuality, who performs the deeds attributed to his name, with Blake simply arousing Milton and providing the opportunity for him to act. To understand *Milton* is to see the events of the poem in this way. To say that Milton's actions are the product of Blake's imagination and exist only in the poem is an accurate observation but accords inadequate ontological status both to the spiritual events themselves and to the imagination. For the events of the poem do not ultimately originate or unfold in the subjectivity of the poet or of the reader, and the imagination—which allows Milton's essential identity to be present and the events to occur—is not primarily and fundamentally a psychological faculty. Rather, the imagination is first of all that dimension of Being by virtue of which non-actual individuals and particulars affect and are affected by actuality. It is by virtue of this dimension of Being that Milton's unique identity continues after his death, and influences and is itself transformed by survivors such as Blake (at the time the poem was written) and the reader (at the present time). The events and exposition of *Milton* both portray and re-enact this truth.

Fulfillment through Posthumous Presence

Blake begins his elucidation of this point by immediately challenging the Satanic notion of death as annihilation of individual identity. He identifies Milton's resurrection precisely with his going to Eternal Death:

> Then Milton rose up from the heavens of Albion ardorous!
> The whole Assembly wept prophetic, seeing in Miltons face
> And in his lineaments divine the shades of Death & Ulro
> He took off the robe of the promise, & ungirded himself from the
>   oath of God
> And Milton said, I go to Eternal Death!
>
> (14:10-14)

The deleterious effect which the Bard's realizations and Milton's subsequent actions will have on the ultimate values of the present epoch is signalled by the Assembly's prophetic weeping. And those effects are manifested immediately in Milton's actions, as he leaves heaven—the orthodox view of infinity as total positive, immediate existence—and renounces this traditional hope of fulfillment signified by "the robe of the promise" and "the oath of God." This action implies that Milton no longer accepts the view of fulfillment promulgated by Christian doctrine—i.e., fulfillment as immediate, positive existence after death, in union with a higher being. The Bard has revealed to Milton the falseness of this view, by showing that this aspect of one's being is doomed to be forever unfulfilled.

In fact, fulfillment is now to be sought precisely in denouncing such positive existence and going instead to Eternal Death. Milton declares:

> I go to Eternal Death! The Nations still
> Follow after the destable Gods of Priam; in pomp
> Of warlike selfhood, contradicting and blaspheming.
> When will the Resurrection come; to deliver the sleeping body
> From corruptibility: O when Lord Jesus wilt thou come?
> Tarry no longer; for my soul lies at the gates of death.
>
> (14:14-19)

Milton laments the ascendancy of positivism manifested in the fact that nations still organize themselves into warring states with despotic systems of government. This system prevails, it is implied, because the "sleeping body" has not yet been delivered from corruptibility—i.e., because the individual's being is still identified with its immediate actuality (the body), which perishes and is therefore counted as nought. And because the being of the individual is seen as nugatory, all Being is held to reside in the supra-individual categories of nations and Gods, which survive individuals' deaths. The deliverance or resurrection of the sleeping body that Milton longs for will bring an end to the denigration of the individual and to the warfare between nations, which is based on the assumption that individuals have no intrinsic being and that being is a homogeneous commodity of which there is a limited amount that all individuals must vie for. In this state of affairs, Milton says, his "soul lies at the gates of death" (14:19)—his intrinsic being, or true identity, is in danger of actually being destroyed by the system which refuses to recognize intrinsic individual being. For although death by itself cannot destroy this intrinsic being, a false vision of individuality by those who remain alive can do so, by failing to value and take account of the unique, intrinsic being of individuals.

To prevent this total destruction of his being, Milton must alter the fundamental vision of Being held by those who are still alive. He resolves to

> Arise and look forth for the morning of the grave.
> I will go down to the sepulcher to see if morning breaks!
> I will go down to self annihilation and eternal death,
> Lest the Last Judgment come & find me unannihilate
> And I be siez'd & giv'n into the hands of my own Selfhood.
>
> (14:20-24)

Jesus' resurrection and second coming are, of course, strongly alluded to here; yet the preservation and fulfillment that Milton seeks is not identical with salvation as understood in the doctrine of atonement. For Milton expects to find renewal in death itself rather than in escape from death: what he fears is not annihilation and Eternal Death, but rather the *failure to attain* annihilation and Eternal Death. Nor is this death that Milton seeks a temporary state (like Rahab's "Spectre of Sleep") from which one soon returns to life (as the popular Christian version would have it); it is rather complete, total, and final annihilation of ego-consciousness or selfhood—that self-presence which we usually assume to constitute our very being. This false identity must, in Milton's view, be totally destroyed by death before one's true individual being can attain fulfillment. For if this limited, immediate, self-conscious identity were not completely destroyed by death, then one's total being would, in the final analysis (i.e., in "the Last Judgment"), be limited to that same immediate actuality—the self-present Selfhood, or ego-consciousness—which controls and thus limits one's being during life. By virtue of death, however, one's intrinsic being is no longer captive of one's immediate actuality (or more specifically, of one's consciousness); it becomes freed of these restrictions, and as we shall see in Milton's entrance into Blake, is able to be actualized through other individuals.

This, in fact, is the authentic meaning of the crucifixion and resurrection of Jesus: one's true being emerges and becomes actualized only after one's immediate existence is destroyed by death. The prevailing vision of the Christ-event, however, constitutes only a dim, distorted, and partial understanding of its true significance: "The Lamb of God is seen thro' mists & shadows, hovring / Over the sepulchers in clouds of Jehovah & winds of Elohim / A disk of blood," another quantity of being ("disk of blood," or bloody coin) that has reverted to its lender (Jehovah or the Elohim) upon foreclosure, and that serves as a ransom allowing Christians to retain their own lease on being, which they identify with their Selfhood—their life, or immediate actuality. This distortion of Jesus' true nature is a result of the

same feudalistic metaphysics that is embodied in the Old Testament conceptions of God (as Jehovah and the Elohim).

After portraying the falsehood of the orthodox view of death and eternal
life—the view in which death is only a temporary state like a "Spectre of
Sleep" which soon gives way once again to ego-consciousness, or the Selfhood—Blake has Milton ask, "What do I here before the Judgment?" (14:28).
Here Blake is challenging, in a humorous bit of staging, the validity of the
popular view that has placed Milton in heaven after his death—and especially
before the Last Judgment. This popular view has, in effect, relegated Milton's
being to a static realm outside of existence where it no longer has any
influence on actuality. This view separates Milton's being from his emanation, which is the objectified or projected counterpart of his being—i.e.,
those others or objects (actual or imagined), including the products of his
labor, his female companions, and the unactualized situations or objects
which conform to or mirror his unique being, and thus constitute the unique
world in which his unique identity could exist in total fulfillment. Without
these others that correspond to his true being, Milton himself is but a cipher.
It is impossible for his unique individual being to be preserved apart from
these unique individual others that provide the occasion or context for Milton's uniqueness to actualize itself. Therefore the popular notion of heaven, in
which Milton is supposed to dwell in independence from these individuals, is
false, and is based on a failure to recognize the inherently relational nature of
individual identity. Blake signals this falsehood by having the newly aroused
Milton leave this heaven.

This popular view of immortality also errs in having Milton dwelling
"with the daughters of memory, & not with the daughters of inspiration"
(14:29). The daughters of memory are the offspring of what has already
happened, the actual, while the daughters of inspiration are the progeny of
what could, should, and will happen—the possible, which embodies the
fulfillment of the actual. In the popular view of eternal life, Milton's being is
limited to its past existence; after death it is preserved in an eternal, static state
in which no further growth or development is possible. Blake's poem asserts,
however, that the individual's intrinsic being continues to grow and develop
after the individual's death—i.e., that one's true being dwells with the
daughters of inspiration, in possibilities that one automatically cedes to one's
successors rather than merely in memories of the actualities of one's past
existence. In fact it is precisely the posthumous growth of the open-ended
possibilities that constitute Milton's identity which is both the subject and the
origin of the poem *Milton*.

Blake/Milton's new understanding of death and individual being also includes insight into the origin of the false popular vision. Most importantly, Milton realizes that Satan and the feudalistic, *quid pro quo* systems that grow out of him are located in the desiring and devouring ego-consciousness, or Selfhood: "I in my Selfhood am that Satan," he says. "I am that Evil One!" (14:30). Satan, the destroyer of individual being, the predator of uniqueness, is identical with the power which causes every individual to view other individuals as mere holders of quantities of being which it can itself expropriate and assimilate. The entire food chain of nature is dependent upon this power (the Miller of Eternity, as we have seen, has an essential role in the process of Being), and in humans, this power manifests itself in greed, envy, jealousy, and even in pity and love, as the Bard's Song has revealed. Thus all desires for self-enhancement at the expense of another individual are based on the tacit assumption that individual being is transferable and hence extrinsic and homogeneous rather than intrinsic and unique.

This predatory aspect of individuals, however—that aspect which reduces other individuals to quantities of homogeneous being—is not itself the true being of individuals. This Satanic aspect, Milton says, "is my Spectre!" (14:31). Satan is an aspect of every individual—even, perhaps, the most readily apparent aspect—but is a false manifestation or unreal appearance (spectre) of the individual's true being. Satan is thus an essential, necessary part of every individual's life but a perverse and destructive obfuscation of one's true being.

Only through death can one escape the Satan element—this desiring, devouring Selfhood—and it is for this purpose, Milton says, that he embraces death: "in my obedience to loose [my Spectre] from my Hells / To claim the Hells, my Furnaces, I go to Eternal Death" (14:31-2). In embracing Eternal Death, Milton reclaims it from Satan, who in the popular view possesses eternal death as his hell—i.e., as eternal torment. Instead of regions of eternal punishment, however, these "hells" of Eternal Death are actually "Furnaces" which purify and refine's one's true being by destroying the impure and Satanic, grasping and devouring ego-consciousness. Through eternal death this spectrous aspect of one's being is annihilated and one's unique intrinsic individual being can emerge purified and tempered.

This new vision of death and individual being has tremendous repercussions for all of Being, including the transcendental dimension: we are told that "Eternity shudderd at the image of eternal death" (14:35). We were told earlier that the Bard's vision of the Satanic destructiveness of the orthodox view of individual being caused a "shaking [of] the roots & fast foundations of the Earth." Now we are told that Milton/Blake's vision of the true nature of individual being and perishing causes Eternity itself to shake. This vision, that is, carries the seeds of destruction of the popular orthodox vision, and the shuddering is the preliminary indication of the collapse of the orthodox metaphysical structure. What is particularly unsettling to Eternity is the fact that Milton "took the outside course, among the graves of the dead / A mournful shade" (14:34-5). Milton, that is, goes to Eternal Death in the real external world of dead bodies and graves, and stays there forever. Such an image of eternal death—as real, actual, physical death—means, to the orthodox view, total destruction of Milton's being, and to contend that such eternal death is not total annihilation of being is to overturn the orthodox view completely and threaten the metaphysics of presence on which it is based. The popular orthodox view fears death, refusing to accept it as eternal, believing instead in a magical return to life after death. This fear of death, taught by one's spectrous, Satanic ego-consciousness, is what Blake/Milton must overcome, by presenting a new vision in which the notion of Being is reformulated and the principle of individual identity is re-formed.

A New Vision of Immortality

Posthumous Mediated Presence in Actuality

Having rejected the popular notion of immortality, Blake now proceeds to develop more fully his vision of the true nature of immortality as the post-humous, *mediated* presence—rather than the immediate self-presence—in actuality of one's unique individual being. As Milton descends to Eternal Death, he encounters his shadow. As an insubstantial projection of the substantial form of an individual, or its outline of identity, a shadow denotes the mediated or indirect presence of an individual's being: Milton's shadow is the mediated presence of his unique individual being where he himself is not actually in existence. More specifically, his shadow is projected by the works he has written and by influence—conscious or unconscious, direct or indirect—which his being has had. As "a mournful form double; her-maphroditic: male & female / In one wonderful body" (14:37-8), this mediated presence is both agent and patient. As male, or agent, the presence of Milton's unique individual being has a seminal effect on that which it touches; for example, Milton's poetry contains seeds that germinate and grow when they encounter fertile minds. And as female, or patient, Milton's presence is itself in a state of growth, development, and productivity—when Milton's works are penetrated by a seminal spirit such as Blake's. Serving as both host and inhabitant of existing beings, Milton's projected being (his "shadow") itself undergoes transformation as it transforms the existing beings. Thus, rather than being fixed and static, Milton's unique identity continues to live and grow after his death, functioning as both male and female, agent and patient, in relation to existing beings.

Entering into his shadow, Milton, in death, thus gives his being over to non-self-presence, non-immediacy. This transition to non-immediacy—i.e., dying—is extremely difficult and painful, for it means total relinquishment of that which we normally take to be our essential identity: self-consciousness or self-presence. Dying thus appears as entrance into the annihilating depths of hell:

> . . . he enterd into it
> In direful pain for the dread Shadow, twenty-seven fold
> Reachd to the depth of direst Hell, & thence to Albions land:
> Which is this earth of vegetation on which I write.
>
> (14:38-41)

It is through this annihilation, however, that the presence of Milton's being reaches the actual world of our experience ("this earth of vegetation"), where it is free to live and grow apart from the limitations and constraints of Milton's conscious Selfhood or self-presence. The absence of this self-presence is indicated by that fact that the Milton who enters his shadow has no consciousness of what is happening to him, no self-awareness: "As when a man dreams, he reflects not that his body sleeps, / Else he would wake; so seem'd he entering his Shadow" (15:1-2). In death, then, consciousness or self-presence is absent, but one's unique individual being continues in mediated actuality in existing beings.

Eternal Forms and Posthumous Presence

The shadowy posthumous presence of Milton draws its sustenance from its connection with Milton's "Sleeping Body"—i.e., "His real immortal Self," the ideal form of Milton's unique identity: "the Spirits of the Seven Angels of the Presence," who enter Milton's shadow with him, "g[i]ve him still perceptions of his Sleeping Body" (15:3-4)—i.e., of his dormant, unactualized identity. This eternal form of Milton's unique identity, consisting of multiple, open-ended possibilities, still endures, reposing in Eden, the realm of origins or possibility, which persists indirectly through present actuality:

> . . . when he enterd into his Shadow: Himself:
> His real and immortal Self: was as appeard to those

Who dwell in immortality, as One sleeping on a couch
Of gold...

(15:10-13)

Ministers of Presence

This eternal form of Milton's unique identity is itself sustained and validated by various powers which support and produce Presence itself. Blake
portrays these powers or principles as the Seven Angels of the Presence, who
weep over Milton's shadow and whose spirits enter the shadow with Milton.
On the basis of these powers, Milton's immortality is then constituted by
"those / Who dwell in immortality," who "gave forth their Emanations /
Like Females of sweet beauty, to guard round him & to feed / His lips with
food of Eden in his cold and dim repose!" (15:13-15). Those who dwell in
immortality are actual, existing individuals, it seems, who attend to the
unique being of those who are in the "cold and dim repose" of the grave, and
nurture, through their own emanations (thoughts, desires, and actions) the
unique individuality of the dead. The emanations or actualizations of the
existing individuals sustain the bygone beings with "food of Eden," i.e.,
with transformation, which is the sustenance that the ultimate nature of
things (Eden) provides for the dead. Those who dwell thus among the
immortal identities or eternal forms of the dead see them "as One sleeping on
a couch / Of gold," their unique and individual identity preserved forever
beyond the growth and destruction of the vegetating world of immediately
actual existence. The fact that the angels are seven connects them with the
Seven Eyes of God (see 13:17-29), which are constituted by various forms of
belief in posthumous existence, or transcendence. These beliefs make posthumous presence possible by inducing actual individuals to conduct themselves in relation to the dormant eternal forms of bygone individuals, and in
so doing, to actualize these individuals indirectly.

Milton's death, therefore, while it destroys his self-presence, does not
constitute the cessation of his being—a fact which the action of Blake's entire
poem asserts. Milton is simply no longer consciously or self-presently direct-
ing his actions, as he did when he was alive; now "to himself he seemd a
wanderer lost in dreary night,...walking as one walks / In sleep" (15:16,
6-7). In death Milton's being continues, only without the reflection and
self-presence of consciousness—those functions which we normally assume
to constitute our true identity. Or so it would seem. But in another sense
Milton's *self-presence* continues as well, for we are told that "*to himself* he
seemed...," and we saw a moment ago that the Seven Angels, the agents of

posthumous presence, "gave him still perceptions of his Sleeping Body" (15:3-4): insofar as Milton has died, his original self-presence has been annihilated, but insofar as his being now resides in other self-conscious individuals, Milton's being is self-present, only not in its original form as Milton's Selfhood.

Posthumous Presence and Interrelatedness

Milton's shadow, then, is the projected presence of his distant, non-actual being, moving "among the Spectres; call'd / Satan, but swift as lightning passing them" (15:17-18), not being encumbered with the weight of actuality but free to move through infinity. This freedom or participation in infinity consists in the ability to enter into relationships with an indefinite number of other individuals. This ability, in fact, is what constitutes infinity itself, as Blake now explains:

> The nature of infinity is this: That every thing has its
> Own Vortex; and when once a traveller thro' Eternity
> Has passd that Vortex, he percieves it roll backward behind
> His path, into a globe itself infolding; like a sun:
> Or like a moon, or like a universe of starry majesty,
> While he keeps onwards in his wondrous journey on the earth
> Or like a human form a friend with whom he livd benevolent.
> As the eye of man views both the east & west encompassing
> Its vortex; and the north & south, with all their starry host;
> Also the rising sun & setting moon he views surrounding
> His corn-fields and his valleys of five hundred acres square.
> Thus is the earth one infinite plane, and not as apparent
> To the weak traveller confin'd beneath the moony shade.
> Thus is the heaven a vortex passd already, and the earth
> A vortex not yet pass'd by the traveller thro' Eternity.
> (15:21-35)

The image of the vortex indicates that everything that exists is ontologically ultimate, or self-moving: it has its own absolute, intrinsic motion which is dependent only upon itself. Each thing, however, exerts a pull on other individuals that pass within its sphere of influence.[1] In a very enlightening analysis of this passage, W.J.T. Mitchell finds, in effect, that the image of the vortex expresses both the sameness and the otherness of an object, and he discovers four phases of perception articulated in this passage, through which this simultaneous sameness and otherness is recognized. The first phase, seeing the object as a globe, involves "recognition of the object as a world with its own unique laws and form. . . ." The second phase entails "recognition of the object as something that has relations with things outside itself, a transmitter and receiver of light 'like a sun: / Or like a moon.' " Phase three occurs when we see the object "as a 'universe,'. . . a system which contains numerous subworlds within itself," and in phase four we see the object "as a human form, a center of consciousness as complex as the perceiver himself. . . ."[2] This simultaneous sameness and otherness (difference) is crucial: it is only on the basis of the difference or multiplicity of unique vortexes or centers of being that there is infinity, for without them there would be only dimensionless homogeneity—which is the same as nothingness. The nature of infinity, that is, is constituted by the simultaneous difference—i.e., the intrinsic uniqueness—of individual beings, and the sameness or mutual influence which these individuals exert on each other. Moreover, these individuals become what they truly are only after their influence has had its effect on another individual, and vice versa: only after its vortex (influence) is passed/past (i.e., only after its influence has occurred) does the individual assume a definite, individuated form. For one thing's act of affecting another thing is constitutive of the form or identity of the first thing (the agent), as well as the second (the patient). This explains why Milton, through his shadow, must enter the realm of actuality. It is only through actuality that he has a real and definite identity, for an individual's identity is a product of mutual influence: of the effect which the individual has on others, and of the perspective (and hence effect) which others have on the individual.

Lifeless Albion: The Dormancy of Interrelatedness

In actuality, however, this mutual interrelatedness barely exists, as indicated by the fact that instead of a realm of mutual influences, the first thing that Milton's presence encounters when it descends is the lifeless Albion, the dormant and unfulfilled unity of individuals. The fact that Albion lies upon the "Rock of Ages" indicates that the only thing preserving the unity of individuals from total destruction is the fact of substantive endurance, i.e., the rock. For lying on the solid rock, Albion is separated from "the Sea of Time & Space," which "thundered aloud / Against the rock" (15:40), protected from its powerful destructiveness. Yet Albion's separation from the destructive process of time and space is really death itself, for apart from these powerful destructive processes there is no change and hence no transformation and development—i.e., no mutual influence among individuals, and thus no life. Thus the very rock which protects Albion is "inwrapped with the weeds of death" (15:40), for it actually destroys the unity of individuals which is his being. This deadly rock is, moreover, the Rock of Ages, which is another name for the despotic deity of orthodox monotheistic Christianity. Albion's death thus coincides with refuge from destruction, which people seek by counting their own existence as nought and attributing being that is intrinsically their own to a being that is unmoving and unchanging. By reposing on such a deity—i.e., by seeing the being of individuals as homogeneous, one preserves a modicum of unity among individuals, since they are all seen to have ultimately the same being. Yet in reality, as we have seen, such a view destroys the true unity of individuals—the unity of mutual influence, which is also the nature of infinity—by destroying its ontological basis, and by precipitating mutual opposition and destruction.

In his journey to Eternal Death, Milton thus encounters, in the orthodox attempt to avoid death—the destruction of self-presence, which the orthodox perceive to be the annihilation of their being—the consequent destruction of humanity's true being by a more profound and fatal type of death. Encountering Albion in this state, Milton is at first drawn into Albion's perspective, which completely inverts Milton's values:

> Hovering over the cold bosom, in its vortex Milton bent down
> To the bosom of death, what was underneath soon seemd above.
> A cloudy heaven mingled with stormy seas in loudest ruin.
>
> (15:41-3)

The Transformation of Posthumous Presence

It is only by virtue of such a unity—i.e., the mutual interaction of different identities having either immediate or mediated (posthumous) actuality—that Blake has any contact with Milton at all. In fact, Milton's descent into the Sea of Time and Space is identical with Blake's encountering Milton's presence: "Then first I saw him," Blake writes, "in the Zenith as a falling star, / Descending perpendicular, swift as the swallow or swift" (15:47-8). Blake first encounters Milton as a falling star, a majestic individual who has perished but whose light or being continues to shine forth in his posthumous presence, which itself approaches Blake and enters into him, "on [his] left foot falling on the tarsus, enter[ing] there" (15:49).

Upon uniting with Blake, Milton's own being is enhanced, benefiting from Blake's unique vision and being. This enhancement takes place first of all as a purification of the false elements of Milton's being, indicated by the fact that when Milton enters Blake's foot, "from [Blake's] left foot a black cloud redounding spread over Europe" (15:50): as an indefinite and obfuscating form, the cloud embodies that aspect of Milton's existence which obscured his true being and prevented it from actualizing itself in definite form. Milton now sloughs off this aspect by virtue of Blake's rejection of it: it is foreign to Blake's being and cannot enter there, where the rest of Milton's posthumous existence is actualized. This aspect of Milton unfortunately does, however, attain an indirect actualization of its own, in the despotic philosophical, political, and religious systems which spread across Europe like a dark cloud.

United with Blake's vision, Milton's being, in addition to this purification, gains added potential for actualization or fulfillment, realizing only now the significance of his wives and daughters:

> Then Milton knew that the Three Heavens of Beulah were beheld
> By him on earth in his bright pilgrimage of sixty years
> In those three females whom his Wives, & those three whom his Daughters
> Had represented and containd, that they might be resum'd
> By giving up of Selfhood....
>
> (15:51-17:3)

Only now, by virtue of his new habitation in Blake, does Milton realize that his three wives and three daughters provided essential avenues of fulfillment for him—ways of actualizing his true being. The Three Heavens of Beulah, which were associated in the Bard's Song with "Foreheads & ...Bosoms & ...Loins" of the daughters of Albion (5:5-9), embody fulfillment through vision (knowledge, insight), love (including emotion and desire), and sexual passion (physical union) and reproduction. During his life Milton had merely used his wives and daughters without being aware of their importance or metaphysical significance to him. Now, however, through Blake's vision, Milton's being is conjoined with this insight, which opens up new possibilities for Milton's posthumous development—specifically, the possibility of "resuming" his wives and daughters and their three Heavens or modes of fulfillment, by giving up his selfhood (self-presence) and thus transcending his desiring and acquisitive ego. With the death of his former conscious desiring, Milton's being is no longer distracted from its true course and can unite with rather than merely exploit his wives and daughters, for he realizes that his true being, his humanity, occurs not through expropriation of, but rather through mutuality and union with, his wives and daughters:

> ...also Milton knew: they and
> Himself *was* Human, tho' now wandering thro Death's Vale

> In conflict with those Female forms, which in blood & jealousy
> Surrounded him, dividing & uniting without end or number.
>
> (17:5-8, emphasis added)

The use of the singular "was" emphasizes that an individual's being is actualized only through its union with other individuals. It is this union with otherness that constitutes Milton's true being, even though his posthumous presence (like his previous, actual identity) is in conflict with other beings in the world of our existence, where conflict, destruction, and transformation of individuals prevail.

Of course, Milton's wives and daughters are literally dead, as he himself is; but like him, they continue to *be*, even though they no longer exist immediately in actuality, and their being both takes account of and is affected by his being: "they distant view'd his journey / In their eternal spheres, now Human, tho' their Bodies remain clos'd / In the dark Ulro till the Judgment" (17:3-5). Milton and his wives continue to *be*, by virtue of the influence (direct and indirect), which they have on actually existing individuals, like Blake—and, more indirectly, Blake's reader. The significance of reading, in fact, cannot be overestimated, for reading is a primary means by which one incorporates the posthumous presence of a dead individual. As when Blake read Milton, when we read Blake or any other writer, the unique being of the writer makes itself present—and also *self-present*—in our being. Blake's account of immortality thus incorporates the insight which George Poulet was later to express (without pursuing its metaphysical significance) when he observed that since reading introduces alien thoughts into consciousness, and "since every thought must have a subject to think it, this *thought* which is alien to me and yet in me, must also have a *subjectivity* which is alien to me."[3] Thus a thought (or even an unconscious response or adjustment) elicited, directly or indirectly, by another being, establishes a new subject within an individual; and this subject is nothing less than a new form of the other being, which now inhabits and (partially) animates the present individual, and thus continues to exist, to grow, and even to be self-present (through the consciousness of the present individual), even if the original self(hood) from which it came has been annihilated.

Overcoming Feudalistic Metaphysics

The continued growth and self-presence of the posthumously present individual are indicated by the fact that Milton now realizes the errors of his former ways—i.e., "he [sees] the Cruelties of Ulro"—and through Blake's pen,

> ...he [writes] them down
> In iron tablets: and his Wives & Daughters names were these
> Rahab and Tirzah, & Milcah & Malah & Noah & Hoglah.
> That sat rang'd round him as the rocks of Horeb round the land
> Of Canaan: they write in thunder smoke and fire
> His dictate; and his body was the Rock Sinai; that body,
> Which was on earth born to corruption: & the six Females
> Are Hor & Peor & Bashan & Abarim & Lebanon & Hermon
> Seven rocky masses terrible in the Desarts of Midian.
>
> (17:9-17)

The Miltonic presence in Blake sees that Milton's wives and daughters—i.e., his emanations, or the objects corresponding to his intentionality—were Rahab, or destructive false fulfillment, and Zelophehad's five daughters, the self-aggrandizing offspring of a tyrannical patriarch. These objects constituted by his goals, desires, and labors surround him like "the rocks of Horeb," and his body, his own actualized self-present identity, is "the Rock of Sinai." As Sinai, the origin of the Decalogue, Milton is the locus of the divine fiat, the establishment of monotheistic despotism which usurped the being of all individuals, and of all other gods and nations, as well—ontologically through the a priori claims of the Decalogue, and actually through the Israelites' wars of conquest. Milton himself embodied this tyrannous power, and his wives embodied the otherness whose being was usurped, being identified with kingdoms of Hebrew conquest: "Hor & Peor & Bashan & Abarim & Lebanon & Hermon." The "Cruelties of Ulro" which Milton/Blake writes down are the acts of tyrannous suppression in which Milton reduced his wives and daughters to mere extensions of his own will. As Milton said earlier (14:30-31), he is himself Satan, the usurping, despotic power that also manifests itself in Yahweh and his monotheistic system—which, moreover, is the death of Albion, the true unity of individuals.

Milton's presence in Blake now realizes that this "conflict with those Female forms" (17:7) was a perversion of his true, human being, the presence of which ("Milton's *Human* Shadow") now "continu'd journeying above / The rocky masses of The Mundane Shell; in the Lands / Of Edom & Aram & Moab & Midian & Amalek" (17:18-20). These lands were all enemies of Israel whose women tempted the sons of Israel, and Milton's presence in them and above the Mundane Shell would indicate that his true, human being has transcended the limitations of the Hebrew monotheistic metaphysics and is now opposed to that system. Such a system or Mundane Shell is composed of a static reflection or projection—a "hardend shadow" (17:22)—of the world of actual existence. It is a realm of immutable forms and principles which seems to transcend the world of experience, but which actually merely limits this world by reflecting back to it in enlarged and absolutized form the limited categories of this world's own immediate form:

> The Mundane Shell, is a vast Concave Earth: an immense
> Hardend shadow of all things upon our Vegetated Earth
> Enlarg'd into dimension & deform'd into indefinite space,
> In Twenty-seven Heavens and all their Hells; with Chaos
> And Ancient Night; & Purgatory.
>
> (17:21-5)

The Mundane Shell is the realm of metaphysics and religion, and of poems like *Paradise Lost*, which account for (i.e., reflect) every facet of actuality by employing the categories of presence and immediacy in which existents present themselves. Such an account confuses and obscures rather than illuminates the existents which it purports to account for: it constitutes "a cavernous Earth / Of labyrinthine intricacy, twenty-seven folds of opakeness" (17:26-7), reducing individuals to components in a meaningless maze of a mysterious and unclarified substance.

The Mundane Shell has its limits, however: it "finishes where the lark mounts" (17:27)—i.e., where (as we shall see later) the unique intrinsic being of one individual goes forth to encounter that of another. Eternity is not found beyond the limits of the Mundane Shell (the circumference of knowledge or speculation), but beneath the Mundane Shell, before one even comes near to this elevated realm of speculation—i.e., in the concrete being of particular individuals, like the lark. Going outward, away from individuality and into the realm of abstraction, one moves toward the seat of Satan, the principle of abstraction itself, which denies the unique, intrinsic being of concrete individuals: "travellers from Eternity. pass outward to Satan's seat" (17:29). In order to reach Eternity, one must pass inward into the concrete uniqueness of individual being: "travellers to Eternity. pass inward to Golgonooza" (17:30). This is the direction in which Milton must move in order to reach eternity; he must embrace the concrete by entering into Eternal Death and thus allowing his own unique being to be preserved and actualized by other unique individuals.

CHAPTER V

Beyond Presence: Metaphysical Ramifications of Milton's Embrace of Eternal Death

Milton versus Enitharmon: The Repercussions of Posthumous Presence on Actuality

In entering the world of experience, Milton's presence has an effect not only on Blake, but on the fundamental powers and principles, evoking an immediate reaction in them. Whatever else they may be, Milton's posthumous presence and his going to Eternal Death are not without profound impact on fundamental aspects of Being. Thus we are told that Urizen, who in Generation is Satan, "[beholds] the immortal Man [Milton]," as do "Tharmas Demon of the Waters & Orc, who is Luvah" (17:36-18:1). The most immediate impact of Milton's posthumous presence, however, is on Enitharmon, who believes that Milton's presence will free her from her bondage to Los:

> Los the Vehicular terror beheld him, & divine Enitharmon
> Call'd all her daughters, Saying. Surely to unloose my bond
> Is this Man come! Satan shall be unloosd upon Albion.
>
> (17:31-3)

As we have seen, it is to achieve mediated preservation and growth through existing individuals that Milton's posthumous presence has fallen down "into the Sea of Time & Space" (15:46), entering actuality and moving inward toward the concreteness of unique individuality—and thus toward Eternity. Enitharmon assumes, however, that such posthumous presence is identical to a static, enduring actuality. Enitharmon, who embodies space and its pure immediacy and actuality, assumes that Milton's purpose in entering actuality is to "unloose" her bond and free Satan. Her bond—that which limits her and restricts her—is the continuous flux of actuality, which destroys something as soon as it is created and thus limits actuality to the immediate present. Her hope to be free of this bond (which is the doing of Los, the principle of change itself) derives from her assumption that the

91

posthumous presence of Milton—who as the author of *Paradise Lost* is the champion of a metaphysics of presence and permanence—signals the instantiation of an eternity based on endurance and permanence: pure, absolute space without time. Such a reality, removing the restrictions on Enitharmon, would also leave Albion prey to Satan: the unity of individuals through mutual interaction would be destroyed by the principle of homogenization and reduction. Pure space without time—i.e., absolute immediacy, actuality, and fulfillment—would destroy the unity of individuals because it is the inherent incompleteness of individuals that constitutes the basis for their unity with each other, by motivating the mutual interaction which is their unity. A static, fully actualized individual is a self-contradictory concept, and the full actualization or presence which Enitharmon and Satan desire is thus equivalent to nothingness.

Los is thus understandably terrified at Enitharmon's words, which if true, would signal his own demise and that of Being itself. To avoid this disaster, Los attempts to stop the entrance of Milton's posthumous presence into actuality: "in fibrous strength / His limbs shot forth like roots of trees against the forward path / Of Miltons journey" (17:34-6). Los firmly enroots himself, anchoring the process of time in, and drawing sustenance from, the ground of past actuality. This enrooting of process and transformation in the past impedes Milton's progress, making it difficult for him to enter time and space—difficult, that is, to insert his own shadowy being into the actualizing process and have an effect on it.

Milton versus the Shadowy Female:
Nature against Individual Desire

The entrance of Milton's posthumous presence into actuality also evokes a reaction from "the Shadowy Female [who] seeing Milton, howl'd in her lamentation / Over the Deeps outstretching her Twenty seven Heavens over Albion" (18:2-3). As the possessor or controller of the twenty-seven heavens—the "twenty-seven folds of opakeness" which constitute the Mundane Shell (17:26)—the Shadowy Female is an instance of Satanic opacity or obfuscation of the internal light (the unique intrinsic being) of individuals. More specifically, she is the vague, obscure power of generation and reproduction—hence, productivity. In her embodiments as the Great Mother or the goddess of Nature, she is credited with producing all individuals, who are thus seen as derivative and subordinate to nature. The Female's lamentation and attempt to counter the entrance of Milton's posthumous presence expresses the threat which such posthumous presence presents to concepts like the Great Mother or Mother Nature. For once the fact of this posthumous presence is recognized, the recognition of the intrinsicness and uniqueness of individual being is close behind: the persisting, posthumous presence of individuals indicates that individual being is not merely a function of its immediate actuality and thus contingent, but is rather self-contained, irreplaceable, and irreducible. Moreover, the posthumous efficacy of this unique individuality further reduces the degree of power that can be attributed to some vague, shadowy, general principle of growth or production, for such transformation is now seen to be the result of the mutual influence of posthumous and actual individuals, rather than of some abstract or general power.

Even more threatening than the fact of posthumous presence, however, is the effect which its reality has on individuals, freeing them from the fear of death and even encouraging self-sacrifice. Such valorization of self-sacrifice completely undercuts the status of the Shadowy Female, which is based on her supposed power to create and destroy individuals. For if individuals now see their own perishing as intrinsic, necessary, and thus desirable, and if they furthermore realize that such perishing is ultimately a creative transformation of their own being and that of the other individuals which they influence, the very being of the Shadowy Female will vanish. No longer will some abstract and general Mother Nature be seen as the origin and goal of individual existence.

The actuality of posthumous presence and the valorization of self-sacrifice embodied in Milton are thus opposed by the Shadowy Female. This opposition is constituted by the simultaneous cruelty and generosity of nature. The Female hopes to make Milton's posthumous presence subordinate to her by "lament[ing] over Milton in the lamentations of the afflicted" (18:5), seeming to show concern for the pain and frustration of individuals so that she will be perceived as a beneficent guardian of individual being and not as the cruel usurper she is. She declares, "I will put on the Human Form & take the Image of God / Even pity & Humanity but my Clothing shall be Cruelty" (18:19-20). Since nature in her immediacy or actuality is cruel and uncaring to the individuals which she supposedly nurtures, some see this cruelty as Nature's true being. The Shadowy Female, however, makes this cruelty seem a mere cover, a garment, while underneath she puts on a Human Form of pity and love that is then perceived as her true being. Her cruelty—the affliction of individual beings—then serves to adorn and ornament this Human Form, providing the occasion for her supposed pity/love to manifest itself to greatest advantage. The greater the affliction of individuals, the more will be appreciated any lack of affliction, and this absence of hardship and oppression will be attributed to the loving care of the Shadowy Female, thus according more power and being to her. In this way the Shadowy Female hopes to get Milton to "come into [her] tents" (18:18) —i.e., to enter her sphere of dominion and submit to her values, worshipping the general powers of nature to the degradation of individual being.

The Shadowy Female's adorning herself with human affliction is thus designed to reduce the power of individuals, as she tells Orc:

> ...I will put on Holiness as a breastplate & as a helmet
> And all my ornaments shall be of the gold of broken hearts
> And the precious stones of anxiety & care & desperation & death
> And repentance for sin & sorrow & punishment & fear
> To defend me from thy terrors O Orc! my only beloved!
>
> (18:21-5)

The appearance of holiness or supremacy which she manages to create for herself serves to protect her from the power of Orc, "who is Luvah" (18:1). As desire, Orc normally approaches nature as an object to satisfy him rather than as an ultimate power and repository of being. But when nature appears to be holy, desire, the actualizing impetus of individuals, is made subservient to its object and is thus deprived ontologically if its intrinsic being and literally of its self-assurance and thus also of its efficacy.

The Shadowy Female's assumption of the Human Form therefore terrifies Orc, who beseeches, "Take not the Human Form O loveliest. Take not / Terror upon thee! Behold how I am & tremble lest thou also / Consume in my Consummation" (18:26-8). When nature attempts to withdraw into unapproachable sanctity, desire reacts in violent self-defense. "When thou attemptest to put on the Human Form," Orc says, "my wrath / Burns to the top of heaven against thee in Jealousy & Fear. / Then I rend thee asunder" (18:31-3). Orc asks why nature must prey on individuals by "creat[ing] and weav[ing] this Satan for a Covering" (18:30) —i.e., by creating an actuality of suffering and affliction for individuals. Why, he asks, cannot the actualities of the physical world satisfy desire rather than frustrate it:

> When wilt thou put on the Female Form as in times of old
> With a Garment of Pity & Compassion like the Garment of God
> His garments are long sufferings for the Children of Men
> Jerusalem is his Garment & not thy Covering Cherub O lovely
> Shadow of my delight who wanderest seeking for thy prey.
>
> (18:34-8)

Why, Orc asks, is nature not pitying and compassionate in actuality, fulfilling individuals as God in eternity does in Jerusalem? Why is desire

frustrated; why is there affliction and suffering? This question, which constitutes the fundamental impetus behind Blake's earlier poetry, motivates the
metaphysical analyses of the present poem as well.

Orc, or desire, thus has an ambivalent attitude toward nature: on the one
hand, he is drawn toward her by her potential to fulfill him, but on the other
hand he is repelled by her actual frustration of attempted fulfillment. Nature,
then, embodies both fulfillment and captivity—it is both Jerusalem and Babylon. And it uses its potential fulfillment (Jerusalem) to lure desire into
captivity (Babylon). This ambiguity of nature is expressed as the seductive
union of Oothoon (the principle of individual fulfillment) and Leutha (the
principle of expropriative self-aggrandizement):

> So spoke Orc when Oothoon & Leutha hoverd over his Couch
> Of fire in interchange of Beauty & Perfection in the darkness
> Opening interiorly into Jerusalem & Babylon shining glorious
> In the Shadowy Females bosom.
>
> (18:39-42)

This unity in Nature of true fulfillment and captivity creates an enormous
conflict between nature and desire. Nature jealously guards her being from
consumption by desire, and accuses desire of transgression when it attempts
to expropriate nature for its own fulfillment:

> Jealous her darkness grew:
> Howlings filld all the desolate places in accusations of Sin
> In Female beauty shining in the unformd void & Orc in vain
> Stretch'd out his hands of fire, & wooed: they triumph in his pain.
>
> (18:42-5)

Nature and her powers triumph in the pain of frustrated desire, "in the
lamentations of the afflicted" (18:5), which demonstrates a literal ascendancy
of the generative force over individual beings and thus argues for the ontological supremacy of that force. The more recalcitrant Nature becomes, however, the hotter desire burns:

> Thus darkend the Shadowy Female tenfold & Orc tenfold
> Glowd on his rocky Couch against the darkness: loud thunders
> Told of the enormous conflict[.] Earthquake beneath: around;
> Rent the Immortal Females, limb from limb & joint from joint
> And moved the fast foundations of the Earth to wake the Dead.
>
> (18:46-50)

Not fulfilled by Nature's actual state, which instead causes affliction and
suffering, desire dismembers Nature's body, or actual state, both in revenge

and in order to reconstitute nature to fulfill desire. This is labor: the destruction and transformation of nature to make it accord with desire. And from a slightly different perspective, this dismemberment of nature is the process of individuation itself, which is the ground and cause of all desire: nature is the jealous, undifferentiated reservoir of homogeneous being out of which individual desire must draw fulfillment and thus actualize the being of the individual.

Milton versus Urizen: Eternal Death and the Re-Formation of Identity

The relation between nature and individual desire is thus thrown into question by Milton's embrace of Eternal Death: the Shadowy Female attempts to reassert her supremacy in the face of the double threat which Milton represents, and desire then redoubles its efforts, revealing the dismemberment or individuation of nature as the ground of desire. At this very instant, the principle of individuation itself emerges into view: "Urizen emerged from his Rocky Form & from his Snows" (18:51). Urizen, as the bounding or limiting principle (his name is perhaps derived from the Greek *ourizein*, to bound or limit) which seeks to establish "a solid without fluctuation" (*The Book of Urizen*, 4:4), is the principle of differentiation or individuation, the power of persistance and sameness—resistance to change—that establishes and preserves individual identities. As such, he, like Los and the Shadowy Female, is also threatened by Milton's descent to Eternal Death, for Milton's act of ultimate self-sacrifice is, it would appear, in direct opposition to Urizen's preservation and consolidation of individual existence. The very nature of the principle of identity thus further impedes Milton's progress toward Eternal Death, with Urizen

> ...freezing dark rocks between
> The footsteps. and infixing deep the feet in marble beds:
> That Milton labourd with his journey, & his feet bled sore
> Upon the clay now changd to marble.
>
> (19:1-4)

Self-sacrifice is thus opposed by self-preservation, the freezing, ossifying, perpetuating power of Urizen. This struggle is both an interior, psychological struggle within Milton's presence (within Blake) and a cosmic event that implicates all things. Furthermore, the two regions are connected, and the events of the microcosm affect those of the macrocosm: Milton, through going to Eternal Death, is re-creating the nature of individual being and marking a new path toward fulfillment which other individuals can follow. His going to Eternal Death, in fact, constitutes nothing less than a re-forming of the very principle of individual identity. This fact is clarified in the description of the conflict between Milton and Urizen:

> Silent they met, and silent strove among the streams, of Arnon
> Even to Mahanaim, when with cold hand Urizen stoop'd down
> And took up water from the river Jordan: pouring on
> To Miltons brain the icy fluid from his broad cold palm.
> But Milton took of the red clay of Succoth, moulding it with care
> Between his palms; and filling up the furrows of many years
> Beginning at the feet of Urizen, and on the bones
> Creating new flesh on the Demon cold, and building him,
> As with new clay a Human form in the Valley of Beth Peor.
>
> (19:6-14)

Although neither posthumous presence (Milton) nor general principle (Demon) acknowledges (or even really apprehends, perhaps) the presence of the other, individual (posthumous) identity and general principle nonetheless have an effect on each other. Urizen attempts to baptize Milton—to give him a rigid identity subject to a higher being, preserving Milton's existence by freezing him into a static, continuously present actuality. Milton, on the other hand, tries to re-form the individuating power and create a new mode of individual being—a new Adam formed from the "red clay" (the literal meaning of "Adam"). Through self-sacrifice, Milton gives individual being a new meaning, a Human form, in which the being of an individual is no longer contingent upon its resistance to destruction but is rather intrinsic, a function of its love and pity—i.e., a function of its contribution to other individual beings, through union with them. Individuation and the fulfillment of individual being can in the future take this new path of self-sacrifice—the path of change and transformation which ultimately leads to becoming other in death, at which point one's being resides in what one has donated to others through all the effects, direct and indirect, which one's unique identify has had and continues to have in other beings.

The creation of this new being is identified with the supersession or burial of the old being by the fact that the new being is created "in the Valley of Beth Peor," the burial place of Moses, who was instrumental in creating the old being that existed as a vassal to Yahweh and his feudalistic metaphysical system. In fact, Milton's act of covering Urizen with clay is literally a burial of sorts at the same time that it creates a new form for individual being. Milton's purpose however, is not to bury but to regenerate Urizen, and this act in itself epitomizes the nature of the new being he is creating, whose means of fulfillment is through the enhancement of what is other than one's own immediate actual being. This mode of being is the direct opposite of that of the old Urizen, who opposes what is other and tries to destroy it to enhance his own being. As Rahab and Tirzah note several lines later, the modes of intercourse of Milton and Urizen are diametrically opposed, "one [Milton] giving life, the other [Urizen] giving death / To his adversary" (19:29-30).[1] Similarly, the new, Human form of individuation through self-sacrifice is life-giving, while the old Urizenic form, as we have seen, ultimately yields death of individual being, with Urizen becoming Satan as the force of self-preservation becomes the power that destroys other individuals.[2]

Milton versus the Fallen Zoas: Posthumous Presence and the Grounds of Being

If the embrace of Eternal Death can re-form the very principle of identity, then its ramifications are literally cosmic. At this point in the poem, Blake indicates the significance which Milton's going to Eternal Death has for the entire cosmos, or the fundamental dimensions of Being, which are described as follows:

> Four Universes round the Mundane Egg remain Chaotic
> One to the North, named Urthona: One to the South, named
>   Urizen:
> One to the East, named Luvah: One to the West, named Tharmas
> They are the Four Zoa's that stood around the Throne Divine!
> But when Luvah assum'd the World of Urizen to the South:
> And Albion was slain upon his mountans, & in his tent:
> All fell towards the Center in dire ruin, sinking down.
> And in the South remains a burning fire; in the East a void.
> In the West, a world of raging waters; in the North a solid,
> Unfathomable! without end. But in the midst of these,
> Is built eternally the Universe of Los and Enitharmon:
> Towards which Milton went, but Urizen oppos'd his path.
>
> (19:15-26)

The Mundane Egg is enclosed by the Mundane Shell—which, we have seen, "is a vast Concave Earth" (17:21), a metaphysical system—which reflects the world of actuality. We now learn that there are four universes around the Mundane Shell, which "are the Four Zoa's that stood around the Throne Divine." These four would constitute the regions, dimensions, or modes of Being that surround and support actuality (the world of existence) and guard and minister to Being itself ("the Throne Divine"). These dimensions of Being, however, are in a chaotic state—they do not have their orderly and proper relation to one another, since all of them have fallen toward the center, losing their differentiation and diversification and moving toward homogeneity. This transcendental disorder was precipitated, we are told, "when Luvah assum'd the World of Urizen to the South: / And Albion was slain upon his mountains, & in his tent." We saw earlier that the slaying of Albion is the destruction of the intrinsic, authentic unity of individuals. We now see that this destruction of the unity of individuals—this death of Albion—involves an improper relation between Luvah and Urizen, which we have identified, respectively, as the powers of love (union and self-sacrifice) and of differentiation or individuation (and hence separation and opposition). The collapse of the four modes of Being and the death of Albion, that is, occur when Luvah, the power of union, "assum[es] the World of Urizen to the South"—i.e., when the power of union takes for granted, and/or moves into the territory of, the power of separation, an event which is very similar to Satan's usurpation of Palamabron's role. This movement constitutes, in the first place, Luvah's abandonment of his own position, leaving a void which signifies an absence of authentic love, the power that respects, preserves, and enhances the sanctity of other individuals while embracing them in union. In addition, the fact that Luvah's movement is into the territory of Urizen indicates either that love has become subservient to the realm of individuation—being used, as in Satan's actions, to destroy other individuals through seduction and assimilation of their being—or that the power of union has usurped the power of differentiation, with all individuals losing their unique and intrinsic being and being reduced to a homogeneous quantity. Both perspectives point to the same end result: the destruction of individual being.

The lesson of this account is clear: the powers of union and separation must maintain a delicate and complex equilibrium, otherwise all will fall "towards the center in dire ruin, sinking down" into the nothingness of non-differentiation. With this dynamic equilibrium no longer intact among the four powers of Being, the absolute modes of Being which surround the actual world become negative and destructive. In the South, which Luvah invaded, there "remains a burning fire": the unifying impulse of desire, together with the force of self-preservation, unites everything by consuming it. In the East, which Luvah vacated, there is a void—pure nothingness—the absolutization of a lack which is at the heart of all love and desire and which motivates the movement toward otherness. In the West, inhabited by "Tharmas Demon of the Waters" (18:1), is "a world of raging waters," the

nothingness of undifferentiated flux or process, while in the North is the
nothingness of undifferentiated stasis or substance, "a solid, / Unfathomable! without end." Apart from its proper relationship to the others, each of
these powers or regions of Being is nothingness, non-being. Actuality occurs
only when these forces or principles are brought together in some form of
dynamic equilibrium. This is precisely the task of Los and Enitharmon, who
build their universe, the world of time and space—actuality—"in the midst of
these" four absolute universes. And it is this universe, we are reminded,
"toward which Milton went" (19:26). Milton's embrace of Eternal Death,
that is, is also a movement toward the equilibrium of the four powers, for
through his self-sacrifice he re-establishes authentic love (union, sameness)
and individuation (separation, difference) in their proper relation. But his
attempt to attain such equilibrium, we have seen, is hindered by various
powers and principles in service to pure presence: by Enitharmon, Los (to a
degree), and the Shadowy Female—and most importantly, by Urizen, the
present form of the principle of identity or differentiation and also, we shall
now see, by Rahab and Tirzah, the inauthentic and spurious forms of union
with otherness.

Milton versus Rahab and Tirzah: Posthumous Presence versus Immediate Fulfillment

Milton's going to Eternal Death challenges, as we have seen, the fundamental assumption that an individual's being is constituted by its immediate
actuality. Contrary to the usual view, Milton's action asserts that an individual's being is constituted by its mediated or indirect actuality that is a
product of the individual's effect on other beings. If Milton's vision is
adopted, then individuals will live for this ultimate fulfillment rather than for
immediate satisfaction of gratuitous desires. Because of this fact, Rahab and
Tirzah, false fulfillment and superficial pleasure, "trembled to behold / The
enormous strife" (19:28-9) between Milton and Urizen, for the defeat or
re-formation of Urizen would mean their downfall as well. This opposition
between ultimate fulfillment and immediate satisfaction—an opposition
implicit in the very definition of temptation—is presented here as Rahab and
Tirzah's attempt to entice Milton across the river:

> . . . they sent forth all their sons & daughters
> In all their beauty to entice Milton across the river,
> The Twofold form Hermaphroditic: and the Double-sexed;
> The Female-male & the Male-female, self-dividing stood

> Before him in their beauty, & in cruelties of holiness!
> Shining in darkness, glorious upon the deeps of Entuthon.
>
> (19:30-35)

Rahab and Tirzah offer Milton the opportunity to be complete unto himself: as hermaphroditic forms, their offspring are completely self-sufficient, relying on nothing outside themselves for fulfillment. Rahab and Tirzah, false fulfillment and superficial pleasure, offer Milton a similar wholeness, in which he expropriates all objects of his desire and makes them mere appendages of his own being that can immediately satisfy his every whim. This strategy is based on the "cruelties of holiness"—on the destruction of other beings which results when one accords holiness, or privileged value and being, to one's own individuality. The course is directly opposite to the route of self-sacrifice which Milton has chosen: it is the route of other-sacrifice, of the consolidation of power within oneself. Rahab and Tirzah's enticement is identical with the Urizenic urge, except that here that urge is presented from the inverse perspective, as a temptation rather than an opposition: rather than trying, like Urizen, to impede Milton's progress to self-sacrifice, Rahab and Tirzah try to lure Milton in the opposite direction from self-sacrifice.

The power of Tirzah, or pleasure, derives from the deficiency of actual existence, which individuals attempt to overcome in immediacy rather than in mediation, embracing pleasure as the solution to their finitude:

> Because Ahania rent apart into a desolate night,
> Laments! & Enion wanders like a weeping articulate voice
> And Vala labours for her bread & water among the Furnaces
> Therefore bright Tirzah triumphs: putting on all beauty.
> And all perfection, in her cruel sports among the Victims.
>
> (19:41-5)

Tirzah offers immediate gratification, but at the expense of ultimate fulfillment, or Jerusalem, which is fulfillment through the mutual enhancement and unity of all individuals which is Albion. To embrace immediate gratification at the expense of other individuals is to destroy Albion, or, in the terms of the present exposition, to offer Jerusalem—true fulfillment in mutuality—up to holiness, or cruelty and exclusivity. "Come bring with thee Jerusalem," Rahab and Tirzah call to Milton. "In Natural Religion! in experiments on Men, / Let her be Offered up to Holiness!" (19:46-7). Such an act assumes that individuals are mere quantities of homogeneous being, which can be transferred to another individual, thus destroying the inherent being of individuals and making them subservient to this ultimate being, or Holiness.

This is the vision of Natural Religion, to which Rahab and Tirzah want Milton to sacrifice Jerusalem, the contrary vision in which the unique intrinsic being of individuals is primary and individuals mutually constitute and enhance each other.

The position of Rahab and Tirzah is positivistic to the core. It assumes that only the immediately present things have being, and that if something cannot be apprehended in actuality—i.e., measured and quantified—it is not real. Thus "Tirzah numbers [Jerusalem]" (19:48), trying to take account of Jerusalem's being as though it were merely a quantity of homogeneous substance. Intrinsic uniqueness is not noticed at all. Nor is possibility or potential counted as part of being: Tirzah "numbers with her fingers every fibre *ere it grow*" (19:49, emphasis added), not making even quantitative adjustments for the additional being which growth will bring. Taking account only of what is immediate, this view asks, "Where is the Lamb of God? where is the promise of his coming?" (19:40). Since the Lamb and the promise are not present in immediacy, but rather in the future and the past, respectively— and, moreover, are never immediately and positively present as such—Tirzah (immediate pleasure) accords them no being.

This view, in discounting the implicit dimension of things, including possibility or potential (which by its very nature is not immediately present), stymies growth and ossifies being: Tirzah's "shadowy Sisters form the bones, even the bones of Horeb: / Around the marrow! and the orbed scull around the brain!" (19:51-2). From the positivist perspective, the being of individuals is limited to their present actuality, in addition to being reduced to an extrinsic homogeneous quantity, and as a result the fulfillment attained in self-sacrifice is completely incomprehensible to positivism. Thus in Rahab's eyes, the image of the Lamb of God promotes war and sacrifice to Tirzah (and it actually does so, we have seen, when linked with a positivist metaphysics), for the fate of the Lamb reminds individuals of the extrinsicness and vulnerability of their own being and thus incites them to war against other individuals in order to preserve their own immediate, self-present actuality. "His images are born for war!" Rahab says, "for sacrifice to Tirzah! To Natural Religion! to Tirzah the Daughter of Rahab the Holy!" (19:53-4). The death of Jesus is seen by Rahab, through the perspective of the doctrine of atonement, as the exchange of one individual's immediate, positive being for that of another individual. Jesus' vulnerability and the supposed substitutability of his being are thus taken as proof that individuals are intrinsically nought, that all being is homogeneous, and that therefore the only fulfillment possible for individuals is in pleasure—i.e., immediate, positive existence—which is thus the offspring of the positivist feudalistic metaphysics: "Tirzah the Daughter of Rahab the Holy" (19:54).

Tirzah, like her progenitor Holiness, elevates one aspect of Being above the others, locating true being in it and making other aspects secondary, epiphenomenal: as pleasure, she invests immediacy with ultimate value. And as the principle that valorizes immediacy, Tirzah is also the more general localizing, specializing, or differentiating power that is virtually identical with an aspect of Urizen, or the power of individuation, for "she ties the knot of nervous fibres, into a white brain! / She ties the knot of bloody veins, into a red hot heart!" (19:55-6). This principle of concentration is an offspring of the principle of holiness, which limits and consolidates Being within a certain region; in the case of Tirzah and Urizen it is simply a quality rather than Being itself which is consolidated in a particular region. The principles of holiness and pleasure are, therefore, as we have already seen, closely related to the power of individuation—i.e., existence itself—and can be viewed as a distortion or disequilibrium of that principle rather than as totally independent powers. This distortion occurs when the unique intrinsic being of individuals is ignored, which simultaneously allows differentiation to become the mere quantitative difference of superiority/inferiority, and individuation to become the warfare of self-preservation.

The immediatizing and localizing function of Tirzah thus also has at its heart (i.e., as both its cause and its effect) the destruction of the intrinsic unity of individuals: "Within her bosom Albion lies embalmed, never to awake" (19:57). Tirzah, that is, is responsible for the limited, positivist perception of reality, forcing individuals to think only within their brains, to love and desire only with their hearts, and to have intercourse only with their genitals. And this fragmentation of individual being both causes and results from loss of the intrinsic unity of individuals. For the three centers of individuals' activity, Rahab says, "are our Three Heavens beneath the shades of Beulah, land of rest!" (20:2). Now we have seen these regions to be the three modes of unity available to fragmented individuals: intellectual, emotional, and sexual union with otherness. These three modes, however, are claimed by Rahab as three "Heavens"—three means of pleasure or self-gratification—and she tries to entice Milton to embrace them as such rather than as three modes of the ultimate fulfillment he seeks, offering him, as Satan did Christ, possession of the entire realm of actuality:

> Come then to Ephraim & Manasseh O beloved-one!
> Come to my ivory palaces O beloved of thy mother!

> And let us bind thee in the bands of War & be thou King
> Of Canaan and reign in Hazor where the Twelve Tribes meet.
>
> (20:3-6)

Milton has realized, however, from the Bard's Song, that fulfillment is ultimately impossible within the realm of immediate presence, for every individual must eventually perish and lose its immediate actuality forever. The only permanence possible, then, must be mediated permanence—a permanence of indirect actualization through incorporation of one's own uniqueness into the unique, intrinsic being of other actual individuals. Milton's route to fulfillment therefore requires re-formation of individual being, a re-creation of the principle of individuation so that it works through authentic love and pity, thus preserving its work, rather than through envy and opposition, which destroy the very intrinsic being that individuation creates.

Hence Milton ignores the temptations of Rahab's proferred fulfillments of immediacy, and concentrates instead on providing for a transcendence of immediacy:

> Silent Milton stood before
> The *darkend* Urizen; as the sculptor silent stands before
> His forming image; he walks round it patient labouring.
> Thus Milton stood forming *bright* Urizen....
>
> (20:7-10; emphasis added)

The present Urizen is "darkened": he has no internal light, indicating that individuality in its old Urizenic form is devoid of intrinsic being. The new Urizen that Milton is creating, however, is "bright," signifying that Milton's labor is restoring intrinsic being to individuality.

We are reminded once again that it is Milton's posthumous presence which is performing this labor, and not the actual living Milton, which is long dead ("his Mortal part / Sat frozen in the rock of Horeb," 20:10-11). This posthumous presence of Milton is called his "Redeemed portion" (20:11), since it is the part of his being which is achieving its authentic actualization—as indirect actualization through other individuals. We are told, in addition, that within this Redeemed portion, "his real Human walked above in power and majesty / Tho darkend; and the Seven Angels of the Presence attended him" (20:13-14). This "real Human" portion, as we have seen, is the not yet fully actualized (therefore "darkend") ideal form of Milton which, if actualized, would constitute complete fulfillment of Milton's being. Though this part of Milton is not actualized even indirectly, it nonetheless continues to *be*, as the open-ended possibility inherent in and motivating the Redeemed portion, which is being actualized indirectly, through Blake and others.

The New Form of Individuality

The Spectrous Vision of Individual Identity

Having analyzed the various forms of inauthentic and ultimately unfulfilling existence, Blake is now prepared to portray a fulfilling form—a form in which individuals achieve liberation, or infinity. But such a portrait, since it must focus on the non-actual, non-immediate aspects of Being, is exceedingly difficult to produce, since language is fixated on actuality and presence. "O how," Blake agonizes, "can I with my gross tongue that cleaveth to the dust, / Tell of the Four-fold Man, in starry numbers fitly orderd / Or how can I with my cold hand of clay!" (20:15-17). The "cold hand of clay" suggests an association with Urizen, whom Milton is still in the process of re-forming, and may indicate that the poet himself has not yet been completely transformed by Milton's re-formation of identity. The comment which the poet makes immediately afterwards reinforces this possibility: "But thou O Lord / Do with me as thou wilt! for I am nothing, and vanity" (20:17-18). This declaration may indicate that the poet himself has not yet been fully liberated by Milton's action, and that he is still unknowingly caught up in the Satanic perspective on individual being, which assumes that the individual is essentially nothing.

On the other hand—or in addition—it is possible that the poet is here making not a metaphysical pronouncement but rather an admission of his existential condition, acknowledging the powerlessness of his own will—as when, for example, it confronts the intractability of language. The possibility that he is proclaiming the nothingness of his ego-consciousness or self-present actuality—his "I" or spectrous form and not his intrinsic being—is reinforced by the rest of his statement:

> If thou chuse to elect a worm, it shall remove the mountains.
> For that portion namd the Elect: the Spectrous body of Milton:
> Redounding from my left foot into Los's Mundane space,
> Brooded over his Body in Horeb against the Resurrection
> Preparing it for the Great Consummation; red the Cherub on Sinai
> Glow'd; but in terrors folded round his clouds of blood.
>
> (20:19-24)

Milton's Spectrous body—the manifestation of his inauthentic being, in his action and his conscious beliefs and values — is here seen to act in opposition to Milton's true being. This inauthentic part of Milton, which is not able to enter Blake along with the authentic part, is the desire for immediacy, which is portrayed as brooding over Milton's dead body, waiting for it to return to life. This expectation, which derives from the valorization of immediate presence, espouses a false view of resurrection and eternal life and actually inhibits the real resurrection, which occurs in the posthumous indirect actualization of Milton's authentic being. This conscious spectrous part of Milton continues to be present in the form of the general belief in a material resurrection, even though Milton's personal consciousness or self-presence has perished. This spectrous being, moreover, is allied with the feudalistic system of Yaweh's Decalogue, appearing as a glowing red Cherub on Sinai: the hope for a material resurrection assumes that individual being is homogeneous, transferable, and under control of a central power. Milton's spectrous being, however, is not completely secure in its illusion, for it "in terrors" tries to protect itself with "clouds of blood," the obscurities and obfuscations of its views of life and death. This insecurity is the result of Milton's descent and of the new principle of identity which his self-sacrifice creates. The emergence of this new being is also expressed as the awakening of Albion, and we are told that "now Albion's sleeping Humanity began to turn upon his couch; / Feeling the electric flame of Miltons awful precipitate descent" (20:25-6).

The new form of individual being appears imminent, then, but it has not yet been established. It is from within this transition state that the poet is speaking: because this new being is partially formed, the poet is able to apprehend it and speak about it, but because it is not yet fully formed, the apprehending and speaking are partial and deficient. Nonetheless, Blake proceeds to sketch the outlines of this new form of being.

The New Form of Individual Identity

The purpose of *Milton* is to promote the actualization of a more fulfilling form of individual being by engendering the vision and the affects necessary to nurture that being. Blake now gives us, in a beautiful lyric passage, an example of the vision of this new form of being; he asks, "Seest thou the little winged fly, smaller than a grain of sand? / It has a heart like thee; a brain open to heaven and hell, / Withinside wondrous & expansive..." (20:27-9). Even the tiniest individual has its own intrinsic being — its own urges and pur- poses, its particular type of awareness or way of taking other things into account. Within this minute being there is a magnificence and grandeur that belies the limitations apparent in its exterior dimensions. Yet despite the fact that its being lies within itself, the individual is not monadic and self-enclosed: "its gates are not clos'd," Blake says; "I hope thine are not: hence it clothes itself in rich array; / Hence thou art cloth'd with human beauty O thou mortal man" (20:29-31). Although its being is intrinsic, the individual manifests and actualizes (i.e., "clothes") itself through interaction with other individuals. Without such intercourse with others, the individual's intrinsic being is dormant, unrealized. Yet despite the fact that its clothes derive from outside, from otherness, it clothes itself: the origin of its actualizing process is internal.

One's being, therefore, lies within oneself and not in some external source. "Seek not thy heavenly father then beyond the skies," Blake says. "There Chaos dwells & ancient Night & Og & Anak old" (20:32-3). The progenitor of an individual is intrinsic to the individual itself, no matter what other external actuality may be causally implicated in the individual's genesis. The answer to all questions of origin and purpose, of meaning and value, must be found within the individual being. Individuals are ends and beginnings as well as means, and apart from individuals there is no order or being—only "Chaos" and "ancient Night": disorder, purposelessness, destruction, non-being.

There is but a fine line between being intrinsic or self-contained, on the one hand, and being self-enclosed and isolated, on the other. And there is only a subtle distinction between being open to otherness and being at the mercy of another. The fulfilling form of individual being is self-contained without being closed off from otherness, and is open to otherness without being either victimized by it or imperialistic toward it. This equilibrium of individuality is expressed through the image of an enclosing wall with gates in it:

> For every human heart has gates of brass & bars of adamant,
> Which few dare unbar because dread Og & Anak guard the gates
> Terrific! and each mortal brain is walld and moated round
> Within: and Og & Anak watch here; here is the Seat
> Of Satan in its Webs; for in brain and heart and loins
> Gates open behind Satans Seat to the City of Golgonooza
> Which is the spiritual fourfold London, in the loins of Albion.
>
> (20:34-40)

The nature of individuality is determined by the nature of its relation to otherness, and in human being there are, as we have seen, three primary modes of intercourse: intellectual, emotional, and sensual (i.e., relation through head, heart, and loins). Emotional intercourse is the rarest, for few dare to risk it, fearing the destruction it might bring: to let another into one's heart is to risk losing one's self-presence. But to keep the gates closed is to deny actualization to one's intrinsic being.

The brain is more open to intercourse with others, because as the seat of thought rather than feelings it is less unique and more general. But this generality of the brain is also an insensitivity to individual uniqueness and is thus destructive of individual being that enters it. It is thus "the Seat / Of Satan in its Webs," the place where the destroyer of individual uniqueness lies waiting to capture individuals in its web of generalities and devour them. As we have seen, however, a degree of such destruction is necessary in order for relatedness and process to occur: Satan is an essential aspect of Being.

This Satanic destructiveness of individuality, however, is not the nucleus of individual uniqueness and its relation to otherness, for behind this destructiveness, deeper within individuality, lies the essence of individual being: "the City of Golgonooza / Which is the spiritual fourfold London, in the loins of Albion." Golgonooza, which is "ever building, ever falling" (6:2), is the process of actualization which forms the core of each individual. It is the activity of Los, which develops and transforms individuals by actualizing new possibilities—i.e., incorporating otherness into their being. This process of actualization is also the locus of the true, authentic community of individuals—"the spiritual fourfold London"—the fundamental, metaphysical process whereby one individual makes contact with and even unites with another. The process is said to lie "in the loins of Albion" because Albion, as the unity or relatedness of individuals, is what engenders novelty: Albion is the mutual interaction of individuals which continuously re-produces them—i.e., transforms them into new and different beings.

CHAPTER VI

Negativity, Eternity, and the Metaphysics of Presence

Metaphysics and the Fall into Abstraction

The ultimate obstacle to the attainment of this new form of being, however, has not been surmounted. In fact, that obstacle is present in the very attempt to articulate this new form of being in the description of the fly. For despite the renovating qualities of the description of the fly's individual being, the poet's account has left the particular reality of the little winged fly and has gone off into that very realm of generalities and metaphysical speculation that usurps the intrinsic being of individuals. In fact, the generality that is inherent in language seems to preclude any other course. Blake recognizes this fact, and proceeds to describe this path of his thinking as the path which Milton takes, suggesting that Milton's presence in Blake is responsible for these thoughts (and for the entire poem as well): "Thus Milton fell thro Albions heart, travelling outside of Humanity / Beyond the Stars in Chaos in Caverns of the Mundane Shell" (20:41-2). Milton-in-Blake moves right through the heart of Albion—the core of the relatedness and unity of individuals, as manifested in the little winged fly—and into the realm of metaphysical speculation, never even pausing within the little winged fly itself. Milton and Blake—and the reader too—thus travel "outside of Humanity" or the concrete individual, beyond all particular individuals, even the stars, ending up "in Chaos," in the emptiness and non-being of metaphysical abstractions ("Caverns of the Mundane Shell"). This movement away from the concrete individual constitutes a fall—indeed, it is in a sense The Fall itself, for it is what makes possible the obliviousness to and consequent destruction of individual being, which is a turning away from the divine or ultimate Being which the individual *is*.

109

Eternals and Individuals:
Possibilities versus Actuality

A specific aspect of this destruction by abstract generalities is presented as the Eternals' reaction to Milton's attempt to rehabilitate individual being:

> But many of the Eternals rose up from eternal tables
> Drunk with the Spirit, burning round the Couch of death they
>   stood
> Looking down into Beulah: wrathful, fill'd with rage!
> They rend the heavens round the Watchers in a fiery circle:
> And round the Shadowy Eighth. . . .

> (20:43-7)

The Eternals—who are both the principles which inhabit the realm of ultimates and the humans who valorize those principles—are outraged at Milton's rehabilitation of individuality, for it deprives them of power. They are nourished by the lack of being of individuals, which they consume at their eternal tables, intoxicated by the power of abstraction ("the Spirit"); it is through the perishing of individuals (on "the Couch of death") that the traditional notions of the ultimate and absolute derive their fiery power: perishing supposedly indicates a lack of power and being, and since all individuals perish, they must be inherently without power and being.

Milton's embrace of Eternal Death, by denying the ultimacy of presence, is intended to demonstrate that perishing does not put an end to an individual's being, and the rehabilitation of individual being that results from this vision diminishes the power of the traditional notion of Eternity and of those who have invested in this notion. But since Milton's mission denies ultimacy to immediate actuality or presence, it plays right into the hands of this Eternity, which is traditionally identified as the realm where non-actualized possibilities reside. It is precisely their supposed control over the non-actualized dimension of Being which constitutes the Eternals' opposition to Milton's attempted rehabilitation of the individual: for if (as Milton's action maintains) the individual's immediate actuality does not constitute the individual's total being or true identity, and if that true identity thus lies in the realm of possibility, then the individual's true being resides, after all, in the universal possibilities of Eternity, and the individual's being is neither intrinsic nor unique. But while denying the ultimacy of actuality and presence, Milton's action also embraces the finitude of actual existence and thus renounces the ultimacy of these universal possibilities; and as a result, these possibilities or

Eternals no longer provide the metaphysical support for the non-actual dimension of the individual. This fact is portrayed as the Eternals' forming a fiery circle around the Watchers—the more traditional notions which preserve Milton's non-actualized individual uniqueness—isolating them from Being and relegating them to a Dantean hell. The Shadowy Eighth, the ideal form or essence of Milton which remains outside the realm of actuality, is also deprived of metaphysical support, as are its seven companions: thus exiled metaphysically from the Eternals and their realm of being, "the Eight [Watchers] close up the Couch [of death] / Into a tabernacle, and flee with cries down to the Deeps" (20:47-8).

The affirmation of the ultimacy of unique, finite, individual being thus entails what seems to be an insurmountable dilemma: in order to affirm individual ultimacy, one must also affirm the non-ultimacy of immediate actuality (since in its immediate actuality the individual is anything but ultimate and absolute); but affirming the non-ultimacy of immediate actuality means that the realm of possibilities receives priority—and possibilities are traditionally taken to be universal and eternal rather than individual and transient. Therefore, to maintain the ultimacy of the individual, this transcendent realm of possibilities must also be denied priority; and this move further entails the transference of non-actual being from an abstract universal realm to the realm of actual, individual being itself. Thus Milton's unactualized form or essence is now seen as being preserved not in some transcendent realm but within the actualizing process of concrete individuals (such as Blake's writing), "where Los opens his three wide gates" (20:49). The unique non-actual being of individuals is thus forced out of Eternity by feudalistic metaphysics, which accommodates only general, abstract being in its transcendent realm. Unique, particular non-actuality is reduced to an aspect of actual individuals, which is (in the view of this metaphysics) the proper realm of the unique and particular: the powers that preserve non-actual particularity thus "soon find their own place & join the Watchers of the Ulro" (20:51).

This reduction of the non-actual to an aspect of the actual, however, threatens to collapse the various dimensions of being into immediate actuality: for how can possibility, or the true being of the individual, reside only within the individual's actuality and yet remain distinct from this actuality? It is this question which terrifies Los when he sees the descent of the non-actual from a transcendent to an immanent realm: "Los saw them and a cold pale horror coverd o'er his limbs" (20:51). For without particularity outside actuality, the actualizing power is neutralized: without transcendent particulars—

i.e., particular possibilities which transcend the present state—entelechy cannot occur, for it is by definition a movement from a particular actual state to another particular, but non-actual, state. And without the movement of actualization caused by the attraction of a distant, non-actual particular, the powers which regulate relation to otherness might also disappear: "Rintrah and Palamabron might depart" (20:52), the powers of wrath and pity, which provide, respectively, for the sanctity or security of the individual and the inter-connectedness or relatedness of the individual with others. Non-actual particularity, or negativity, is thus an absolute prerequisite of Being itself, and the elimination, by metaphysical abstraction, of non-actual particulars thus threatens the very process of Being.

Countering the Eviction of Negativity from Eternity

Freeing Orc: Eros as Conscious Entelechy

The denial of transcendent status to non-actual particularity, however, does not necessarily render entelechy impossible, as Los finally realizes:

> At last when desperation almost tore his heart in twain
> He recollected an old Prophecy in Eden recorded,
> And often sung to the loud harp at the immortal feasts
> That Milton of the Land of Albion should up ascend
> Forwards from Ulro from the Vale of Felpham; and set free
> Orc from his chain of Jealousy, he started at the thought.
>
> (20:56-61)

It is possible, Los realizes, that the entelechic, actualizing power can derive its impetus from the intrinsic dynamism of individuals—namely, through conscious eros, or Orc. Of course, for eros to function as the vehicle of the authentic actualization of Being, it must be set free from the Chain of Jealousy—i.e., it must not be restricted to self-aggrandizement of the ego, the self-preservation of the self-present, actual state of existence. Desire must become true eros: it must free itself from slavery to the actual existence of the individual and instead serve the less limited form of the individual which is present in the individual as its own intrinsic open-ended possibilities to become other than it now is. Eros must motivate and impel the sacrifice of the present, actual form of the individual in favor of what the individual can become—including, ultimately, the individual's Eternal Death, or non-self-presence.

This new form of identity formation is dimly perceived by Los as inherent in the origin or ground of existence (i.e., as "an old Prophecy in Eden recorded"). The dimness of Los's perception indicates the novelty of this possibility. For actualization of individual being usually proceeds without the support of the individual's self-presence or consciousness: the individual comes into existence, grows and changes, and dies—all without consciously (self-presently) desiring these transformations and in many instances even consciously opposing them. This is the case because desire is devoted to the perpetuation and enhancement of that aspect of actual existence which is taken by conscious desire to constitute the individual's identity. In most instances, this aspect is desire itself, and desire thus desires the perpetuation of conscious desiring and satisfaction. Thus in most cases eros actualizes the intrinsic being of the individual only fitfully and as a by-product of perpetuating itself.

But if eros is freed from this chain of jealousy—which is itself grounded in a metaphysics of presence—and serves the less limited form of the individual rather than eros itself, it can provide the impetus and guidance for the power of actualization (Los). The actualization of the intrinsic possibilities of the individual will thus coincide with the individual's self-conscious goals and activities, and the individual's being will then be truly intrinsic.

The way in which eros can be set free from the chain of jealousy is to turn it away from the metaphysics of presence—i.e., to reveal to it that the most fulfilling form of the individual lies not in its immediate, actual state, but in the process of actualizing the forms of particularity that are its own intrinsic, but perhaps hitherto unimagined, possibilities. These forms, moreover, lie not only within the individual itself, but in others as well. Thus not all of the forms which the individual actualizes will be actualized immediately, i.e., through its own existence; it can itself embody only a small number of such forms. Rather, the vast majority of particular possibilities will be actualized indirectly by an individual, and it is this indirect, or mediated actualization which eros must come to see as its purpose. Such a vision is possible only if the metaphysics of presence is overcome.

This re-formation of desire (analyzed more fully in the descent of Ololon) is effected by the overcoming of the metaphysics of presence, through Milton's going to Eternal Death: in giving up his own immediate actuality—i.e., in dying—Milton is training conscious desire to serve the greater being of individuality rather than merely to perpetuate itself. Milton's action thus provides a paradigm for the desires of other individuals as well—blazes a trail, as it were, for them to follow. In going to Eternal Death, Milton implicitly asserts that there is an element of individual being that is greater than the immediate self-presence of desiring consciousness. And the very success of Milton's effort to embrace Eternal Death proves that there *is* such an element—that individual being consists not in the immediate state of existence (self-presence) but in the process that achieves that unique state and then discards it in favor of another unique actuality, and so on, ultimately discarding its own existence in favor of indirect, mediated actuality in other individuals. In this realization, the metaphysics of presence is overcome, both theoretically and practically, and the individual actualizes its own absoluteness.

We are now given a hint of how this transformation might actually come about in the realm of experience. When the possibility of this transformation is apprehended by Los, "he started at the thought / And down descended into Udan-Adan" (20:61-21:1), into the world of experience, where one (self-present) conscious desire struggles against another. Here, where desires of one individual destroy another individual, Los encounters Satan, the power which reduces individual uniqueness: "it was night / And Satan sat sleeping upon his Couch in Udan-Adan: / His spectre slept, his shadow woke; when one sleeps th'other wakes" (21:2-3). The Shadow, the non-immediate, non-actual presence of individual reduction (Satan) is active, but the false embodiment of reduction of individual uniqueness (i.e., total negation of unique individual being) is dormant, inactive. In such a situation, where the individual's self-present actuality is destroyed, but individual being is not (since the destroyer of that being is dormant), eros can be freed from the Chain of Jealousy and serve Los. Such a situation occurs at night, when the ego-consciousness, or self-presence, the spectrous Satanic aspect of existence, sleeps and the authentic function of Satan, the destruction of individual differences, is invisibly, imperceptibly present (as his shadow), allowing the individual desire to move (as for example in the widening of the boundaries of identity which occurs in dreams) beyond the demands of self-preservation and into actualization of otherness.

The Role of Blake and Milton in the Freeing of Orc

Before these events can occur, however, they must be grasped by individual consciousnesses as the most fulfilling possibilities of the individuals. This step is made possible by Blake's articulation of these possibilities in *Milton*, and Blake now returns to this fact and recalls the ground and provenance of his own vision:

> But Milton entering my Foot, I saw in the nether
> Regions of the Imagination; also all men on Earth,
> And all in Heaven, saw in the nether regions of the Imagination
> In Ulro beneath Beulah, the vast breach of Miltons descent.
> But I knew not that it was Milton, for man cannot know
> What passes in his members till periods of Space & Time
> Reveal the secrets of Eternity: for more extensive
> Than any other earthly things, are Mans earthly lineaments.
>
> (21:4-11)

Blake's vision of "Milton entering [his] Foot . . . in the nether / Regions of the Imagination" indicates that Blake is vaguely aware of the fact that somehow Milton's unique individual being has entered his own. He is aware of this fact, however, only as a change in his own being, for he says, "I knew not that it was Milton." When the change took place in Blake, he was not aware that it was due to the presence of Milton: he had the experience, but he missed the meaning, "for," as he says, "man cannot know / What passes in his members till periods of Space & Time / Reveal the secrets of Eternity." Many moments and perspectives are needed in order for an individual to become aware of its own unique being, "for more extensive / Than any other earthly things, are Mans earthly lineaments." Here in Blake's experience is a specific manifestation of the very point which eros must realize: that an individual's being greatly exceeds its ego-consciousness—i.e., its own self-presence or immediate actuality. In fact, the individual so exceeds its own immediate actuality, Blake asserts, that every individual is in some way affected by (i.e., takes account of) Milton's descent into actuality in Blake: ". . . all men on Earth, / And all in Heaven, saw in the nether regions of the Imagination / In Ulro beneath Beulah, the vast breach of Miltons descent." The point here is, as Whitehead was later to declare, that everything is in a sense everywhere at all times: Milton's posthumous presence has an effect, however minute and indirect, on every individual that exists.

The immediate effect of Milton's presence on Blake is that "all this Vegetable World appeard on [his] left Foot, / As a bright sandal formd immortal of precious stones & gold" (21:12-13). Milton's influence has caused Blake to see the phenomenal or "vegetable" world in a new way: instead of seeing it as a conglomeration of physical objects, he now perceives it as something supporting his journeying—a form tailored to his needs ("a bright sandal") and composed of intrinsically valuable things ("precious stones and gold"). This new perception is identical with Milton's rehabilitation of individuals, the re-establishment of their intrinsic being by affirming, through his desire to die, that perishing does not destroy an individual's being—that an individual's being is not limited to its actual existence. It is this new vision of actual individual entities that opens the way to infinity and immortality, as indicated by the fact that it allows Blake to enter Eternity: "I stooped down & bound [the sandal] on to walk forward thro' Eternity" (21:14). Blake—and hopefully his reader as well—now realizes that since individual entities of the phenomenal or vegetable world have intrinsic being, and since these individuals indirectly actualize and thus preserve the unique being of other individuals, these individual beings provide the means to encounter the infinite aspect of Being (i.e., Eternity, which is constituted by the process of actualization which each individual is) and, through participating in the process of this actualization, "to walk forward thro' Eternity"—i.e., to progress in infinity, and thus to achieve immortality.

The Metaphysics of Presence and the Denial of Negativity

This new vision of individuals entails the acceptance of negativity—i.e., of non-actualized particularity in all its forms, including desire, frustration, pain, and destruction—as an essential dimension of Being. Such acceptance, however, runs contrary to a certain aspect of Eternity—i.e., to a certain system of thought and to the principles conceptualized in that system. As we have already seen, this notion of Eternity, called Ololon, rejects the stationing of non-actual particulars in Eternity. For Ololon, ultimate Being consists of full immediacy, or presence—a fact now made clear by the description of Ololon as "a sweet River, of milk & liquid pearl" (21:15). From this description, Ololon appears to be a rich, nourishing and seminal force lying in the origin of existence. Ideally, this continuously flowing munificence meets every desire as soon as it arises, and no frustration or deficiency of any kind is ever experienced. For this form of Eternity, the negativity and non-being that is part of all desire and striving—indeed of all change and progress—has no meaning. Hence Ololon (i.e., those who inhabit this form of Eternity) are[1] presented as having had no idea that Milton's non-actualized particularity was an essential dimension of Being—i.e., that it constituted the pole of possibility which gave the actual its dynamic force. Only after they have driven this non-actualized particularity of Milton into the realm of mere actuality do they realize its essentiality. Hence

> ...they lamented that they had in wrath & fury & fire
> Driven Milton into the Ulro; for now they knew too late

> That it was Milton the Awakener: they had not heard the Bard,
> Whose song calld Milton to the attempt. . . .
>
> (21:31-4)

The necessity of such non-actual particularity is expressed in the image of the sun's refusal to rise (21:20-23). In order for the world to turn, or the sun to rise—i.e., for the process of Being to unroll—there must be a final cause or goal (inherently particular) to elicit any movement whatsoever, as well as to give the movement direction. Without a goal—i.e., without a non-actual particularity—the process of Being would stand still. Such is the situation when negativity—i.e., non-actualized particularity—is expelled from the transcendent realm of Being (Eternity).

When such transcendent particular possibilities are denied, the process of being is seen as carried on through the blind desire of instinct:

> Luvahs bulls each morning drag the sulphur Sun out of the Deep
> Harnessd with starry harness black & shining kept by black slaves
> That work all night at the starry harness, Strong and vigorous
> They drag the unwilling Orb. . . .
>
> (21:20-23)

Since it has been said that "Orc . . . is Luvah" (18:1), the motive force provided by Luvah's bulls must be closely related to Orc's power, which Los, as we have seen, hopes to harness when it is freed from the Chain of Jealousy. Luvah's bulls are the blind desires of instinct with which abstract philosophy keeps the process of actualization going when a transcendent goal or final cause is denied. Without a transcendent goal the process of actualization is seen to proceed through the slavery, bondage, and compulsion of individuals' self-aggrandizing desire, with no real fulfillment occurring. In such a situation everything experiences unmitigated deficiency, negativity, non-being; thus all those in Ololon "wept in long resounding song / For seven days of eternity, and the rivers living banks / The mountains wail'd & every plant that grew, in solemn sighs lamented" (21:17-19). When internal, intrinsic deficiency is perceived as mere abstract negativity rather than as particular possibility that draws actuality forward, individuals are in a state of lamentation rather than labor. Such is the situation of Ololon, whose very name suggests the Greek word for lamentation: Ololon, immersed in the metaphysics of presence, experiences deficiency as totally without value. This perception derives from Ololon's metaphysical perspective: Ololon has not accepted negativity (or non-actuality, non-presence) as an aspect of Being. For Ololon's lamentation to become productive and negate deficiency, the deficiency in actuality must be seen not as mere nothingness but rather as a definite particular possibility to be actualized. But for that to occur, negativity or non-presence (which is the essence of possibility) must first be admitted as a part of Being.

It is thus necessary for Eternity to include this negativity and give it its due. Eternity does so in the concept of Providence, we are shown, but the ultimate effect of this concept is further repression of the negative: when the sun is dragged out of the deep—i.e., when brute desire is seen to actualize Being— "all the Family / Of Eden heard the lamentation and Providence began" (21:21-4). This image expresses the point that when desire actualizes something it proves the reality of desire's power—and the reality of the negativity on which it is based. It is in recognition of this fact that Eternity has acknowledged the significance of need, or deficiency, which motivates individuals. However, Eternity's inclusion of negativity manifests itself as the concept of Providence, which is a recognition of deficiency that denies ultimate significance to that deficiency. Here the fact of negativity has become explicit to consciousness and to the powers of Eternity, but the establishment of the universal principle of Providence emphasizes not the significance of negativity in and of itself, but rather the fact that deficiencies are filled and desires satisfied from time to time: the sun does, by whatever means, rise, and the credit is given to "Providence." The crucial significance of negativity is itself again ignored.

This denial of the negative is also expressed by the fact that when there is full and immediate actuality—i.e., during the day, as it were, when the sun is out—the deficiency or negativity is drowned out by the impact of immediate actuality: "when the clarions of day sounded they drownd the lamentations" (21:25). The denial is even more pronounced, however, when actuality is in abeyance, i.e., at night: "when night came all was silent in Ololon: & all refusd to lament / In the still night fearing lest they should others molest" (21:26-7). The cessation of Ololon's lamentation, it is clear, is due not to the cessation of the cause for lamentation (negativity), but rather to a refusal to lament deriving from a fear of producing more negativity. For fear of molesting others is actually fear of negativity—fear of producing frustration, dissatisfaction, and pain. And this fear derives from the failure to recognize that negativity, in its various manifestations as frustration, pain, and even destruction, is a necessary and fundamental dimension of Being itself.

We are now reminded once again that this metaphysical denial of ultimacy to negativity—this failure to grasp negativity as non-actualized particularity—stymies Los, the very principle of actualization:

Seven mornings Los heard them, as the poor bird within the shell
Hears its impatient parent bird; and Enitharmon heard them;
But saw them not, for the blue Mundane Shell inclos'd them in.
                                                    (21:28-30)

Los, the entelechic power which guides and directs the process of actualization, is restricted and cut off from the transcendent particularities by the
Mundane Shell, the abstract metaphysical system which accommodates no
individuality and particularity whatsoever, much less non-actualized particularity. This system denies access to an ultimate individual purpose or transcendent particular telos, and leaves the entelechic power in an embyronic
state, without the power to effect the actualization of the possibilities whose
call it dimly perceives, or even fully envision those possibilities. Entelechy
thus, for the most part, apprehends possibilities only as a nothingness or lack
in actuality—i.e., as Ololon's lament, which, as well as being a reaction
against negativity, is also an appeal to positivity, or presence, to fill the
deficiency: "Los heard these laments. / He heard them call in prayer all the
Divine Family" (21:34-5).

This devotion to presence and denial of negativity, we are now shown, is
identical with the spectrous, self-perpetuating, self-present aspect of Milton.
For at this moment, Los "beheld the Cloud of Milton stretching over
Europe" (21:36). This cloud, we recall, is "the Spectrous body of Milton
[which] / Redound[ed] from [Blake's] left foot into Los's Mundane Space
[and] / Brooded over [Milton's] Body in Horeb against the Resurrection"
(20:20-22): it is Milton's "narrow doleful form," which seeks fulfillment by
trying to perpetuate past actuality, i.e., trying to re-actualize Milton's dead
body. This misdirected effort, which spreads all across Europe—as the Christian notion of life after death—is the result of the restriction of Los by the
Mundane Shell through the refusal to admit negativity or non-actuality,
deficiency, into Being. For the denial of the negative results in fear of death
(which Milton must overcome) and in identification of fulfillment with
restitution of past actuality to immediate presence—that is to say: literal
resurrection of the dead.

This denial of the negative is also expressed as the movement of the Divine
Family—the pantheon of ultimate powers and principles—toward pure presence and positivity:

...all the Family Divine collected as Four Suns
In the Four Points of heaven East, West & North & South,
Enlarging and enlarging till their Disks approachd each other;
And when they touch'd closed together Southward in One Sun

> Over Ololon: and as One Man, who weeps over his brother,
> In a dark tomb, so all the Family Divine. wept over Ololon.
> Saying. Milton goes to Eternal Death! so saying, they groan'd in
>   spirit
> And were troubled! and again the Divine Family groaned in spirit!
> (21:37-44)

The merging of the Four Suns is very similar to the Four Universes' falling toward the center, which, we saw (19:15-24), constituted the destruction of the intrinsic unity of individuals (the death of Albion). The Four Suns, the fundamental dimensions or aspects of Being, now merge together and lose their differentiation, becoming pure immediacy, pure presence: all these aspects of Being gravitate toward Ololon, the notion of Eternity as pure presence and positivity. Ololon, in fact, is the cause of this gravitation. For as we have seen, those who dwell in the munificence of Ololon identify Being with full presence and complete lack of deficiency, and when they experience lack or desire—negativity—they reject it as having no part in the process of Being. This refusal of the negative, this lamentation, has the effect of gathering all aspects of Being—the past, the future, appearance, possibility, etc.— together over the single aspect of Being which Ololon absolutizes: pure presence. All Being is thus made to weep over death, need, desire, absence, and mediation—over any kind of negativity or non-presence.

This reduction of Being to presence makes unbearable the tension and flux of desire which deficiency causes. The inhabitants of Ololon yearn for the stasis of full presence, and find the stasis of death to be more like presence than the strife of existence is:

> And Ololon said, Let us descend also, and let us give
> Ourselves to death in Ulro among the Transgressors.
> Is Virtue a Punisher? O no! how is this wondrous thing:
> This World beneath, unseen before: this refuge from the wars
> Of Great Eternity! unnatural refuge! unknown by us till now!
> Or are these the pangs of repentance! let us enter into them.
> (21:45-50)

The flux of Eternity is unbearable to those who identify Being with presence, and they prefer to be non-actual rather than to endure the strife of actualization. Or rather, their yearning for full presence *is* a yearning for death, stasis, nothingness, for the two states are ultimately indistinguishable.

This movement of Ololon is opposed, however, by the Divine Family, all the other deposed principles and powers of Being, who tell Ololon that death or negativity is "The Universal Dictate"—a necessary part of the process of

Being. They urge Ololon not to abandon the struggle of negativity:

> ...the Divine Family said. Six Thousand Years are now
> Accomplish'd in this World of Sorrow; Milton's Angel knew
> The Universal Dictate; and you also feel this Dictate.
> And now you know this World of Sorrow, and feel Pity. Obey
> The Dictate! Watch over this World, and with your brooding
> wings,
> Renew it to Eternal Life: Lo! I am with you alway
> But you canot renew Milton he goes to Eternal Death.
>
> (21:51-7)

The world, says the Divine Family, can be renewed to Eternal Life, i.e., it can achieve infinity. Milton, however, can never be renewed or actualized, and Ololon must accept this fact. Yet although the Divine Family seems to be accepting the negative, in saying that Milton cannot be renewed it is tacitly embracing the positivist assumptions of Ololon: namely, that Being consists in presence, and that when an individual is no longer immediately actual or present (i.e., is dead), that individual's being is lost and can never be actualized. This assumption unites the Divine Family with Ololon in a virtual apotheosis of presence, the *parousia* itself:

> So spake the Family Divine as One Man even Jesus
> Uniting in One with Ololon & the appearance of One Man.
> Jesus the Saviour appeard coming in the Clouds of Ololon!
>
> (21:58-60)

The pronouncement by the Divine Family is identical with the message of Jesus' coming as it is traditionally interpreted: a promise of fulfillment through restoration of full presence at the end of labor rather than fulfillment in the very working of the negative or non-present itself. Here Jesus appears "in the Clouds of Ololon" — i.e., obscured by the metaphysics of presence — his significance identified as the denial of the reality of negativity and death. This is a false vision. The Divine Vision, Blake tells us in summary, has been "driven away with the Seven Starry Ones into the Ulro" (22:1): i.e., the truth of ultimate Being has disappeared with the expulsion of the negative. Nonetheless, Blake asserts, this truth of Being in a sense remains intact everywhere, intrinsic in all things, even in Ololon, the complete devotion to presence — implicit, that is, in the very fact of lamentation, which is the bemoaning of a lack of presence: "Yet the Divine Vision remains Everywhere For-ever. Amen. / And Ololon lamented for Milton with great lamentation" (22:2-3).

PART THREE

Mediated Presence
and Individual Identity:
Los and The Process of Actualization

CHAPTER VII

Negativity, Mediation, and Actualization

Blake and Los: The Role of the Individual
in the Process of Actualization

Blake is now prepared to examine further the role which negativity or non-presence has in Being. This investigation takes the form of an exploration of the various modes of negativity encountered in the phenomenal world. Before Blake engages in this analysis, however, he pauses to remind the reader of the function which this analysis itself has within the process of Being. As Blake is binding on the sandals—i.e., engaging the finite phenomenal world as a means of exploring the infinity of Being—he becomes aware of the entelechic power, the dynamism of the actualizing process itself, behind him. He realizes, that is, that his visionary activity is backed by the very principle of actualization that he is setting out to investigate:

> And Los behind me stood; a terrible flaming Sun: just close
> Behind my back; I turned round in terror, and behold.
> Los stood in that fierce glowing fire; & he also stoop'd down
> And bound my sandals on in Udan-Adan; trembling I stood
> Exceedingly with fear & terror, standing in the Vale
> Of Lambeth: but he kissed me, and wishd me health.
> And I became One Man with him arising in my strength:
> Twas too late now to recede. Los had enterd into my soul:
> His terrors now possess'd me whole! I arose in fury & strength.
>
> (22:6–14)

Los himself, the principle of entelechy, helps Blake understand the phenomenal world (bind on the sandals) as preparation for exploring Being, and when this occurs, Blake's conscious intention coincides with the principle itself, such that his unique being is in total accord with the entelechic power. At first the power and the otherness of the principle terrify Blake, but then he recognizes it as an element of his own greater being—as opposed to his

125

immediate actual identity—and arises in strength, in full actualization. Through becoming wholly possessed by Los—i.e., realizing that the cosmic entelechic power is his own inmost being as well as a universal principle— Blake encounters the possibility of his wholeness (expressed by Los wishing him health).

When Blake realizes that his unique individual being is united with the very principle of actualization, he achieves further insight into the nature of individual being and its ontological status in the total scheme of things. In a statement that seems at first to be spoken by Blake—and is, since Blake the poet has written it and Blake the character has united with Los—Los declares:

> I am that Shadowy Prophet who Six Thousand Years ago
> Fell from my station in the Eternal bosom. Six Thousand Years
> Are finishd. I return! both Time & Space obey my will.
> I in Six Thousand Years walk up and down....
>
> (22:15–18)

The entelechic power, which in existence (the six thousand years since creation) has fallen from the metaphysical ascendancy which it occupies in the Eternal scheme of things, is now prepared to resume that position in the company of Blake—i.e., by means of Blake's writings, which are themselves part of the process of actualization which Los is. The reascendance will occur through the acceptance of negativity and the establishment of the fact that individual being is unique, intrinsic, and inherently indestructible.

Time as Negativity and Mediation

Los now asserts this indestructibility of the individual and explains that it derives from the mediated presence of the past:

>   ...for not one Moment
> Of Time is lost, nor one Event of Space unpermanent.
> But all remain: every fabric of Six Thousand Years
> Remains permanent: tho' on the Earth where Satan
> Fell, and was cut off all things vanish & are seen no more
> They vanish not from me & mine, we guard them first & last[.]
> The generations of men run on in the tide of Time
> But leave their destind lineaments permanent for ever & ever.
>
> (22:18–25)

Los here directly contradicts the view of Ololon, which accords being only to that which is continuously and immediately present. Being thus does not reside primarily in ideal forms or objects (as it does for the idealist views of Ololon), or in immediate actuality, as empiricism assumes. Rather, Being resides in, and is intrinsic to, individuals, and the being of these individuals is imperishable, whether the individual still actually and immediately exists or not. Although in actuality "all things vanish & are seen no more," ultimately these actual individual things which have perished remain in being, guarded by the process of actualization itself. For even though all things perish— vanish from the world of existence—their unique being ("destind linea- ments") is preserved by the process of actualization, which in its transforma- tion of the actual into the non-actual, and vice versa, retains the non-actual in the newly actualized: as the basis, cause, or occasion of the newly actualized, that which has perished remains, indirectly actualized in that which super- sedes it.

This notion of preservation through supersession is a crucial insight of Blake's vision, and it is thus important that its full significance be apprehended at this point. Hegel and Whitehead (whose own organicist philosophies have many points of similarity with Blake's vision) offer obser- vations that help to illuminate Blake's notion of preservation. Hegel explains the notion in the following way:

> Immediate actuality is in general as such never what it ought to be; it is finite actuality with an inherent flaw, and its vocation is to be consumed. But the other aspect of actuality is its essentiality. This is primarily the inside which as a mere possibility is no less destined to be suspended. Possibility thus suspended is the issuing of a new actuality, of which the first immediate actuality was the presupposition.... This new actuality thus issuing is the very inside of the immediate actuality which it uses up. Thus there comes into being quite another shape of things, and yet it is not an other: for the first actuality is only put [set forth] as what it in essence was. The conditions which are sacrificed, which fall to the ground and are spent, only unite with themselves in the other actuality. Such in general is the nature of the process of actuality. The actual is no mere case of immediate Being, but, as essential Being, a suspension of its own immediacy, and thereby mediating itself with itself.[1]

Whitehead names this preservation of a superseded individual "objective immortality," which he explains as follows:

> ... The relatedness of actualities ... is wholly concerned with the appropriation of the dead by the living—that is to say, with

'objective immortality' whereby what is divested of its own living immediacy becomes a real component in other living immediacies of becoming.... Actual entities 'perpetually perish' subjectively [i.e., in the form of immediate self-presence], but are immortal objectively. Actuality in perishing acquires objectivity, while it loses subjective immediacy. It loses the final causation which is its internal principle of unrest, and it acquires efficient causation whereby it is a ground of obligation characterizing the creativity [of its successor].[2]

Time's very negation or destruction of individuals thus ensures that the unique being of every individual is necessarily preserved. The inimitable, inherent being of each individual process of actualization continues to live and grow in new individuals where it is actualized indirectly through the influence (immediate or mediated) which it has on their unique actualizations. Everything remains because ontologically everything is interwoven with everything else from the beginning of time.

Rintrah and Palamabron's Critique
of Milton's Religion

Having asserted the metaphysical significance of the destructive/ productive process of actualization, Blake is now prepared to explore this process of actualization itself, here expressed as the activity of Golgonooza. As he approaches this topic he is once again confronted with the invalidity of the metaphysics of presence, perceived this time through the eyes of Rintrah and Palamabron. Taking Blake with him, Los returns to Golgonooza, the source and center of the process of actualization, where, at the Gate of Golgonooza, they meet Rintrah and Palamabron, the powers, respectively, of wrath or self-preservation and of pity or mutuality. These powers, seeing the presence of Milton and Blake, are "clouded with discontent. & brooding in their minds terrible things" (22:28). They demand:

Whence is this Shadow terrible? Wherefore dost thou refuse
To throw him into the Furnaces! knowest thou not that he
Will unchain Orc? & let loose Satan, Og, Sihon & Anak,
Upon the Body of Albion? for this he is come! behold it written
Upon his fibrous left Foot black! most dismal to our eyes.

(22:30-35)

Rintrah and Palamabron's opposition to Blake's entrance into the very center of actualization derives from their fear that Blake/Milton, in prophetically embodying this process, will cause individual desire to be set free and that such unchecked desire will release monstrous, Satanic forces that will destroy the unity of individuals (Albion). Rintrah and Palamabron (mistakenly) identify the release of individual desire —which will result from Blake's entering into and portraying the process of actualization—with unmitigated self-aggrandizement and its concomitant anarchy. They also mistakenly identify the aspect of Milton which is present in Blake with Milton's religious beliefs. They correctly identify these beliefs, however, as being the cause of the present state of turmoil and destruction:

> Miltons Religion is the cause: there is no end to destruction!
> Seeing the Churches at their Period in terror & despair:
> Rahab created Voltaire: Tirzah created Rousseau;
> Asserting the Self-righteousness against the Universal Saviour,
> Mocking the Confessors & Martyrs, claiming Self-righteousness;
> With cruel Virtue: making War upon the Lambs Redeemed;
> To perpetuate War & Glory. to perpetuate the Laws of Sin.
> (22:39-45)

The ethic of war, glory, virtue, and self-righteousness is, as we have seen, based on a feudalistic metaphysics of centralized being such as that which Milton espoused during his life. This cruel and self-righteous ethic results because where individuals are seen as having no intrinsic being, but rather as competing for a limited quantity of homogeneous being, the only way for an individual to increase its being is through opposing and destroying other individuals—rather than through the development of its own intrinsic possibilities in mutuality with others. The Voltaires and Rousseaus, promulgators of ego-centrism ("self-righteousness"), are created by Rahab and Tirzah, the false, immediate fulfillments offered by a feudalistic metaphysics. These forces

> ...destroy Jerusalem as a Harlot & her Sons as Reprobates;
> [And] raise up Mystery the Virgin Harlot Mother of War,
> Babylon the Great, the Abomination of Desolation!
> (22:47-9)

True fulfillment, that is (Jerusalem), is branded as false fulfillment (a harlot) and thus destroyed, and individuals who draw sustenance from true fulfillment are called evil. In place of the true fulfillment of mediated actualization, a vague, undefined false satisfaction of immediate presence is erected, a satisfaction which always beckons but never yields fulfillment (Virgin Harlot). It is this false, obscure promise of fulfillment which breeds War, engendering a conflict among individuals which has no other cause than an obscure and oppressive feeling of frustration, dissatisfaction with the status quo. This obscure image of false fulfillment is "Babylon the Great," the great enslaver—the feudalistic metaphysics which enslaves all things by denying them their being, through denying the being of the non-actual, or the negative.

Ironically, the true significance of the Christ-event—i.e., of love and self-sacrifice—is lost in this religious system, which sees all action in terms of debits and credits which ransom one being for another:

> Shewing the Transgressors in Hell, the proud Warriors in Heaven:
> Heaven as a Punisher & Hell as One under Punishment:
> With Laws from Plato & his Greeks to renew the Trojan Gods,
> In Albion; to deny the value of the Saviours blood.
>
> (22:51-4)

The ontological status of individual being is thus severely threatened by this system, the "Covering Cherub [which] advances from the East" (23:10), and Rintrah and Palamabron fearfully ask,

> How long shall we lay dead in the Street of the great City
> How long beneath the Covering Cherub give our Emanations
> Milton will utterly consume us & thee our beloved Father[.]
> He hath enterd into the Covering Cherub, becoming one with
> Albions dread Sons. . . .
>
> (23:11-15)

The whole entelechic process is threatened by this feudalistic system of Milton's, and Rintrah and Palamabron therefore ask Los to destroy Milton—to negate that which negates authentic actualization (i.e., that which destroys their emanations).

Negating the Negative versus
Tolerating the Negative

Immediacy versus Deferral of Action

Los recognizes the danger which Milton's false vision presents; in fact, the speech of Rintrah and Palamabron is also the speech of Los, since Rintrah and Palamabron (wrath and pity) are offspring or aspects of Los. Los's involvement in the speech is evident from his stormy appearance during the speech:

Like the black storm, coming out of Chaos, beyond the stars:
It issues thro the dark & intricate caves of the Mundane Shell
Passing the planetary visions, & the well adorned Firmament
The Sun rolls into Chaos & the stars into the Desarts:
And then the storms become visible, audible & terrible,
Covering the light of day, & rolling down upon the mountains,
Deluge all the country round. Such is a vision of Los;
When Rintrah & Palamabron spoke; and such his stormy face
Appeard, as does the face of heaven, when coverd with thick
    storms
Pitying and loving tho in frowns of terrible perturbation.

                                                    (23:21-30)

The entelechic power is inclined to oppose and destroy that which opposes actualization; the entire movement of the entelechic force is toward greater fulfillment of individuals, and consequently it must oppose and overcome whatever opposes such actualization. Los is thus urged to destroy precipitously this false religion which hinders actualization.

Yet at the same time, Los feels the need to wait to let the false vision be overcome more by intrinsic means and less by violence and external force. He therefore pleads, "O noble Sons, be patient yet a little[.] / I have embracd the falling Death, he is become One with me / O Sons we live not by wrath. by mercy alone we live!" (23:32-4). It is Los as Blake and Milton who is speaking here, for it is Blake who has united with Milton, "the falling Death," and Los has embraced Blake. This aspect of Los has a broader, deeper vision than do his sons, and he can see the distant ramifications of the present situation:

I recollect an old Prophecy in Eden recorded in gold; and oft
Sung to the harp: That Milton of the land of Albion
Should up ascend forward from Felphams Vale & break the Chain
Of Jealousy from all its roots; be patient therefore O my Sons.

                                                    (23:35-8)

Los/Blake is aware of what Hegel called the working of the negative, the necessary function of the non-actual, the false, and the perverse in the process of actualization. He understands that the feudalistic vision of actuality has a (provisional) truth of its own that is a prerequisite for the fuller truth of a later stage of actualization. He thus recognizes, for example, that even "the Daughters of Los... [who] in deceit / ... weave a new Religion from new Jealousy of Theotormon" (22:37-8), and "Gwendolen & Conwenna [who

surround Milton] as a garment woven / Of War & Religion" (23:16–17), act
out of necessity:

> These lovely Females form sweet night and silence and secret
> Obscurities to hide from Satans Watch-Fiends. Human loves
> And graces; lest they write them in their Books, & in the Scroll
> Of mortal life, to condemn the accused: who at Satans Bar
> Tremble in Spectrous Bodies continually day and night
> While on the Earth they live in sorrowful Vegetations.
>
> (23:39–44)

The mysteries and obfuscations of religion ("sweet night and silence and
secret / Obscurities") serve a necessary purpose in preserving "Human
loves / And graces," those values and modes of behavior which actualize less
limited forms of being but which could not survive outside the protection of
a (limited and limiting) metaphysical system. That is, if love and kindness
were not taken to be mysterious or magical means (authorized by God) for
protecting one's existence "from Satans Watch-Fiends," these virtues might
almost cease to exist, and the process of actualization would be even further
stymied. For the general consciousness is not yet powerful enough to
apprehend the fact that love and kindness are in and of themselves modes of
fulfillment (through actualizing one indirectly, in others); rather, people
conceive of fulfillment only as a positive and present enhancement of their
being, obtained by opposition to and destruction of others, and they accept
love as a means to fulfillment (salvation) only because of its supposed value as
a mysterious currency which can buy off their own destruction and effect
such positive enhancement of their being (in the full presence of the hereafter). Because this system of mystery and supernaturalism provides the sole
means whereby many individuals are able to go on living and being productive, it has value in the process of actualization and should not be perempto-
rily destroyed, even though it is based upon false assumptions and itself
embodies a large degree of falsehood.

Los/Blake is thus torn between the two courses of actualization—
evolution and revolution—a tension also present in such diverse (and similar)
systems as Marxism and Christianity, both of which believe, on the one
hand, in inevitable amelioration, and yet preach, on the other hand, conscious intervention in the process of history. Recognition of the falseness,
inadequacy, and destructiveness of the present state of affairs brings a yearning for immediate destruction of the present actuality in an attempt to
achieve greater actualization and fulfillment. Thus Los cries: "O when shall
we tread our Wine-presses in heaven and Reap / Our wheat with shoutings

of joy, and leave the Earth in peace" (23:45-6). Yet at the same time, this desire for revolution is countered by the realization that revolution is perhaps ultimately more destructive than the falsehood and injustice that persist in the course of evolution. "Remember," Los responds to himself, "how Calvin and Luther in fury premature / Sow'd War and stern division between Papists & Protestants / Let it not be so now!" (23:47-9). Calvin and Luther tried to destroy falsehood directly, short-circuiting the process of time instead of letting the labor of the negative take place. Los realizes that total fulfillment cannot be reached in a single leap, and that although the ultimate purpose of actualizing all individuals may be clear, the best course for that actualization is not always apparent, and the work of the negative must be allowed to continue:

> We were plac'd here by the Universal Brotherhood & Mercy
> With powers fitted to circumscribe this dark Satanic death
> And that the Seven Eyes of God may have space for Redemption.
> But how this is as yet we know not, and we cannot know:
> Till Albion is arisen....
>
> (23:50-54)

The function of the entelechic power is not completely to destroy Satanic destruction but to circumscribe it, limit its area of control—i.e., to give direction, limit, determination to the working of the negative. This tentative, provisional, holding action, moreover, is dictated by the fact that the precise path of fulfillment is not preordained; the path of fulfillment will not become clear, Los says, till such fulfillment has actually occurred—"till Albion is arisen" and individuality assumes its true form as union with otherness.

But although Los is not sure precisely how fulfillment will come about, he is convinced that Milton's embrace of Eternal Death holds the answer:

> Six Thousand years are passd away the end approaches fast;
> This mighty one is come from Eden, he is of the Elect,
> Who died from Earth & he is returnd before the Judgment. This
> thing
> Was never known that one of the holy dead should willingly return
> Then patient wait a little while till the Last Vintage is over:
> Till we have quenchd the Sun of Salah in the Lake of Udan Adan.
> (23:55-60)

The fact that Milton's voluntary embrace of Eternal Death has never been known before is an indication to Los that it will bring about radical change, and that the process of actualization should follow the ramifications of

Milton's embrace of the negative rather than effect a cataclysmic revolution. Los is willing to be patient because he understands the working of time, which he explained to Blake when he united with him: Los realizes that fulfillment must be achieved through incremental actualization of many generations of individuals—that fuller actualization can only arise from the ground of antecedent lesser actualizations and cannot be imposed from a realm of pure presence or eternal possibility above or beyond actuality.

The Consequences of Embracing Immediacy

Los therefore begs Rintrah and Palamabron not to leave him—not to desert the incremental labor of the process of actualization. For wrath and pity to separate themselves from the entelechic power would be for them to be generated—i.e., to become natural, merely contingent (psychological) powers immersed in the immediate exigencies of existence—rather than to retain their essential ontological status as principles governing, respectively, the inviolability and the mutuality of individuals, functions necessary for the preservation and advancement of the very process of Being. Wrath and Pity will no longer serve this function if they leave Los, the principle of actualization, and become autonomous psychological forces. This fact is explained in the fate of the auxiliary powers which left the service of Los during the events described in the Bard's Song:

> Twelve Sons successive fled away in that thousand years of sorrow
> Of Palamabrons Harrow, & of Rintrahs wrath & fury:
> Reuben & Manazzoth & Gad & Simeon & Levi,
> And Ephraim & Judah were Generated, because
> They left me, wandering with Tirzah. . . .
>
> (23:62-24:4)

These forces, which apparently became autonomous following Satan's usurpation of Palamabron's function and Satan's subsequent declaration of autonomy, did so because they sought immediate actualization. By leaving the service of Los, who guides the total, interconnected actualizations of all individuals, these forces lose sight of their ultimate goal and wander—i.e., desert their telos and move aimlessly about—with Tirzah or pleasure, following immediate satisfaction wherever it leads. No longer in the service of the ontological entelechic principle, they become mere natural forces engaged in the struggles of the world of existence. And as a result, existence itself becomes disrupted: immediate actuality itself, Enitharmon, "wept / One thousand years, and all the Earth was in a watry deluge" (24:4-5). When immediate actuality becomes paramount, it is inadequate even to itself, and collapses into non-differentiation, deluging existence with its own amorphous homogeneity.

Despite the disequilibrium and destruction, however, the forces of actualization are protected—by "the Seven Eyes of God [who] continually / Guard round them" (24:7-8): those various visions of ultimacy which have guided human behavior through history. In this way Los, the entelechic power which guides the process of Being, is also preserved, and thus Being is not rendered totally chaotic by the defection of the auxiliary forces. Los explains:

> . . . I the Fourth Zoa am also set
> The Watchman of Eternity, the Three are not! & I am Preserved
> Still my four mighty ones are left to me in Golgonooza
> Still Rintrah fierce, and Palamabron mild & piteous
> Theotormon filld with care, Bromion loving Science
> You O my Sons still guard round Los. O wander not & leave me.
> (24:8-13)

Although three other primary aspects of Being no longer function, Los can continue to guard Eternity—i.e., preserve the infinite aspect of Being—through actualizing individual beings (the work in Golgonooza). Los is able to perform this function by means of four primal modes of interrelatedness among individuals: the forces of wrath, pity, care, and knowledge. It is through these modes of mutual influence among individuals that actualization—i.e., transformation and development—occurs. Thus if these powers were disconnected from Los, the creative advance of Being would cease.

Los therefore continues to plead with Rintrah and Palamabron to remain with him, reminding them of the fate of other forces which abandoned or were exiled from their origins. "Rintrah," he says, "thou well rememberest when Amalek & Canaan / Fled with their Sister Moab into that abhorred Void / They became Nations in our sight beneath the hands of Tirzah" (24:14-16). All forces, be they social, political, or psychological, should work in concert with the entelechic power, marshalling their resources in support of this fundamental principle. All beings, both individual and collective, should be like Israel, which considered itself the chosen people who heard God's call and did his will. All should avoid the path of Amalek and Canaan, which, following only their own immediate concerns and ignoring the entelechic urge, were thus ignorant of the ultimate ramifications of their action and suffered destruction. For such preoccupation with the immediate rather that the ultimate—i.e., ignoring the direction of the entelechic power, which takes all other things and other times into account—results in failure to achieve full actualization. Involuntary separation from the entelechic force (through ignorance of that force, for example) has the same effect, as Los reminds Palamabron with the case of Joseph. Los then concludes:

> And if you also flee away and leave your Fathers side,
> Following Milton into Ulro, altho your power is great
> Surely you also shall become poor mortal vegetations
> Beneath the Moon of Ulro: pity then your Fathers tears.
>
> (24:22-5)

If love and wrath strive for immediate gratification rather than follow the general course of the process of Being, they will not fully actualize Being but will merely subsist in a state of illusory being ("beneath the Moon of Ulro").

But this appetite for immediacy is powerful, and it has even been institutionalized in orthodox Christianity—in particular, in the doctrine of the resurrection of the body, which sees eternal life as restitution of an individual to immediate actuality. Los describes this doctrine through the symbol of the resurrection of Lazarus:

> When Jesus raisd Lazarus from the Grave I stood & saw
> Lazarus who is the Vehicular Body of Albion the Redeemd
> Arise into the Covering Cherub who is the Spectre of Albion
> By martyrdoms to suffer: to watch over the Sleeping Body.
> Upon his rock beneath his Tomb.
>
> (24:26-30)

The symbol of Lazarus represents in truth "the Vehicular Body of Albion the Redeemd," which is the efficacious presence of the posthumously transformed (i.e., "Redeemd") individuals (Lazarus, like Milton, arising in his true being only after his death). Orthodox Christianity, however, tacitly assumes that the true being of an individual is constituted by the individual's most immediate actuality—i.e., its physical body—and the Lazarus story is thus taken as proof of physical resurrection (i.e., Lazarus is seen to "arise into the Covering Cherub"). Christian orthodoxy takes the risen Lazarus into itself, "the Covering Cherub," which is supposedly the locus of the divine presence but which is in truth the Spectre of Albion: the Cherub is an image of the homogeneous presence or substance which constitutes the false form of the unity of individual beings. This doctrine—Lazarus in the Covering Cherub—thus broods over the dead physical body, just as the Spectre of Milton did (20:20-22), with its fixation on immediacy.

This orientation to immediacy, of which the doctrine of the resurrection of the body is the most obvious manifestation, also reveals itself as the urge to establish immediate political dominion in the temporal world, as in the cases of Paul, Constantine, Charlemagne, and Luther. At the arising of Lazarus, Los says, he "saw the Covering Cherub / Divide Four-fold into Four Churches / Paul, Constantine, Charlemaine, Luther..." (24:30-32). Since these different forms of devotion to immediacy pervade western civilization — "behold they stand before us," Los says, "Stretchd over Europe & Asia" (24:32-3) — Los warns his sons that the effects of such devotion are deadly:

> ...come O Sons, come, away
> Arise O sons give all your strength against Eternal Death
> Lest we are vegetated, for Cathedrons Looms weave only Death
> A Web of Death....
>
> (24:33-6)

The Function of Mediation and Destruction

The Necessity of Mediation

Immersion in immediate actuality yields only death, for the present moment — the actuality woven by Cathedron's Looms — is continuously perishing. Immediacy is thus tantamount to non-being; and were it not for the various mediative processes, everything would be one amorphous mass of mere being, or simple presence:

> ...were it not for Bowlahoola & Allamanda
> No Human Form but only a Fibrous Vegetation
> A Polypus of soft affections without Thought or Vision
> Must tremble in the Heavens & Earths thro all the Ulro space[.]
> (24:36-9)

The Human Form, in contrast to mere vegetative existence, is constituted by non-immediacy, or negativity; it is characterized by thought and vision, relations of mediation and indirectness, as opposed to the immediacy of sensation or affections. Without such mediation, the process of Being would be inchoate and amorphous, because it would have no *telos* or final cause to give it form. All individuals would be like a polypus, which is largely amorphous and unarticulated, a mere subsistence which is actualized blindly, in all directions, without taking into account what is beyond its immediate spatial and temporal presence, simply reacting to what is immediately present.

The Human Form, the differentiated individual whose being is actualized in mediation—i.e., through its mediating other individuals and being mediated by them—is thus made possible by Bowlahoola and Allamanda. For the moment, however, we are not given an explanation of these functions; we are simply made to focus on the difference between the Human Form of existence and the largely undifferentiated form of the Polypus, and to ponder the condition of the possibility of this difference: i.e., how it is possible that there is a Human Form at all and not simply "Fibrous Vegetation," or a Polypus.

After thus urging his sons to resist capitulation to immediacy, which, he says, will result in eternal death, complete destruction of actualization, Los agrees to let Rintrah and Palamabron discard or destroy all individuals immersed in immediacy ("all the Vegetated Mortals"); however, he reaffirms Milton's importance as a signal that ultimate actualization or consummation is imminent:

> Throw all the Vegetated Mortals into Bowlahoola
> But as to this Elected Form who is returnd again
> He is the Signal that the Last Vintage now approaches
> Nor Vegetation may go on till all the Earth is reapd.
>
> (24:40-43)

The ultimate consummation, the Last Vintage, is fulfillment through destruction, the process by which one form of being is destroyed in order that another form may be actualized. The harvest thus symbolizes the process of actualization in general, which always destroys one actuality to put another in its place. But the purpose of the harvest is not simply to destroy the grain so that new grain can be grown; rather, it is to make grain available as nourishment for more complex, less immediate forms of being—Human Forms, which actualize themselves only by virtue of the unique being of the grain, and thus in some way preserve the unique individuality of the grain in their unique human form. For as we have seen, all actualization of one individual proceeds only by virtue of the unique being of antecedent individuals.

This self-overcoming which occurs in all actualization is virtually identical with the "objective immortality" which Milton achieves in embracing Eternal Death. Objective immortality, as we have seen, involves the indirect actualization in an existing being of another being which has perished, this indirect actualization being constituted by whatever effect or influence (direct or indirect) the perished entity has had on the actual entity. Thus Milton's embrace of Eternal Death is essentially the same occurrence as the Last Vintage. The fact that this Vintage is said to be the last does not mean simply that there will be no more vintages and hence no more destruction and suffering. Rather, "last" here signifies ultimate (as in Blake's phrase, "the Last Judgment"): Milton's descent signals the *Last* Vintage because his desiring Eternal Death is the ultimate instance of self-overcoming.

Although Los thus explains the necessity of the moment of negation for the creation of forms other than vegetative forms—"Nor Vegetation may go on till all the Earth is reapd," he declares—Rintrah and Palamabron are not persuaded to abandon immediacy:

> So Los spoke. Furious they descended to Bowlahoola &
>   Allamanda
> Indignant. unconvincd by Los's arguments & thun[d]ers rolling
> They saw that wrath now swayd and now pity absorbd him
> As it was, so it remaind & no hope of an end.
>
> (24:44-7)

Rintrah and Palamabron descend because they can see no satisfaction at all in the entelechic process, only an endless oscillation between pity and wrath, mutuality and opposition. They conceive of fulfillment not as an ongoing process of self-transformation, but rather as a state of presence which they can attain. This view of fulfillment, in fact, itself constitutes their descent from the transcendental principle of Los to the mere immediacy of the interaction and struggles of Allamanda and Bowlahoola.

The Establishment of Identity through Destruction

Allamanda and Bowlahoola, however, are themselves essential to the process of actualization. We are now told that "Bowlahoola is namd Law. by mortals, Tharmas founded it: / Because of Satan, before Luban the City of Golgonooza" (24:48-9). As law, Bowlahoola is the principle which safeguards identity, preserving the sanctity of an individual by circumscribing or delineating its being and by preventing incursion on its being. Bowlahoola is the counter to the Satanic principle, which overruns the boundaries of individuality and expropriates the unique being of individuals, reducing that being to a homogeneous quantity. This transcendental principle which Bowlahoola is manifests itself in the realm of experience as law—as the law of nature and the law established by society, both of which determine the proper roles and relationships among different individuals.

The fact that Bowlahoola is in Golgonooza, which "is namd Art & Maufacture by mortal men" (24:50), reveals that it is part of the productive, constructing, form-giving process of actualization — that process at the heart of Being which is embodied most clearly in the activities of art and manufacture. As a more specific indication of Bowlahoola's nature, we are told that "in Bowlahoola Los's Anvils stand & his Furnaces rage; / Thundering the Hammers beat & the Bellows loud / Living self moving" (24:51-3). Bowlahoola is thus the force which transforms the indefinite, inchoate, and amorphous into definiteness, actuality, and existence; it has its own intrinsic dynamism (it is "self-moving") that ineluctably imposes form on intractable amorphousness.

At the organic level this power manifests itself as the means by which individuals give new form to matter by incorporating and assimilating it into their own unique being. Thus we are told that "the Bellows are the Animal Lungs: the Hammers the Animal Heart / The Furnaces the Stomach for Digestion" (24:58-9), and that the process of digestion epitomizes this principle's instantiation in the biological realm: "Bowlahoola is the Stomach in every individual man" (24:67). Ordinarily we do not see digestion as terrible, but if we look closely at the phenomenon, we must conclude that in a way it is terrible, for by eating we deny existence to the other which we consume. Any giving of form, in fact, does violence to the matter on which the form is imposed. All actualization is thus destructive and painful to the antecedent individuals which it supersedes, evoking an incessant howling, as it were, from that which it is incessantly destroying, and a mourning and lamenting from those that remain: "Living self-moving mourning lamenting & howling incessantly / Bowlahoola thro all its porches feels" (24:53-4). Bowlahoola is the universal process of life living on death, revealed now as the source of all actualization.

A Redemptive Vision of Destruction

From another perspective, however, this violence and destructiveness of the process of actualization is seen to be pleasant and comforting:

> ...softly lilling flutes
> Accordant with the horrid labours make sweet melody.
> . . . .
> Thousands & thousands labour. thousands play on instruments
> Stringed or fluted to ameliorate the sorrows of slavery

Loud sport the dancers in the dance of death, rejoicing in carnage
The hard dentant Hammers are lulld by the flutes lula lula
The bellowing Furnaces['] blare by the long sounding clarion
The double drum drowns howls & groans, the shrill fife, shrieks &
  cries:
The crooked horn bellows the hoarse raving serpent, terrible but
  harmonious.

(24:56-7, 60-66)

The music is the pleasing interpretation or meaning that is given to these
events of destruction. By themselves these events are horrible, but in relation
to each other they are seen to constitute a larger whole which is pleasant and
reassuring. This "music" thus "ameliorates the sorrows of slavery"—i.e., the
sorrow resulting from making (through destruction) one individual a mere
means for another's actualization and fulfillment. This amelioration is
effected by a process of synthesis, giving a context to the individual acts of
destruction and making us see these acts in a larger temporal context, as notes
in a melody. Ultimately this music—this pleasant interpretation of destructive events—is the vision of the process of actualization itself: the incessant
howling of the brute fact of destruction is overlaid with the melodious
interpretation of destruction as preservation and even fulfillment, comforting us with the thought that this destruction is necessary and even good.
Blake thus presents actualization as that interminable process of striving,
overcoming, being destroyed, and (perhaps) surviving which is both terrible
and beautiful—beautiful, however, only when we apprehend each moment,
as in music or melody, through its mediated presence in other moments, and
theirs in it.

The Process of Actualization
and Productive Destruction

The Negating Function of Time

This destructive, negating process of actualization, we now see, is identical
with the process of time itself:

Los is by mortals nam'd Time Enitharmon is nam'd Space
But they depict him bald & aged who is in eternal youth
All powerful and his locks flourish like the brows of morning
He is the Spirit of Prophecy the ever apparent Elias.

(24:68-71)

What we call time is actually the process of actualization, or Los. This principle of time or actualization is the pre-eminent power in the universe, and all powers and forces of the world of existence are offspring—aspects or instantiations—of this power: "All the gods of the Kingdoms of Earth labour in Los's Halls," we are told; "every one is a fallen Son of the Spirit of Prophecy" (24:74-5). The power of actualization is the aspect of Being which completes and makes whole all the other aspects; "he is the Fourth Zoa, that stood arou[n]d the Throne Divine" (24:76).

The way in which time makes whole, however, is not through uninterrupted aggrandizement or positivity. Rather, it moves toward fulfillment by a continual negation of immediate, present actuality. We normally see time in terms of duration or endurance, and thus we depict it as "bald & aged." But in truth time is entelechy—continuous change and transformation and eternal renewal; it is a continuous morning (and mourning) or new beginning, that creative power through which novelty enters the world. As such it is the mediation between the actual and the non-actual, the "Spirit of Prophecy," which grasps the possibility at the heart of actuality and realizes that possibility. Because of this constant transformation which it produces, "time is the mercy of Eternity; without Times swiftness / Which is the swiftest of all things: all were eternal torment" (24:72-3). Since the very nature of existence is based upon finitude and incompleteness, which manifest themselves as torment, without time—i.e., change—these torments would never be mitigated in any respect. Thus the negation or destruction produced by the process of actualization is never merely destruction pure and simple: it is also the destruction of deficiency—the negation of negativity—and is thus positive or productive.

Productive Destruction

As we have already seen, this destructive/productive process of actualization is symbolized by the harvest and the vintage, in which the perishing of individuals of one type provides for the actualization of other individuals. This process is now made more graphic, with the image of the wine-press, in which individuals are literally crushed:

> Loud shout the sons of Luvah, at the Wine-presses as Los descended
> With Rintrah & Palamabron in his fires of resistless fury.
> The Wine-press on the Rhine groans loud, but all its central beams
> Act more terrific in the central Cities of the Nations

> Where Human Thought is crushd beneath the iron hand of Power.
> There Los puts all into the Press, the Opressor & the Opressed
> Together, ripe for the Harvest & Vintage & ready for the Loom.
>
> (25:1-7)

The cruelty and destructiveness of some paths of actualization is shown to be unmistakable. The inexorable process of actualization destroys all which is gathered into it, good and bad alike, especially "in the central Cities of the Nations," the regions where individual being is devoured by centralized, feudalistic systems. Here everything is reduced to a homogeneous, amorphous substance to be woven into the fabric of existence on Cathedron's Loom and given over to the brutal struggle between predator and prey ("the Opressor & the Opressed").

From a certain perspective, this process is fulfilling. Those who attend to the wine presses, for example—the Sons of Luvah, who are the offspring of love, the urge toward wholeness, unity, and fulfillment—rejoice that the moment of fulfillment is at hand:

> They sang at the Vintage. This is the Last Vintage! & Seed
> Shall no more be sown upon Earth, till all the Vintage is over
> And all gatherd in, till the Plow has passd over the Nations
> And the Harrow & heavy thundering Roller upon the mountains.
>
> (25:8-11)

The Sons say this is the last vintage, implying that the new actuality which grows up after the destruction of the present actuality will be final and ultimate, never to be superseded. Henceforth there will be only growth, no destruction. Such a state seems paradoxical, for we have seen that life and growth depend upon death. It may be, therefore, that the Sons of Luvah are deluded by the ecstasy of fulfillment into thinking that this fulfillment is ultimate, not aware that its actuality too must pass away.[3]

But the present vintage is, in fact, last—in another sense, as we have already seen (although it is questionable whether the Sons of Luvah are themselves aware of this sense). It is last because it constitutes, through Milton's voluntary embrace of Eternal Death, the ultimate instance of self-overcoming, freeing desire from self-perpetuation (i.e., freeing Orc from the Chain of Jealousy) and allowing it to will its own supersession, or fulfillment through self-destruction. When conscious desire takes this form, there is in a sense no more annihilative destruction as we understand it: there is only supersession, or productive destruction. Such a vision is constituted by a comprehensive embrace of all elements of actuality, past and present, seeing everything as interconnected with and mutually supportive of everything else, and as ultimately constitutive of oneself.

Los proceeds to describe this comprehension, first pausing to rebuke those who would attempt immediate self-aggrandizement:

> . . . loud the Souls howl round the Porches of Golgonooza
> Crying O God deliver us to the Heavens or to the Earths,
> That we may preach righteousness & punish the sinner with death.
> But Los refused, till all the Vintage of Earth was Gatherd in.
>
> (25:12-15)

These souls are apparently possibilities of individual being which are about to enter the process of actualization, Golgonooza. The possibilities have an urge to become actual and to acquire immediate completion or satisfaction, which proceeds through the exercise of power and control over others. The howling of the souls is the *élan* of individuals which motivates the quest for full realization of intrinsic possibilities and inevitably takes the form of suppressing those possibilities which lie outside the path of its identity, a suppression which constitutes the preaching of righteousness and the punishing with death. This quest for immediate satisfaction that bypasses and even suppresses the rest of reality is opposed by Los: he refuses to allow these souls to be actualized "till all the Vintage of Earth was gatherd in" — i.e., till all of actuality is taken into account and given its due.

Los now describes this comprehensive unity of individuals, which constitutes the fulfillment of each of them:

> Fellow Labourers! The Great Vintage & Harvest is now upon Earth
> The Whole extent of the Globe is explored: Every scatterd Atom
> Of Human Intellect now is flocking to the sound of the Trumpet
> All the Wisdom which was hidden in caves & dens, from ancient
> Time; is now sought out from Animal & Vegetable & Mineral
> The Awakener is come. outstretchd over Europe! the Vision of
>   God is fulfilled.
>
> (25:17-22)

The Great Vintage & Harvest which Los speaks of is the actualization of every individual through the mediation of the Human Intellect. This actualization is effected through the realization of the uniqueness and intrinsic value of all the previously ignored or imperceptible beings and attributes — "all the wisdom which was hidden in caves & dens." By acknowledging the intrinsic being of "Animal & Vegetable & Mineral" beings, the Human Intellect indirectly actualizes that being—in the changes which it undergoes itself as a result of its new awareness, and in the changes which this new awareness effects in being which it acts upon or influences. In the first place, the simple acknowledgement by one individual of another's being constitutes an indirect or mediated actualization of the acknowledged individual. And when all these acknowledgements are brought together and account is taken of the intrinsic being of all individuals, the Great Harvest occurs, which is a gathering and assimilation of all the intrinsic being of other individuals, without, however, negating the uniqueness of that being, but rather preserving it. This is the fulfillment of the "Vision of God," the reunion of the multiplicity of individual existents in the One, the ground of beings from which they all sprang.

The unity of individuals achieved through the expansion of the Human Intellect is expressed as the awakening of the Ancient Man, the dormant authentic being of individuals which is constituted by the mediated unity of all individuals: "The Ancient Man upon the Rock of Albion Awakes" (25:23). The actuality which he encounters, however, is a perversion of the authentic unity of individual beings which he is: "He listens to the sounds of War astonishd & ashamd; / He sees his Children mock at Faith and deny Providence" (25:24-5). His Children, the instantiations of the unity of individuals, do not truly embody this unity, and hence Albion does not yet arise: the true unified form of individuals—in which each individual takes account of all other individuals and thus gives them mediated actuality in itself—does not yet become actual, even though it has now been made possible through being envisioned by Blake/Los.

Immediacy, Perishing, and the Three Classes of Individual Being

Because of this inauthenticity, Los tells the labourers, the harvested individuals must be judged regarding their degree of authenticity:

> Therefore you must bind the Sheaves not by Nations or Families
> You shall bind them in Three Classes; according to their Classes
> So shall you bind them. Separating What has been Mixed.
>
> (25:26-8)

Each individual must be judged and classified according to its own inherent actual being rather than on the basis of its contingent proximity with other individuals or its association with extrinsic realities (e.g., nations). This classification is necessary because of the perversion of authentic individuality which has occurred "since Men began to be Wove into Nations by Rahab & Tirzah / Since Albions Death & Satans Cutting-off from our Fields" (25:2-30): the inauthenticity, or the death of Albion, is constituted by self-aggrandizement—individuals' seeking fulfillment in false satisfaction and immediate pleasure. This embracing of false fulfillment, in turn, is the result of a false vision of the nature of individual being: it is the result, that is, of the separation of Satan, the reductive principle, into an autonomous, absolute principle that denies intrinsic being to individuals and thus precludes their retention of being after perishing and makes immediate, actual fulfillment the only type conceivable.

This embrace of false fulfillment is also expressed as the ascendance of the Elect aspect or type of identity—i.e., as the event "when under pretence of benevolence the Elect Subdud All / From the Foundation of the World" (25:31-2). The Elect are those who "cannot believe in Eternal Life / Except by Miracle & a New Birth" (25:33-4). For them, the destruction of an indi-vidual's actuality is the destruction of its being; in their view, being is identi-cal with immediate total self-presence, and whatever is not immediate *is not*. Thus Eternal Life means the restitution and perpetuation of immediacy. This positivist vision, under pretence of espousing the truth, has subjugated everything, including the notion of Being itself, to immediacy or presence, a subjugation which, as we have seen, is essentially identical with the death of Albion, the usurpation by Satan, and the dominance by Rahab and Tirzah.

There are two other classes of individuals, however, constituted by two other visions of individual being: "the Reprobate who never cease to Believe, and the Redeemd, / Who live in doubts & fears perpetually tormented by the Elect" (25:35-6). The Reprobate are those whose ways are considered sinful and thus damning by the Elect but who do not attempt to change their ways because they do not worry about destruction: i.e., they do not cease to believe—instinctively or implicitly—that destruction is not ultimate. The Redeemed are those who do try to change, because they believe the conten-tion of the Elect that improper actions will lead to their annihilation. The Reprobate and the Redeemed thus reject, at least implicitly, the positivist view of the Elect—the Reprobate by affirming (through their indifference to self-reform) the continuation of their being after death, and the Redeemed by manifesting the recognition that their real being (seen as what they should be) is not identical with their actual immediate identity, which they are trying to change. Because of their common rejection of immediacy or pure presence as the ultimate principle, the Reprobate and the Redeemed should be combined in the same category, Los says: "These you shall bind in a twin bundle for the

Consummation" (25:37). "But the Elect," he says, "must be saved [from] fires of Eternal Death, / To be formed into the Churches of Beulah that they destroy not the Earth" (25:38-9). The Reprobate and Redeemed can be classified as destroyed or consumed because such destruction of existence does not destroy their being. The Elect, however, must be spoken of and dealt with as if their existence did not end, for if they once thought that they would perish, these positivists, for whom immediate presence alone constitutes being, would ravage the earth in a mad rush for immediate fulfillment.

The fundamentality of these three classes or aspects of individual identity is indicated by the fact that these three types are not limited to the realm of human being. Los says that "in every Nation & every Family the Three Classes are born / And in every Species of Earth, Metal, Tree, Fish, Bird & Beast" (25:40-41). In every sphere of being, individual entities exist according to these three fundamental modes, corresponding to three different ontological perspectives. The Reprobate, as we have seen, is that individual (or aspect of individuals) which is immersed in its immediate existence, yet attributes no ultimate value to this immediacy, and thus conducts itself without great circumspection or regard to self-preservation. The Redeemed is the individual (or aspect) which gives precedence to the non-immediate—of the future, on the one hand, and of its own intrinsic being, on the other—yet acknowledges the essential role of the immediate (i.e., of actualization) in uniting the two non-immediates of the future and its own essence: although immediate actuality is not taken to be ultimate, it is nevertheless accepted as the only means of achieving ultimate fulfillment. Finally, the Elect is the individual for which immediacy or presence is all there is, and which, therefore, will do whatever is necessary to preserve or guarantee the perpetuation of its own immediacy.

It is difficult to imagine the difference between, say an Elect bar of iron and a Reprobate bar. But when we consider the organic realm, the distinction begins to make sense—an Elect oak (or aspect of an oak) tenaciously clings to existence, devouring and assimilating otherness; a Reprobate oak (or aspect) opposes whatever it encounters, resisting otherness; and a Redeemed oak or aspect grows and develops by accommodating otherness. The point is that for every individual, regardless of genus or species, there are three fundamental modes of relatedness to other individuals, to its own existence, and to perishing. The recognition of these three aspects of identity is crucial if one is to distinguish between authentic fulfillment and spurious, delusory gratification.

Immediate Gratification versus True Fulfillment

In view of these various aspects of an individual's being, Los and his forces take care to maintain the difference between the individual's true intrinsic being and the immediate present actuality of that individual. "We form the Mundane Egg," he says, "[so] that Spectres coming by fury or amity, / All is the same, & every one remains in his own energy" (25:42-3). The Mundane Egg is the idea of all the unactualized portions of an individual's being—the unhatched embryo—which is present implicitly in the individual and in mediation in the human intellect (in the metaphysics which is the Mundane Shell). This unactualized form or image of the true individual preserves the authentic being of the individual in the face of the appearance of Spectres, the false embodiments or manifestations of its being. Thus the individual "remains in his own energy"—i.e., its own intrinsic being—even when its immediate actuality is inauthentic, or spectrous.

This distinction between true identity and immediate actuality—i.e., between being and presence—is of utmost importance, and Los thus continues to urge the laborers to acknowledge this difference and resist the lure of immediacy:

> Go forth Reapers with rejoicing. you sowed in tears
> But the time of your refreshing cometh, only a little moment
> Still abstain from pleasure & rest in the labours of eternity
> And you shall Reap the whole Earth from Pole to Pole! from Sea to
> Sea.
>
> (25:44-7)

The reaping shall begin, Los says, "at Jerusalems Inner Court, Lambeth [which is] ruin'd and given / To the detestable Gods of Priam, to Apollo: and at the Asylum / Given to Hercules" (25:48-50). That is, the destruction of present actuality which makes way for new actuality will focus on the ideal of fulfillment itself (Jerusalem), which has been given over to the powers of immediacy—Apollo and Hercules, the Gods of Priam, "who labour in Tirzah's Looms for bread. / Who set Pleasure against Duty: who Create Olympic crowns / To make Learning a burden & the Work of the Holy Spirit: Strife" (25:50-52). Jerusalem, that is—the ideal form of ultimate fulfillment—has been captured and destroyed by the positivist view, which sees individual gratification as a pleasure which conflicts with one's obligation to others (duty), that is falsely seen as a requirement imposed by some higher external power. This positivist view also debases authentic—i.e., non-immediate, or spiritual—fulfillment, by emphasizing and rewarding physical achievement (creating "Olympic crowns"). The orientation toward immediacy does not bring fulfillment, however, as we see from the fact that "Lambeth mourns calling Jerusalem. she weeps & looks abroad / For the Lords coming, that Jerusalem may overspread all Nations" (25:54-5).

Los ends his speech with an explicit exhortation to the laborers not to yield to the lure of the immediate. First he tells them not to be caught up in pleasure. "Crave not for the mortal & perishing delights," he admonishes, "but leave them / To the weak, and pity the weak as your infant care" (25:56-7). Pleasure, however, is not the only lure of immediacy; there is also wrath, which, as the attempt to immediately destroy that which is an obstacle to one's fulfillment, is simply the obverse of pleasure. This capitulation to immediacy embodied in wrath is ultimately just as counterproductive in the quest for fulfillment as pleasure is, and Los consequently tells the laborers, "Break not / Forth in your wrath lest you also are vegetated By Tirzah" (25:57-8). Capitulation to wrath or pleasure results in the reduction of an individual to a vegetative state, in which there is virtually no extension of one's being beyond immediacy, or self-presence.

For this reason Los urges patience; by deferring immediate gratification, one can achieve true fulfillment:

> Wait till the Judgement is past, till the Creation is consumed
> And then rush forward with me into the glorious spiritual
> Vegetation; the Supper of the Lamb & his Bride; and the
> Awaking of Albion our friend and ancient companion.
>
>   (25:59-62)

True fulfillment and the activation of authentic individuality will occur only after the present actuality is destroyed and "the Judgement is past." Present actuality, that is, achieves fulfillment only in being assimilated into another actuality which supersedes it. An individual's greater being is actualized only in what it effects, and certain effects of an individual are a function of its perishing. For example, the greater being of the grape—that which all its effort of growth prepares it to become—is wine, and the grape actualizes this being only in perishing. The situation is similar with regard to grain and flour, or more obviously, a bud and a flower. In this process of consummation, an individual is simultaneously consumed and consummated. The actuality which supersedes an individual passes judgment on that individual, preserving and appropriating certain portions of the individual's being (in different ways) and discarding other portions, thus (hopefully) refining the individual by preserving the greater being and destroying the inauthentic. In this way the individual achieves "the glorious spiritual / Vegetation" which is the immediate presence of its essential being in another being apart from its actual existence.

Such, at least, is the *vision* of true fulfillment. We are once again reminded, however, that this is not the actual state of things: Los's plea is not entirely successful, for "lightning of discontent broke on all sides round / And murmurs of thunder rolling heavy long & loud over the mountains / While Los calld his sons around him to the Harvest and Vintage" (25:63-5). The Great Harvest and Last Vintage are taking place, but only in an incipient and partial manner, for not all powers and individuals are participating.

CHAPTER VIII

The Sons of Los: Identity and The Intrinsic Interrelatedness of Individuals

Identity and Mutuality

After establishing the necessity of mediation, Blake proceeds to present several concrete instances of the manner in which such mediation or mutuality constitutes the unique identities of the individuals involved, showing how the being of the individual exceeds the individual's immediacy. Blake here addresses the reader directly, focusing our attention on our own experience of the Sons of Los—i.e., the various particular instantiations of the actualizing, mediating principle:

> Thou seest the Constellations in the deep & wondrous Night
> They rise in order and continue their immortal courses
> Upon the mountains & in vales with harp & heavenly song
> With flute & clarion; with cups & measures filld with foaming wine.
> And the calm Ocean joys beneath & smooths his awful waves!
> These are the Sons of Los, & these the Labourers of the Vintage.
> (25:66-26:1)

We view the Sons of Los—offspring of the principle of actualization—whenever we perceive order in the universe or whenever we observe fulfillment and calm repose. The enduring, orderly movement of the constellations is a tremendous structured process in which numerous forces have combined in harmonious mutual actualization. What might normally be seen as instances of Newtonian mechanics are here seen to be a fulfilled actualization which is at bottom the same fulfillment that we ourselves experience through listening to music or drinking wine: it is constituted through the intercourse and union of powers previously alien to each other. Different forces no longer merely oppose each other but rather each reflects in itself the other's fulfillment: "the streams reflect the Vision of beatitude, / And the calm Ocean joys beneath & smooths his awful waves!"

151

We also observe manifestations of the mediation performed by the actualizing process when we view the organic realm. Blake declares:

> Thou seest the gorgeous clothed Flies that dance & sport in
>   summer
> Upon the sunny brooks & meadows: every one the dance
> Knows in its intricate mazes of delight artful to weave:
> Each one to sound his instruments of music in the dance,
> To touch each other & recede, to cross & change & return
> These are the Children of Los. . . .

> (26:2-7)

We see here that the intricately and complexly structured process effected by the actualizing principle reveals itself both in the relation of the individual to itself from one moment to the next—i.e., in the relation of one step to the others in the dance, or of one note to the others in the music—as well as in the relation of one individual to another. In both cases, each element actualizes its intrinsic being only in the process of interacting with other elements. And this interaction is based not on mutual antagonism but rather on mutual respect of each for the sanctity of the other's intrinsic being: the flies "touch each other and recede," in one moment moving beyond their own sphere of identity and achieving unity and communion, without impinging upon the being of the other, and in the next moment returning to their own sphere of being. In this vision of individuals moving in harmony with other individuals and in accord with the music which the totality of individuals produces, we see the offspring of the actualizing, form-giving power: taking account of the larger pattern through which one's greater being is ultimately manifested and in which one's immediate actuality (spatial and temporal) is but a moment. Even beings such as the flies embody, though without self-consciousness, that vision or synthetic power by means of which the individual differentiates between its being and its immediate actual state, and conducts itself in accordance with the totality of being rather than only in relation to immediate actuality. It is this capacity which makes possible the mutual respect among individuals and which creates the unity of diverse moments or actions, weaving the intricate mazes of delight that constitute ultimate fulfillment.

Behavior like that of the flies thus embodies implicitly the truth that an individual's being exceeds both the immediate temporal moment and the individual's immediate actualization (in the totality of its temporal moments), and that to achieve full actualization it must take account of its own immediate actualization in other temporal moments and of its mediated, or indirect actualization through other beings (e.g., as Milton is indirectly actualized by Blake). Such is a truly ec-static existence, the opposite of the relative self-enclosure of mere vegetation.

Other individuals, in fact, are necessary for one to achieve direct actualization as well as indirect, and Blake proceeds to make us aware of this point:

> ...thou seest the Trees on mountains
> The wind blows heavy, loud they thunder thro' the darksom sky
> Uttering prophecies & speaking instructive words to the sons
> Of men: These are the Sons of Los!
>
> (26:7-10)

The wind needs the trees in order to actualize aspects of itself, for wind is what it is only insofar as it, among other things, thunders through the trees. The trees likewise, although to a lesser extent, depend upon the wind to actualize them. The thunder manifests this mutual actualization (fulfillment) of the wind and the trees ("*they* thunder": without both, there is no thunder), and the instructive words that it utters are the words of Blake: "These are the Sons of Los! These are the Visions of Eternity" (26:10). The wind blowing through the trees, like the other visions, is a dim manifestation of infinity (i.e., of Eternity), which is constituted by the actualization of unique individuals in and through the process of their mutual interaction. Individuals are what they are only by virtue of transcending their immediacy and interacting with other individuals. Seeing the trees respond to the wind, the wind react to the trees, and their interaction produce thunder should make us aware of this togetherness of all things: the simple occurrence of contact and mutual influence between things such as wind and trees points to the much deeper truth that all individual beings are together, related to each other at an ontological level. For if there were no fundamental, ontological contact between the wind and the trees, neither would affect the other—even in the most superficial or external manner—and there would be no thunder manifesting interaction.

In these visions, then, of the cosmic, organic, and physical order and interaction, we perceive infinity, or Eternity. "But," Blake says, "we see only as it were the hem of their garments / When with our vegetable eyes we view these wound'rous Visions" (26:11-12). In order to see their true being and total form rather than just a part of their external appearance, we ourselves must move beyond the immediacy present to our physical vision and take account of the implicit and hidden aspects of these beings, as we have here attempted to do in our reflection on these visions. This is what Blake expects us to do, and what, indeed, we do naturally, in a small way, without even realizing it. In fact, we move beyond the immediate in reading this very passage, when we assume that the wind and the trees interact, for there is no explicit reference to the wind and the trees being together—i.e., no statement of cause and effect. It is we who must supply the connection, and we do, without even being aware of our action, since we take this type of connection for granted. The lack of syntactic connection here should emphasize to us that we always assume such connectedness, even when we actually perceive the wind blowing, the trees swaying, and the thunder rumbling, and therefore assume that the events are interrelated. Blake asks us to ponder this fact and to realize the ontological import of this assumption and recognize that this ontological truth lies beyond the immediate phenomena.

Blake's presentation here of interconnection and causality is especially interesting in contrast with Hume's treatment of causality, for Hume's assumptions are diametrically opposed to Blake's. Hume assumes that since we can never directly experience causality—i.e., since causality is never present in immediacy—we have no right to assume that there is such a thing as causality. This opinion follows directly from the positivism of empiricism, its belief that only that which is immediately—i.e., sensuously—present has being. For Blake the assumption is the opposite: what is immediate is only a small aspect of Being, and to see all of what really is—to attain a vision of Eternity—one must look beyond the immediate, beyond presence.

Relatedness and the Intrinsicness of Individual Being

The Origin of Determinate Identity in Interaction

After establishing that individual being is constituted by mediation—through temporal projection and ecstatic interrelatedness with other individuals—Blake gives an account of the nature of intrinsic individual being and the manner in which that being is actualized by the Sons of Los, the powers generated by the entelechic principle. We are told that

> There are Two Gates thro which all Souls descend. One
>   Southward
> From Dover Cliff to Lizard Point. the other toward the North
> Caithness & rocky Durness, Pentland & John Groats House.
>
> (26:13-15)

These Souls, the unactualized individual being, descend at birth from the realm of pure possibility into the body, or immediate actuality, and then at death descend out of the body into mediated actuality, or "objective immortality." "The Souls descending to the Body," we are told, "wail on the right hand / Of Los; & those delivered from the Body, on the left hand" (26:16-17). Los, the power of actualization, receives individuals into actuality on the one hand and issues them out of immediate actuality into mediated actuality on the other. In addition,

> ...Los against the east his force continually bends
> Along the Valleys of Middlesex from Hounslow to Blackheath
> Lest those Three Heavens of Beulah should the Creation destroy
> And lest they should descend before the north & South Gates
> Groaning with pity, he among the wailing Souls laments.
>   (26:18-22)

Los continually tries to move toward the east, where Jerusalem, fulfillment, lies; in moving toward Jerusalem, Los prevents the Three Heavens of Beulah from destroying all creation by encountering the non-actual souls and deluding them into an inauthentic actualization (direct or indirect) in their false fulfillments of head, heart, and loins (intellectual, emotional, and sensual).

The souls are "piteous Passions & Desires / With neither lineament nor form but like to watry clouds" (26:26-7). They are unactualized beings, mere abstract potentialities, and thus as yet indeterminate. They are therefore not truly individual but are merely dormant possibilities inclining to and yearning for actuality, which they attain only through interaction with other individuals: "such[—]alone[—]sleepers remain[:] meer passion & appetite" (26:29). The souls or possibilities are actualized by being brought into interaction with actual individuals through the continuous flux of Becoming, the insubstantial force which transforms and devours actuality. In Blake's words, "the Passions and Desires descend upon the hungry winds" (26:28), and as Los receives these possibilities into actuality, "the Sons of Los"—actual individuals, which are always also, through interaction, auxiliary powers of actualization—"clothe them & feed & provide houses & fields" (26:30)—i.e., instantiate concrete interactions between the new individuals and the world, thereby producing definite, determinate individuality.

Intrinsic Being

As we have seen, an individual is what it is only by virtue of other individuals, most obviously in eating other beings and taking physical refuge in them (by means of clothes and houses). Yet despite its essential relatedness to other beings, each actualized individual has its unique intrinsic being and its own inherent value and beauty:

> ...every Generated Body in its inward form,
> Is a garden of delight & a building of magnificence,
> Built by the Sons of Los in Bowlahoola & Allamanda
> And the herbs & flowers & furniture & beds & chambers
> Continually woven in the Looms of Enitharmons Daughters
> In bright Cathedrons golden Dome with care & love & tears[.]
>
>   (26:31-6)

Each natural being is a construction ("building of magnificence"), an impressive unity of many parts, constituted by a continual synthesizing process that weaves together the warp of actualities with the woof of possibilities to constitute the fabric of existence. But despite the fact that it is composed of smaller elements and is a component of larger entities, every individual is an end in itself; its mere being is valuable and fulfilling, a "garden of delight" both for itself and for others. Although it exists and, in fact, *is*, only in relation to other individuals and is a result of the universal process of Being, it is not a derivative or secondary phenomenon; it is itself the heart of reality — the good, the beautiful, the goal of all desire.

In this actualization of individuals the type or class of identity is also determined: "the various Classes of Men are all marked out determinate / In Bowlahoola" (26:37-8). The path of actualization, that is, determines the nature of an individual's mode of relationship with otherness and with itself, and the way in which it will attempt to achieve fulfillment. Moreover, the delineation of an individual which occurs when it is actualized also determines the inauthentic aspect, or Spectre, of the individual — the specific inauthentic mode of actualization or the type of false fulfillment which the individual is susceptible to. For we are told that "as the Spectres choose their affinities / So they are born on Earth" (26:38-9): the type of affinities which the Spectre has — i.e., the types of pleasure or false fulfillment which the inauthentic aspect is attracted to — also achieves actualization.

Causality

This determinacy of the individual, however, is not determinism as we normally conceive of it:

>   ...every Class is determinate
> But not by Natural but by Spiritual power alone. Because
> The Natural power continually seeks & tends to Destruction

Ending in Death: which would of itself be Eternal Death
And all are Class'd by Spiritual, & not by Natural power.
(26:39-43)

The power which determines the individual's class, or mode of attempting
fulfillment, is not an actual power or presence which confronts the individual
as an external force: such would be a "Natural power" — efficient and/or
material causality, which is destructive rather than constructive, working
through the extrinsic, external relatedness of mere random collision and
compulsion. The determining Spiritual power, on the other hand, is more
akin to the mediated power of formal and final causality. It is a synthesizing or
constructive power that works through the intrinsic, internal relatedness of
individuals for their mutual benefit. As the mediated power of intrinsic
relatedness, it is that synthesizing, actualizing power which preserves one
individual through the creation of another, and vice versa. Since the Natural
power, the power of immediacy, restricts and reduces the (immediate) actuality of individuals (through their mutual opposition), it leads inexorably to
the perishing or death of individuals. This death, or termination of existence,
would be Eternal Death — total annihilation of the individuals' being — were
it not for the Spiritual power, which preserves dead individuals in the
mediated actuality of posthumous presence which is itself constituted by the
intrinsic relatedness of all individuals. The Class of individuals, or the general structure of their identity, is thus determined by their intrinsic relations
or affinities rather than by contingent, external encounters: in Blake's words,
"all are Class'd by Spiritual, & not by natural power."

All events, in fact, are ultimately determined by the mediated power of
intrinsic relatedness rather than by the immediate power or proximate causality of contingent actual encounters: "every Natural Effect has a Spiritual
Cause, and Not / A Natural: for a Natural Cause only seems, it is a Delusion" (26:44-5). A Natural Cause is not the real cause of events in the natural
world; it is only the immediate occasion for such events. For example, when
it rains and the grass grows, the real cause of growth is not the contingent
occurrence of rain but rather the inherent relatedness between (among other
things) the unique intrinsic being of the grass and that of the rain. The actual
instance of rain is only the contingent immediate occasion or proximate
cause of the grass's growth. If such contingent and immediate occurrences
were the only powers, then there would be no Eternity or preservation of
individual being (or even any mutual interaction at all, as we have seen). The
Spiritual Cause, however, as the intrinsic relatedness of individuals, preserves the rain's unique being in the unique being of the grass, which is

intrinsically related to that of the rain. And when the grass, in turn, is devoured or dies and decays, its unique being is preserved in the being of the earth or the cow, both of which are intrinsically and essentially related to the grass.

The natural cause is thus said to be "a Delusion / Of Ulro: & a ratio of the perishing Vegetable Memory" (26:45-6): it is a misapprehension resulting from attention devoted exclusively to immediacy, the memory which continuously perishes—i.e., forgets—and thus retains only the immediate actuality of the immediate past which it perceives in connection with the immediate actuality of the present. Like Hume, Blake thus dismisses efficient causality as an invalid fabrication of the memory. However, while Hume's skepticism derived from the non-presence of the cause itself—a positivist objection—Blake's objection is precisely the opposite: he objects to the exclusion of mediation (in the form of final and formal causality), an exclusion which ignores the aspect of Being which constitutes the eternity or infinity of individuals.

Interrelatedness and Destruction

Destruction and Fundamental Connexity

Such, then, is the nature of actualization, the activity of Los and his Sons which constitutes the unique, intrinsic being of individuals. Blake now moves to consider once again the opposite moment of being—the moment of destruction, which is also an essential aspect of actualization. This moment is symbolized by "the Wine-Press of Los [which] is eastward of Golgonooza, before the Seat / Of Satan" (27:1-2). Here the being of individuals is reduced to a more homogeneous state, in which it can be assimilated by other individuals. The location of the wine-press, eastward of Golgonooza, expresses the relation of the destructive to the constructive aspects of actualization. The exact significance of the eastward location is somewhat ambiguous, however; it may signify that destruction is prior to or presupposed by construction, but it also indicates that this destructiveness is located in the abandoned realm of "Luvah [who] laid the foundation," and whose "sons & daughters...here...tread the grapes" (27:2-3). This connection between destruction and Luvah indicates that destruction effected by the wine-press is made possible by the ontological principle of love, the principle of connexity of individuals or intrinsic relatedness of individuals which partially constitutes spiritual causality, as we have seen. Here this intrinsic relatedness is seen to be the condition for the possibility of destruction of entities, as well as of their construction. It is so because without some intrinsic connectedness, some essential common ground, one individual could not have any effect at all on another and thus individuals could not destroy each other. The very existence of destruction thus points to a fundamental, intrinsic connectedness of individuals as its basis—a connectedness which is most fully manifest and authentically actualized in love. Destruction or perishing is also based on love because it is, like love, a giving of one's being to another. When one individual passes out of existence, it contributes its being to those who remain behind, although not, as we have seen, in a merely quantitative sense: these surviving individuals are enhanced by the posthumous presence of the perished individual, and they in turn transform and develop the posthumous presence in their own actuality.

While Luvah, or intrinsic connectedness, thus forms the foundation of the wine press, we are told that "Urizen finish'd it in howling woe" (27:2). The actual destruction of individuals is effected through the inherent opposition between individuals which derives, as we have seen, from Urizen, the principle of individuation. This destruction occurs "before the Seat / Of Satan" (27:1-2), the Miller of Eternity who reduces individuals to a relatively homogeneous state so that their being may be assimilated by other individuals. And because the most obvious instance of this destruction is found in violent aggression, "this Wine-press is call'd War on Earth" (27:8).

The winepress is also the "Printing-Press / Of Los; and here he lays his words in order above the mortal brain / As cogs are formd in a wheel to turn the cogs of the adverse wheel" (27:8-10). Events of destruction—especially cataclysmic events such as war—are the means whereby the power of actualization impresses itself upon finite understanding, for adversity moves human awareness with the ineluctability of mechanical motion. Such events are Los's printing press because they present a text which, if read correctly, describes Los as the power which creates a new order through the destruction of the old.

This view of destruction as the prerequisite for generation has affinities with the views of natural religion, and Blake employs images of Bacchic revelry and ceremony to evoke the connection and reveal the valid aspect of the Dionysian mysteries:

> How red the sons & daughters of Luvah! here they tread the grapes.
> Laughing & shouting drunk with odours many fall oerwearied
> Drownd in the wine is many a youth & maiden: those around

Lay them on skins of Tygers & of the spotted Leopard & the Wild
    Ass
Till they revive, or bury them in cool grots, making lamentation.
                                                        (27:3-7)

The great achievement of the Dionysian vision was, as Nietzsche noted, its apprehension of the intimate relation between living and dying, and between rejoicing and lamentation. The rejoicing and dancing are indications of the productive and transforming aspect of actualization, which transforms individuals to the point at which they are completely beside themselves — ec-static.

The individuals that rejoice are those who are drinking the wine made of the destroyed individuals. Blake finds this aspect of destruction epitomized in those species which are most obviously parasitic and live most obviously by the destruction of other individual beings:

Timbrels & violins sport round the Wine-presses; the little Seed;
The sportive Root, the Earth-worm, the gold Beetle; the wise
    Emmet;
Dance round the Wine-presses of Luvah: the Centipede is there:
The ground Spider with many eyes: the Mole clothed in velvet
The ambitious Spider in his sullen web; the lucky golden Spinner;
The earwig armd: the tender Maggot emblem of immortality:
The Flea: Louse: Bug: the Tape-Worm: all the Armies of Disease:
Visible or invisible to the slothful vegetating Man.
The slow Slug: the Grasshopper that sings & laughs & drinks:
Winter comes, he folds his slender bones without a murmur.
The cruel Scorpion is there: the Gnat: Wasp: Hornet & the Honey
    Bee:
The Toad & venomous Newt; the Serpent clothd in gems & gold:
They throw off their gorgeous raiment: they rejoice with loud
    jubilee
Around the Wine-presses of Luvah, naked & drunk with wine.
There is the Nettle that stings with soft down; and there
The indignant Thistle: whose bitterness is bred in his milk:
Who feeds on contempt of his neighbor. there all the idle Weeds
That creep around the obscure places shew their various limbs.
Naked in all their beauty dancing round the Wine-presses.
                                                        (27:11-29)

Although it has the form of a catalogue and seems to shed little light on the subject at hand, this passage subtly recapitulates several important ideas. First, the list includes a short description of each individual species that serves to emphasize its unique intrinsic being. The multiplicity of these species compels us to realize that the world itself and all of reality is nothing other than these myriad individual species in their unique and diverse characters. We are also subtly reminded that it is through destruction that individuals are preserved: we are told that "the tender Maggot," which is normally an emblem of mortality, is "an emblem of immortality." Finally, the acknowledgement of the beauty of all these beings dancing around the winepress affirms both the intrinsic value of each being as well as the value of the process of actualization through destruction.

Negative Aspects of Interrelatedness

The winepress is quite different, however, when it is seen from the inside, from the point of view of the individuals who are being destroyed by the process of actualization:

> But in the Wine-presses the Human grapes sing not, nor dance
> They howl & writhe in shoals of torment: in fierce flames consuming,
> In chains of iron & in dungeons circled with ceaseless fires.
> In pits & dens & shades of death: in shapes of torment & woe.
> The plates & screws & wracks & saws & cords & fires & cisterns
> The cruel joys of Luvahs Daughters lacerating with knives
> And whips their Victims & the deadly sport of Luvahs Sons.
> They dance around the dying, & they drink the howl & groan
> They catch the shrieks in cups of gold, they hand them to one another:
> These are the sports of love, & these the sweet delights of amorous play
> Tears of the grape, the death sweat of the cluster the last sigh
> Of the mild youth who listens to the lureing songs of Luvah.
>
> (27:30-41)

The process of actualization is terrible to those individuals who are being destroyed by it. Their existence is consumed by the "fierce flames" of the actualizing process and circumscribed, restricted, and deformed (since all transformation is a deformation, from the perspective of the status quo) into "shapes of torment & woe" by the various forces and exigencies of the process. The joys and gratifications of those who dance around the wine come by virtue of the destruction of the perishing individuals, to whom this relationship seems a sadistic vampirism. In fact, sadism and vampirism are but the absolutization of an essential aspect of actuality, in which, as the *quid pro quo* metaphysics maintains, the immediate actualization of one individual is directly proportionate to the immediate suppression or destruction of another. Even love itself is a manifestation of this inverse reciprocity, in which one individual gains at the expense of another, getting nourishment from another and filling its own needs through the other. The delight of love is that one's being is enhanced by means of another individual, and the pain of love is due to the fact that one loses part of one's being to the other. And in extreme cases the "lureing songs" of love can squeeze out the last drop of one's being.

Productive Aspects of Interrelatedness

We have seen, however, that love—the intrinsic connectedness of individuals—is also constructive and productive. We are now given an account of this productive aspect of connectedness, or "Allamanda [which is] calld on Earth Commerce" (27:42). As the interrelatedness among individuals which makes all interaction and interchange possible, Allamanda manifests itself on earth—i.e., in the immediate, phenomenal world—as commerce, the interchange of goods among individuals. Allamanda "is the Cultivated land / Around the city of Golgonooza in the Forests of Entuthon" (27:42-3): it is the productive, nourishing ground of the process of actualization, the intrinsic relatedness of individuals which makes growth and transformation possible, as well as destruction. Actualization, the construction of individual identities, is thus seen once again to occur in the region of relatedness.

Immortality is also seen to be a function of interrelatedness. "Here the Sons of Los labour against Death Eternal" (27:44), we are told, for the posthumous presence that is effected through the process of actualization is made possible only by virtue of the intrinsic, essential relatedness of individuals, which preserves the unique identities of individuals who have perished. This labor against Eternal Death takes place "through all / The Twenty-seven Heavens of Beulah in Ulro" (27:44-5)—i.e., in every historical form of belief in some sort of posthumous existence. This preservation of individual uniqueness, moreover, is accomplished on the basis of Satanic destruction of individuals, as we see from the fact that this region of Being is said to constitute the "Seat of Satan, / Which is the False Tongue beneath Beulah" (27:45-6): it is by virtue of Satanic reduction and homogenization of individuals that other individuals are able to assimilate them and thus preserve their being. This assimilation is accomplished through the False Tongue—both the literal consumption of individuals and the ontological consumption which occurs through the general categories of language, which completely disregard individual uniqueness. The False Tongue and the Seat of Satan are also said to be "the Sense of Touch" (27:46)—mere external relatedness, simple contact, with no acknowledgement of the interior or intrinsic being of the object of awareness. Yet when this mere contact is activated—i.e., when its essence is allowed to become active—it produces eternal life, through the preservation of one individual in another. Of course, despite its beneficence, this action is violent and cruel: "the Plow goes forth in tempests & lightnings & the Harrow cruel / In blights of the east; the heavy Roller follows in howlings of woe" (27:47-8).

Interrelatedness and Differentiation

In this same region where the Sons labor to preserve perished individuals by integrating them into other individuals in the process of actualization, the counter forces of separation and differentiation are also at work: "Urizens sons here labour also," we are told; "& here are seen the Mills / Of Theotormon, on the verge of the Lake of Udan-Adan" (27:49-50). The differentiating forces work against the forces of integration and synthesis, reducing conglomerates and organisms to atomic units, much in the way Satan destroys individuals. The mills of Theotormon are the primal, chaotic, tormenting forces of undifferentiated being: "These are the starry voids of night & the depths & caverns of earth / These mills are oceans, clouds & waters ungovernable in their fury" (27:51-2). This nothingness of violence and chaos is creative as well as destructive, however, for we are told that "here are the stars created & the seeds of all things planted / And here the Sun & Moon receive their fixed destinations" (27:53-4). This chaotic flux of non-being is the ground of all beings, that which, through the powers of Urizen, becomes differentiated into unique individuals, which are the heart of Being. All the individuals which make up actuality have their origin in this amorphous flux, and their being is the work of Urizen's sons, the powers of differentiation, individuation, separation, and isolation. The intrinsic relatedness which serves as the basis for eternal life takes its origin from this differentiation in which the unique identity of the individual is established, and which is thus as essential as the labor of Los's sons: the work of integration and synthesis presupposes a labor of differentiation and separation, and the process of actualization is constituted by the interaction of these two processes.

CHAPTER IX

Being Form'd: The Creation of
Unique, Determinate Individuals

Modes of Actualization

Having portrayed the ontological significance of relatedness or mutuality among individuals, Blake now proceeds to elucidate the other dimensions of the process by which individual identity is actualized. He begins by outlining the fundamental modes of actualization, which are only partially active in the present dispensation. "In Eternity," Blake says, "the Four Arts: Poetry, Painting, Music, / And Architecture which is Science: are the Four Faces of Man" (27:55-6). These four fundamental types of form-giving or synthesis constitute the true nature of human being. But "not so in Time & Space," we are told. "There Three are shut out and only / Science remains thro Mercy" (27:57-8). The poetry, painting, and music that we know are therefore not what they should be according to their intrinsic possibilities. Poetry as we know it is usually defined as pleasing and instructive discourse. But (as Heidegger has noted more recently) the greater function of poetry—a function it perhaps only rarely performs—is to gather disparate and diverse particulars together, revealing their intrinsic and essential interrelatedness and thus allowing their full being to stand forth and become actualized by virtue of the account which humans now take of that being. True poetry is a synthetic and productive act that produces new actuality rather than simply reflecting the actuality at hand.

Much the same may be said of painting. While poetry reveals the mediated, universal relatedness of individuals, true painting reveals the intrinsic relatedness of different entities in their immediate and spatial interaction. True painting is thus also synthetic and productive and not merely representational. By gathering physical aspects of different things together in a coherent whole, painting causes the viewer to take account of—and thereby causes to be actualized—the full being of the individuals it

165

portrays, a being which was previously suppressed because the mutuality among its parts and that between itself and other individuals was not taken into account.

True music, likewise, is a synthesis. Its harmonic aspect combines several simultaneous particulars (tones) in the interrelatedness of their unique being, and its melodic aspect synthesizes numerous individual temporal moments (notes) in a meaningful *Gestalt* based on the complex intrinsic relatedness among them all.

Finally, architecture synthesizes—in immediate, enduring, material actuality—numerous individual entities into a new actuality that arises out of the intrinsic relatedness of all the constituent elements. Architecture is the only one of the four arts which exists in its true nature, because, like science, it embodies (although often only implicitly and unconsciously) an understanding of the unique being of every element and of the intrinsic relatedness of each element with each other element. A building stands, for example, only by virtue of the intrinsic natures of wood, stone, and mortar, and their interrelationships.

It is "by means of Science [that] the Three [other arts] / Become apparent in Time & Space, in the Three Professions / Poetry in Religion: Music, Law: Painting, in Physic & Surgery" (27:58-60). It is only through Science, the abstract, linguistic categories of the understanding, that the other types of synthesis exist at all. The synthesis of particulars and universals that true poetry creates is found in the abstract metaphysical dogmas of religion. Music's synthesis of individuals (in the abstract) manifests itself in law, which lays out the particular intrinsic relations that hold sway between one universal individual and another (i.e., between individuals in the abstract). And painting's synthesis by means of immediate physical aspects of individuals finds expression in the knowledge of the relations obtaining between the various physical organs of the body and the actualization or restitution of those proper relations through the exercise of physic and surgery.

Authentic human activity is thus an extension of the process of actualization itself, bodying forth the implicit and invisible—the forms of things unknown—rather than merely reflecting the immediate and the actual. But the power of the positivist view prevents full realization of human being. And the deformed modes of actualization that survive this positivism— Religion, Law, and medicine—are sufficient only to ensure "that Man may live upon Earth till the time of his awaking" (27:61); they provide for humans' moral, social, and physical subsistence, but no more. Yet despite their debased nature, they do embody to a degree the authentic human being—the process of actualization. In fact, we are told that "from these Three, Science derives every Occupation of Men" (27:62): all human activities ultimately derive from these fundamental "Four Faces of Man," the basic modes of the conscious, voluntary actualization of human individuals.

"Science," or theoretical understanding, which is thus the basic mode of all existing actualization, "is divided into Bowlahoola & Allamanda" (27:63), or analysis and synthesis. Bowlahoola, we recall, is named law by mortals. It is thus concerned primarily with delineating the identity or limits of the individual—i.e., defining the individual's rights and privileges. It is "the Stomach in every individual man" (24:67)—the organ which breaks down complexity into its elements—and is thus related to the Urizenic power of differentiation, as well as to the Satanic power of reduction. Allamanda, on the other hand, is "calld on Earth Commerce" (27:42); it is the intrinsic relatedness of individuals and thus the ground of actualization or productivity, the creation of new actuality which Los and his sons are engaged in.[1] All activities that occupy humans thus embody either the analytic or the synthetic—i.e., either the destructive or the constructive—aspects of the actualizing process which is the heart of all Being.

Identity and the Formation of Determinate Passions

Productive Identity

The actualizing process as a whole has now been described, with the Sons of Los constructing the "building of magnificence" (26:32) which each actualized soul is. Blake now proceeds to describe in greater detail the actualization of particular aspects of the individual—namely, those formless passions and desires which constitute each soul or individual:

> Some Sons of Los surround the Passions with porches of iron &
>   silver
> Creating form & beauty around the dark regions of sorrow,
> Giving to airy nothing a name and a habitation
> Delightful! with bounds to the Infinite putting off the Indefinite
> Into most holy forms of Thought....
>
> (28:1-5)

The passions are "dark regions of sorrow," mere lacks or deficiencies that are completely unarticulated and amorphous. They exist as vague yearnings, moods, and feelings of dissatisfaction, and it is only through the labor of actualization that they emerge, in "forms of Thought," as clear desires with definite goals. This emergence into definiteness is effected through the porches which the Sons of Los provide, which give the inchoate passions form and beauty by establishing interaction with otherness. Porches serve as zones of transition between inner and outer, and as such they govern access to and egress from the interior, thus giving form and determination to the modes of intercourse between inner and outer, or between one individual and another. And this establishment of definite modes of intercourse is a determination of the passion itself, which takes on form only when it is directed to a specific, unique other. By creation of such bridges between internal and external, desire and world, the state of vegetation is overcome—i.e., the individual's self-enclosure and lack of commerce with others, a state of indeterminate identity.

This work of the Sons of Los is carried on most evidently by poets, who, in Blake's paraphrase of Shakespeare, give "to airy nothing a name and a habitation / Delightful." The poet takes an inchoate passion and gives it form by articulating its intrinsic, merely implicit object and enunciating the essential mode of intercourse between the passion and its object. By giving "bounds to the Infinite [and] putting off the Indefinite / Into most holy forms of Thought," the poet enhances the actualization of both the individual and the object. "Such is the power of inspiration" (28:5), we are told: the poet receives direction from beyond the actual that allows him to move the actual beyond itself toward fulfillment, toward greater actualization of its implicit intrinsic being.

Destructive Identity

Other Sons of Los actualize the insubstantial, inauthentic, spectrous aspects of an individual:

> Others, Cabinets richly fabricate of gold & ivory;
> For doubts & fears unform'd & wretched & melancholy
> The little weeping Spectre stands on the threshold of Death
> Eternal; and sometimes two Spectres like lamps quivering
> And Often malignant they combat (heart-breaking sorrowful &
>   piteous).
>
> (28:8-12)

The wretched unformed doubts and fears are the aspects of an individual which fear death as the annihilation of the individual's being, a fear which often leads to combat as a means of self-preservation. By articulating these doubts and fears, the Sons of Los allocate them a legitimate sphere of influence in which they can find satisfaction, thus keeping them from expanding their combat to the individual as a whole. This delimitation is the work of Antamon, who

> ...takes them into his beautiful flexible hands,
> As the Sower takes the seed, or as the Artist his clay
> Or fine wax, to mould artful a model for golden ornaments.
> The soft hands of Antamon draw the indelible line:
> Form immortal with golden pen; such as the Spectre admiring
> Puts on the sweet form; then smiles Antamon bright thro his
> windows.
>
> (28:13-18)

The combat between spectrous aspects of individuals derives from the indefiniteness of their identity—they both want the same territory for a part of their being. Antamon stops the combat by establishing an indestructible boundary between the spectres, in the "form immortal" which he gives to them. This definite identity overcomes the threat of Death Eternal, because it establishes the unique, indelible individuality of the passion, a uniqueness which can never be replaced or done away with. After Antamon thus articulates the intrinsic form which the passion then puts on or actualizes, this embryonic actuality receives a protective covering or exterior embodiment from "the Daughters of beauty [who] look up from their Loom & prepare / The integument soft for its clothing with joy & delight" (28:19-20), by weaving the form into the web of interrelationships that constitute an individual's actual identity. Beauty, that is, draws the passion into definite actuality through the passion's attraction to the beautiful object.

The spectrous, inautheneic aspects of individuals—i.e., the mutually destructive elements—do not always achieve proper articulation, however. The weaker spectres, unable to achieve satisfaction by straightforward opposition and combat with other spectres, resort to covert opposition and subversion:

> ...Theotormon & Sotha stand in the Gate of Luban anxious
> Their numbers are seven million & seven thousand & seven
> hundred
> They contend with the weak Spectres, they fabricate soothing
> forms
> The Spectre refuses. he seeks cruelty. they create the crested Cock
> Terrified the Spectre screams & rushes in fear into their Net
> Of kindness & compassion & is born a weeping terror.

> Or they create the Lion & Tyger in compassionate thunderings[.]
> Howling the Spectres flee: they take refuge in Human lineaments.
>   (28:21-7)

The spectre "seeks cruelty"—i.e., seeks to assume a form of cruelty—to enhance his being, for self-preservation is based on cruelty. But when he himself becomes cruel he must also face the cruelty of others. Being weak, he cannot withstand such cruelty, and thus he flees from the ethic of cruelty to an ethic of pity and compassion: he "take[s] refuge in Human lineaments." This compassionate, Human form is only a facade, however, which serves as a base for covert operations of cruelty; it is the slave morality which, as we saw in Leutha's case, the weak use to survive and prevail against the strong.

Cruelty and mutual destructiveness, however, are possible only by virtue of the limitation of perception so that one individual takes account only of the exterior or extrinsic aspects of another, ignoring the other's intrinsic beauty and value. For only on the basis of such restricted vision can one individual make the attribution of nugatoriness to another that is a prerequisite of its devouring the other being. This limitation of perception, which Blake calls Ozoth, is thus responsible for the predatory and scavenging aspect of beings: "He Creates / the speckled Newt, the Spider & Beetle, the Rat & Mouse, / The Badger & Fox: they worship before his feet in trembling fear" (28:41-3). Ozoth's sons—his manifestations or subordinate principles—work "within the Optic Nerve" (28:29), where "they give delights to the man unknown; artificial riches / They give to scorn, & their possessors to trouble & sorrow & care" (28:31-2). The delights given by the Sons of Ozoth are the brute delights of killing and devouring, delights of the natural world which are "to the man unknown"—i.e., totally foreign to those who are truly human. The limited vision instituted by the Sons scorns "artificial riches," the treasures created by the form-giving art and artifice of culture, and constantly opposes those who value anything other than the brutal natural. This vision "shut[s] the sun. & moon. & stars. & trees. & clouds. & waters. / And hills. out from the Optic Nerve & harden[s] it into a bone / Opake" (28:33-5). Perception becomes hard and inflexible, seeing only one aspect or dimension of things—taking account only of the shell of the things it views and being oblivious to their interiors, or non-present being. This hardened vision makes both the perceiver and the perceived

> . . . like the black pebble on the enraged beach.
> While the poor indigent is like the diamond which tho cloth'd

> In rugged covering in the mine, is open all within
> And in his hallowd center holds the heavens of bright eternity.
> (28:35-8)

The true, intrinsic being of both the perceiver and the perceived is shut up within an inpenetrable hull, each unable to actualize itself, because actualization proceeds through enactment of the intrinsic relations between one individual and the other. This limited vision does have a legitimate function, which is to protect the perceiver from the barrage of being that would otherwise assault him and render him immobile, bereft of the singleness of purpose which is required to survive in the natural world: "Ozoth here builds walls of rocks against the surging sea / And timbers crampt with iron cramps bar in the joys of life / From fell destruction in the Spectrous cunning or rage" (28:39-41). Unfortunately, such limitation also precludes experiencing the myriad joys of interaction with others—which experience is itself a mode of actualizing both the perceiver and the perceived.

The Integrity of Individual Being

Temporal Integrity

This separation and isolation is nonetheless, as we have seen, an essential moment of the process of actualization, for it establishes the intrinsic and self-contained nature of the individual. And in order that each individual have an intrinsic and inalienable being, it is also necessary that the various denominations of time itself should have intrinsic and immutable value. As we have already seen, Los works to assure that not one moment of time is lost (22:18-19) so that all individuals or actions occurring in any period will retain their being. But before moments can be preserved, they must first be established, a function performed by "others of the Sons of Los [who] build Moments & Minutes & Hours / And Days & Months & Years & Ages & Periods; wondrous buildings" (28:44-5). This constructing activity indicates that time is not a homogeneous, undifferentiated stream of changes; it is rather a complex of structures, each of which is itself constructed by the synthesizing aspect of actualization. As a result of this complexity, even the moment, the smallest unit of time, is an end in itself, offering intrinsic actuality and fulfillment: "every Moment has a Couch of gold for soft repose" (28:46). Now a moment, we are told, "equals a pulsation of the artery" (28:47), a single complete action without repetition: a moment is the minimum time required for actualization to occur. Each moment, moreover, is separated and held intact apart from other moments: "between every two Moments stands a Daughter of Beulah / To feed the Sleepers on their Couches with maternal care" (28:48-9). Each moment is separated from others by means of the Beulahic illusion of pure presence—the notion that it is possible for there to be such a self-contained and self-sufficient moment. But each moment is itself only by virtue of its connection with other moments; and individuals which have perished—the "Sleepers"—remain intact within the moment in which they were actual, because the daughters of Beulah (immediate presence) mediate between that moment and the next, thus giving it indirect actuality, nourishing the posthumous presence and allowing it to grow.

The larger dimensions of time radiate out from the moment in concentric circles. Each has its center and origin in the (fictional) moment, and each offers additional protection to the refuge and fulfillment provided by the moment:

> And every Minute has an azure Tent with silken Veils.
> And every Hour has a bright golden Gate carved with skill.
> And every Day & Night, has Walls of brass & Gates of adamant,
> Shining like precious stones & ornamented with appropriate signs:
> And every Month, a silver paved Terrace builded high:
> And every Year, invulnerable Barriers with high Towers.
> And every Age is Moated deep with Bridges of silver & gold:
> And every Seven Ages is Incircled with a Flaming Fire.
> Now Seven Ages is amounting to Two Hundred Years
> Each has its Guard. each Moment Minute Hour Day Month & Year.
> All are the work of Fairy hands of the Four Elements
> The Guard are Angels of Providence on duty evermore.
>
> (28:50-61)

Each denomination of time is a realm for dwelling; what occurs in a moment has inalienable being and value, and so do the events of an hour or an age. Each has an intrinsic value and being which nothing can destroy. This principle is crucial, for without the intrinsic value of every period of time, no duration, whatever its dimensions, would have assured value, and passing out of immediacy would be equivalent to annihilation. The value of each period of time, moreover, is a function not of its duration—its size—but rather of the actualization, the creativity or transformation, that it holds:

> Every Time less than a pulsation of the artery
> Is equal in its period & value to Six Thousand Years.
> For in this Period the Poets Work is Done: and all the Great
> Events of Time start forth & are concievd in such a Period
> Within a Moment: a Pulsation of the Artery.
>
> (28:62-29:3)

Beginning happens in an instant which has no dimension, and it is beginning—i.e., creativity and change, the act of synthesis or reduction—that is the essential moment of actualization and thus of Being. Mere duration is nothing—inertia, stasis, non-being. Real being is dynamic, self-differing movement, and the dynamism lies in the occurrence of difference, the arising of otherness—the instant of beginning, after which all else is mere inertia until a new beginning occurs. Immediate actuality itself is no more than this beginning, the mere point of the present instant. This durationless point, itself a construct, is the unit out of which all the durations of time, from the moment to the Seven Ages, are constructed through the synthetic activity of Los's Sons.

Spatial Integrity

Like time, space is also a construct of the Sons of Los, constructed anew in each center of actualization—i.e., each individual:

> The Sky is an immortal Tent built by the Sons of Los
> And every Space that a Man views around his dwelling-place:
> Standing on his own roof, or in his garden on a mount
> Of twenty-five cubits in height, such space is his Universe;
> And on its verge the Sun rises & sets. the Clouds bow
> To meet the flat Earth & the Sea in such an orderd Space:
> The Starry heavens reach no further but here bend and set
> On all sides & the two Poles turn on their valves of gold:
> And if he move his dwelling-place, his heavens also move.
> Where'er he goes & all his neighbourhood bewail his loss.
>
> (29:4-13)

Space is thus not a universal and objective grid subsisting apart from all individual uniqueness; rather, it is a construct of the unique actualizing process of each individual, and is thus not a single, homogeneous space but a multiplicity of unique spaces—or vortexes, to employ the image Blake used earlier in the poem (15:21-35). Space is actualized—and *is*—only insofar as an individual constitutes it, through the appropriation of other things in his unique individuality. Thus when an individual moves his dwelling-place, the actuality of those beings which no longer fall within his purview is reduced, and they bewail their loss of him — a loss resulting from his diminished awareness of them, as well as theirs of him. This is the true nature of spaces, and the homogeneous space of science is a delusion of reason:

> Such are the Spaces called Earth & such its dimension:
> As to that false appearance which appears to the reasoner,
> As of a Globe rolling thro Voidness, it is a delusion of Ulro
> The Microscope knows not of this nor the Telescope. they alter
> The ratio of the Spectators Organs but leave Objects untouchd.
>
> (29:14-18)

The microscope and telescope, which scientific reason uses to try to prove the universality and homogeneity of a single space, reveal nothing about the ultimate nature of space or the individual entities that inhabit it, for these instruments reveal only what the "Spectators Organs" are prepared to perceive. Those who are attuned only to what is immediately manifest can never perceive the truth of space, no matter what instruments they use, "for every Space larger than a red Globule of Mans blood. / Is visionary: and is created by the Hammer of Los" (29:19-20). All visible space, that is, is the product of a synthesizing act, which combines elemental units into a meaningful and valuable structure. The units, however, as in the case of time, are not themselves without value — on the contrary, for "every Space smaller than a Globule of Mans blood. opens / Into Eternity of which this vegetable Earth is but a shadow" (29:21-2). As with time, the value of space is independent of its exterior magnitude. The tiniest of spaces has infinite being that is intrinsic, for it forms the irrefragable refutation of nothingness, the most distant outpost of Being in the realm of non-being. The minute, the inner, the non-manifest, is thus the core of actuality, and as such it is the truly eternal, the unlimited, the infinite.

These miniscule spaces which lie at the heart of actuality constitute the red Globule, the elemental actual individual entity of which all other individuals are constructed: "the red Globule is the unwearied Sun by Los created / To measure Time and Space to mortal Men, every morning" (29:23-4). The red globule is the immediate actuality, the new beginning which Los continually creates. It is the absolute, the zero degree by which all other being — and time and space — are measured. But it too, paradoxically, is a construct, a creation of the power of actualization, and it is constantly being synthesized into a larger complex, on the one hand, and analyzed or reduced to its elements on

the other. These two opposing functions are performed by "Bowlahoola &
Allamanda [which] are placed on each side / Of that Pulsation & that
Globule, terrible their power" (29:25-6). Bowlahoola reduces units of time
and space so that certain parts or aspects can be reconstituted by another
individual and incorporated into a successive actuality, while Allamanda
provides the intrinsic relatedness among units that allows the creation of
larger, more complex beings. This is the same process of differentiation and
union which we discussed above, and is essentially the process of arising and
perishing.

Integrity and Relatedness

The analytic and synthetic functions of Bowlahoola and Allamanda are
thus crucial to the maintenance of the individual's integrity and the simultaneous preservation of its relatedness to other individuals. This is also the
work of Rintrah and Palamabron, who, we are told, "govern over Day &
Night / In Allamanda & Entuthon Benython where souls wail" (29:27-8):
Rintrah, as the power of wrath, which holds individuals apart, presides
during the day, when distinctions among individuals are evident. Palamabron, the power of pity, which draws individuals together, holds sway at
night, when distinctions are suppressed. This simultaneity of separation/
opposition and union/love occurs "where Orc incessant howls burning in
fires of Eternal Youth, / Within the vegetated mortal Nerves" (29:
29-30)—i.e., in desire. For desire is both opposition (the other is seen as an
object of prey) and an attachment (the other is seen as an essential part of one's
own being). Desire, while the source of opposition among individuals, is
also the basis of their union: "every Man born is joined / Within into One
mighty Polypus, and this Polypus is Orc" (29:30-31). One individual is
united with another by desiring it, and is, moreover, at bottom the same
dynamic process of desire that the other is.

Integrity, Negation of Otherness,
and Satanic Metaphysics

It is also desire, however, which is responsible for the destruction of individual being, as we see in the next passage:

> But in the Optic vegetative Nerves Sleep was transformed
> To Death in old time by Satan the father of Sin & Death
> And Satan is the Spectre of Orc & Orc is the generate Luvah.
>
> (29:32-4)

Orc, or desire, is the manifestation in existence of the transcendental principle of union, Luvah. And the inauthentic form of desire—the Spectre of
Orc—is Satan, the source of destruction of individual being. This destruction occurs because of the transformation which desire works on perception:
when one individual desires another, the intrinsic being—the internal
dynamism—of the desired individual is ignored, making the individual
appear to be a mere passive, or dormant, object. This dormancy, or "Sleep,"
is equated with death or non-being by the Satanic desire and is subsequently
literally transformed into death when the individual is destroyed by the
devouring desire. Satan, the destroyer of otherness or difference, reduces
perception to an awareness of only the immediate, external manifestation of
an other's being, and thus when that other is dormant—i.e., passively subject
to the will of the desiring individual—it is taken to have no intrinsic being.
As we have seen, however, such a positivist view ignores the true being of an
individual—being that remains even when the individual's immediate actuality is expropriated or destroyed.

This positivism infects all relations between individuals and perverts our
very notion of individual being: "In the Nerves of the Nostrils," we are
informed, "Accident [was] formed / Into Substance & Principle, by the
cruelties of Demonstration" (29:35-6). "The Nerves of the Nostrils" take
account of the most immediate and evanescent—and thus accidental—
manifestations of a thing. And it is this aspect of a thing which positivism
makes into the essential reality of the thing—its "Substance & Principle"—by
making demonstration (i.e., immediacy, or presence) the criterion for reality.
This criterion is cruel because it denies being to that which is not
immediately present or manifest—i.e., to the intrinsic being of individuals.
In being identified with immediacy, the being of individuals "became Opake
& Indefinite" (29:37): opaque because there is nothing (no "internal light")
beyond their immediacy or exterior, and indefinite because the immediacy,
and thus also the individual (according to this view), varies from one
moment to the next.

Foundations of Individual Integrity

Such a state of being would be total chaos without some mitigating force,
which is provided by "the Divine Saviour, [who] / Formed it into a Solid by
Los's Mathematic power. / He named the Opake Satan; he named the Solid
Adam" (29:37-9). "Los's Mathematic power" adds together the separate
attributes or immediacies of an individual and thus creates a product which is

stable and unvarying—a substance or a solid which underlies and sustains all the immediacies. The opacity of individuals is named Satan because it is constituted by Satan's obfuscation and suppression of individuals' unique, intrinsic being. And the solidity is named Adam because it guarantees a modicum of being to an individual and provides a stable base, however inadequate, from which further development can occur. The Solid is also the homophonous "atom," the irreducible, indestructible individual out of which all other beings are constructed. This Adamic (or atomic) identity is a necessary fiction that gives individuals the sense of self-presence, by virtue of which they are able to act in reference to their own being.

That such a dimension of presence or substance underlies Los's actualizing process is indicated by the fact that it is "on Albions Rock [that] Los stands creating the glorious Sun each morning" (29:41). A definite, present, elemental unit is presupposed by the process of actualization, for process in general requires some thing which undergoes process, and synthesis presupposes pre-existing elements which are synthesized. The very concept of the actualizing process thus demands the concepts of substance and immediate presence.[2] Truly enduring or solid identity, however, is not mere duration or immediacy. Rather, it is a function of repetition. Thus we are told that it is "in the Nerves of the Ear, (for the Nerves of the Tongue are closed) / [that] On Albions Rock Los stands creating the glorious Sun each morning" (29:40-41). Los's stance in the "Nerves of the Ear" indicates that his activity constructs presence out of repetition, for the ear attunes itself to periodicity: language, music, and mere sound itself are constituted by the synthesis of repetitions into an immediately present, unified form. It is on this basis—the capacity to apprehend repetition and periodicity—rather than on the basis of some originary immediate presence, that sameness and identity are established: the identity or intrinsic being of an individual is thus a construct, formed of distinct elements residing in discrete moments of time, rather than an unmediated, continuous presence or self-sameness.

We thus see that an individual's intrinsic being or identity is not constituted by undifferentiated sameness, nor can identity be located solely in immediacy: the intrinsic being of an individual is located within a period of time, and to look at less than this entire period is to find only one aspect of an individual's identity—only one tone of the melody or one vocable of a sentence. And to look at mere immediacy is to find nothing at all, not even a tone, or element of the whole, for below a certain period there is no sound at all. Individuals, like tones and melodies, are thus syntheses of elements and moments, rather than monolithic solids. Such a synthesis transcends the immediate and includes that which has perished and that which has not yet emerged; both these non-actual moments are reflected in the moment of the immediate present, which indirectly actualizes the non-present. This, then, is the moment "when unwearied in the evening [Los] creates the Moon / Death to delude" (29:42-3): the immediate present, like the moon, reflects the light (intrinsic being) of past and future beings—the sun which has set or has not yet risen—thus actualizing indirectly the non-immediate. And it is this indirect actualization which conquers Death, "who all in terror at their splendor leaves / His prey while Los appoints" (29:43-4); for as long as perished individuals receive indirect actualization, their being is not annihilated.

As Los deludes Death, "Rintrah & Palamabron guide / The Souls clear from the Rock of Death that Death himself may wake / In his appointed season when the ends of heaven meet" (29:44-6). Rintrah and Palamabron, the forces of analysis and synthesis, or separation and union, keep the souls away from the nugatory stasis of non-being which Death seems to be: the reductive and synthetic process which individuals undergo when they perish contradicts this view of Death and will someday cause Death to be seen as what it really is. And when Death thus awakes, and its implicit nature becomes actual, it will be accepted as part of the process of Being; individuals will realize that passing away is not passing into nothingness but rather into otherness, an otherness intrinsic in an individual's identity and thus the ful-fillment of its destiny.

Preservation of being thus occurs through indirect actualization. This point is now made explicitly, for we are told that when Los deludes death and Rintrah and Palamabron keep the souls away from annihilation,

> Then Los conducts the Spirits to be Vegetated, into
> Great Golgonooza, free from the four iron pillars of Satans Throne
> (Temperance, Prudence, Justice, Fortitude, the four pillars of
>   tyranny)
> That Satans Watch-Fiends touch them not before they Vegetate.
>   (29:47-50)

Golgonooza, the locus of actualization, is based upon the death of the actual-ity which it is continuously superseding: in order for actualization to occur, individuals must perish, yielding to a new actuality. Such self-sacrifice was the essence of Jesus' act at Golgotha (which is perhaps a linguistic component of "Golgonooza"), and like Golgotha, Golgonooza is the place where one's true being is separated from one's immediacy, the immediate actuality being given over to death so that one's true being may be more fully actualized. This transcendence of the immediate is the opposite of Satan's action, which reduces all things to their immediate actuality, rather than freeing them from it. The "four iron pillars of Satans Throne / (Temperance, Prudence, Justice, Fortitude...)" are all derived from the positivist view that one's being is constituted by one's immediate identity and that one must resist all forms of otherness. To preserve one's being one must resist all change of oneself—any impingements by another and all alien (internal or external) impetuses. In such a system an individual can never become more than it already is in actuality.

Immediacy and Perverse Forms of Actualization

Although the actual identity which Los constructs for individuals is thus an identity that is unique and intrinsic and based on mediated presence in otherness rather than on immediate self-presence, this identity often takes itself to be otherwise, and as a result, engages in perverse, counterproductive forms of actualization. Blake portrays this perversion as Rahab and Tirzah's perversion of the fulfillment provided by Enitharmon. Enitharmon and her daughters have the pleasant task of giving the Spirits "to their lovely heavens till the Great Judgment Day" (29:52). Since Enitharmon is space, or immediate actuality, her heavens would be the immediate experience of infinity or fulfillment—i.e., the immediate experience of unity with others through head, heart, and reins, or intellectual, emotional, and physical union. Such union is the legitimate immediate experience of the ultimate fulfillment constituted by ecstatic transformation into otherness, but when this union becomes perverted into mere pleasure—i.e., when "Rahab & Tirzah pervert / [The] mild influences" of Enitharmon and her daughters (29:53-4)—this experience of immediate fulfillment becomes destructive instead of fulfilling. Rahab and Tirzah produce this destruction of the being of individuals by ignoring the mediated presence embodied in union with otherness and absolutizing the value of immediacy, making immediate fulfillment the only true being. For this reason, "the Seven Eyes of God," the various historical (supernaturalist) modes of preserving the vision (and therefore the mediated actuality) of that which is no longer immediately actual, are necessary to safeguard the being of what has passed away: because of the action of Rahab (false fulfillment) and Tirzah (pleasure), that is, "the Seven Eyes of God walk round / The Three Heavens of Ulro, where Tirzah & her

Sisters / Weave the black Woof of Death upon Entuthon Benython"
(29:54-6).

The destruction of individual being through the valorization of
immediacy reaches its peak with the conjunction of pleasure and feudalistic
metaphysics. This "black Woof of Death" is woven "in the Vale of Surrey
where Horeb terminates in Rephaim" (29:56-7)—the place where feudalistic
metaphysics (Horeb, associated with the Decalogue and the sacrifice to Baal)
culminates in immersion in immediate gratification (Rephaim, known for its
fertility). The loom is operated by Zelophehad's daughters, and "the stamp-
ing feet of Zelophehads Daughters are covered with Human gore / Upon the
treddles of the Loom: they sing to the winged shuttle" (29:58-9). These
daughters, who made the unprecedented demand for an inheritance when
their father died, symbolize the enhancement of one individual through the
destruction of another, and the daughters' singing to the shuttle, which
carries the Woof of Death, indicates their worship of death—the death of
others which brings them riches, and their own death, the fear of which is the
ultimate motive of self-aggrandizement. This predatory attitude is a direct
result of the feudalistic metaphysics, which itself derives from destruction of
individual being through the absolutizing of immediacy. In this system, the
only relief mortals have from death and finitude is death itself—inundation
by the passage of time, which cleanses the Woof of Death: "The River rises
above his banks to wash the Woof: / He takes it in his arms: he passes it in
strength thro his current" (29:60-61). The Woof of Death constitutes the veil
of human miseries and covers the entire realm of undifferentiated being:
"The veil of human miseries is woven over the Ocean / From the Atlantic to
the Great South Sea, the Erythrean" (29:62-3). That is, the pain caused by the
perishing of individuals is universal and cannot be avoided. And the fact that
the veil of miseries occurs over the ocean indicates that it derives from or rests
on the undifferentiated aspect of Being: death is seen as the process by which
an individual loses its uniqueness, its differentiation, and remits its being to
the reservoir of homogeneous being. In this view of Death the individual is
totally annihilated, and thus death constitutes the ultimate misery and the
focal point of all concern—an object of worship.

Los thus keeps the souls free from Satan's Rock of Death—the immediacy
of mere stasis—only to have them covered by the Woof of Death, the veil of
misery woven by Rahab and Tirzah through their valorization of immediacy.
"Such," we are informed, "is the World of Los the labour of six thousand
years. / Thus Nature is a Vision of the Science of the Elohim" (29:64-5). The

world of actuality which has developed during the six thousand years since creation is actually the product of Los's activity; but instead of being seen as such, it is seen as nature, a world of immediacy in which mutual destruction prevails. This view of actuality is "a Vision of the Science of the Elohim," for it derives from the system in which all being belongs to the tyrannous Elohim, shadowy God of Adam, Noah, and Abraham. As we have seen, the feudalistic metaphysics underlying the concept of the Elohim results in a *quid pro quo* view in which one individual can benefit only at the expense of the other. Such a view takes the existential fact that life lives on death and makes it into the dominant ontological principle, which reinforces rather than mitigates the predation in existence. This view of existence, like the Elohist view of nature, is a delusion deriving from the assumption that individuals have no intrinsic being and that Being is identical with presence or immediacy. It will be the function of *Milton* to overthrow this falsehood in Book II.

PART FOUR

Desire and Presence:
The Descent of Ololon
and the Reconciliation with Finitude

CHAPTER X

Presence and Process:
Beulah, Eternity, and Ecstasis

Beulah, or Immediate Presence

The second book of *Milton* reveals the ultimate origin of the valorization of immediacy by elaborating the dialectical relation between immediate presence and mediated presence, or between substance and process. Presence, we are shown, is required by mediated presence, or process; but when one valorizes immediate presence apart from mediation or process (as Rahab and Tirzah do), the first step is taken on the road to the tyrannic *quid pro quo* systems in which the being of the individual is denied. Blake presents the valorization of presence as the realm of Beulah, which represents the first step away from infinity (Eternity) toward the restricted vision of nature which derives from "the Science of the Elohim." Beulah, as its name suggests (it means "married"), is a state of affairs in which no deficiency or frustration occurs and individuals coexist in harmony and union with each other. In Beulah, there is no conflict or opposition, even between opposite forces or principles: it is "a place," we are told, "where contrarieties are equally true" (30:1-2). The reason for this harmonious, peaceful state, however, is that Beulah is a state not of actual existence, but rather of latent, incipient, or dormant existence—an ideal realm. Blake makes this point when he characterizes Beulah as "a pleasant lovely shadow / Where no dispute can come. Because of those who Sleep" (30:2-3). Beulah's shadowy character indicates that it is insubstantial and derivative, a world of dreams and ideals rather than of actuality. Its harmonious nature (the fact that no dispute can occur there) is due to "those who Sleep"—i.e., it is due to the fact that here there are no actual individual entities which could come into conflict: the individuals are dormant ("asleep"), unactualized.

Beulah, then, is the ideal state in which all an individual's needs and desires are immediately satisfied, where there is no gap or deferral between the appearance of desire and its satisfaction. And such a state is possible only where there are no definite, independent, individual identities, for where there are independent individuals, there is inevitably conflict, as we have seen. The individual in this state is like an infant with its mother, where a virtual symbiosis prevails, with the infant drawing whatever it needs directly and immediately from the mother. Thus "Beulah to its Inhabitants appears within each district / As the beloved infant in his mothers bosom round incircled / With arms of love & pity & sweet compassion" (30:10-12). In such a state, of course, the individual is not truly individuated; its individuality is merely incipient, not yet actual.

Eternity, or Process

Beulah, then, is the state or moment of presence—i.e., of stasis, permanence, passivity—and thus also of non-individuation or non-existence. As such, it is in contrast with the primal, originary state of being, Eden, where individuals dwell in the continuous, primordial activity of individuation. Thus we are told that "to / The Sons of Eden the moony habitations of Beulah, / Are from Great Eternity a mild & pleasant Rest" (30:13-14). Eternity—that dimension of Being in which the descendants ("sons") of the authentic, originary state of existence ("Eden") continue to dwell—is a realm of dynamic possibility, conflict, and process, in contrast to the (imagined) immediacy and continuity of Beulah.

The nature of Eternity is described more fully in the following passage:

> Lo the Eternal Great Humanity
> To whom be Glory & Dominion Evermore Amen
> Walks among all his awful Family seen in every face
> As the breath of the Almighty. such are the words of man to man
> In the great Wars of Eternity, in fury of Poetic Inspiration,
> To build the Universe stupendous: Mental forms Creating.
>
> (30:15-20)

Eternity is the center of energy and activity—"the great Wars of Eternity" which constitute the process of differentiation and actualization of individuals. In Eternity, the state of infinite being, "the Eternal Great Humanity" (i.e., the infinite essence of humanity) manifests itself in each individual as ultimate Being—"as the breath of the Almighty." Each individual, that is, is seen as divinely inspired, having a vision and purpose of ultimate value and validity. The relatedness among these unique, independent individuals is one of tension and benign strife; the "words of man to man" constitute "the great

Wars of Eternity," in which each individual struggles with otherness in attempt to make it compatible with himself (assimilation), or himself compatible with it (accommodation). In this struggle, the individual and the other are both transformed and joined together in a single structure, "the Universe stupendous." It is such taking account of otherness and being transformed by it and united with it which builds universes, both microcosms and macrocosms. And only through such conflict does the very process of Being itself occur.

Poetic Inspiration is perhaps the ultimate instance of this constructive process. Inspiration is in a very real sense invasion by otherness, which one struggles with until it reveals itself and becomes actualized through articulation. This other also struggles with other others, fighting for its rightful place in the structure of the whole. In this way, Poetic Inspiration builds a universe of Mental Forms: it articulates new structures of being, new forms of interrelatedness, that individuals can actualize directly—by imitating them, using them as a blueprint for actions—or indirectly, by resisting them or simply by being aware of them.

But the struggles of Eternity also create another type of mental form—namely, forms of mentality, or beings having mind or spirit (such as the Urizen which Los creates). For mind is essentially a taking account of possibilities—i.e., a struggling with otherness, with states not actual (i.e., not present) or with other individuals. These forms of mentality, then, as well as the mental forms they create, are the result of conflict and struggle between an actual individual and various forms of otherness. Such struggle, moreover, is the process of Being; "the great Wars of Eternity" are Eternity, or the infinite aspect of Being on which existence is grounded, and Beulah, the ideal of pure presence, is a state of near non-differentiation and thus virtual non-existence.

The Dialectic of Presence and Process

But pure process, as we have seen, is impossible and even inconceivable, for process or change requires some thing (which is not pure process) to undergo process or transformation. Each instance of process or becoming presupposes one definite, static state as the ground of its origin and another such state as its goal. Thus it is that "Beulah is evermore Created around Eternity; appearing / To the inhabitants of Eden, around them on all sides" (30:8-9): ideals of substance and permanence, which restrict that flux of becoming which is Eternity, also support that flux as its *terminus ad quem* and *terminus a quo*. Presence or permanence (Beulah) thus makes eternal activity possible by constituting the goal or telos of such activity. Without these ideals or illusions of Beulah, not only would there be no such thing as continuity of identity through time; there would be no such thing as process or change either.

The presence or stasis of Beulah is thus in a sense the ultimate goal of all individuation, the true purpose or telos of all actualization, manifestation, and production. Blake expresses this goal of individuation as the urge of the emanations—i.e., of all the products or manifestations of individuals:

> ...the Emanations trembled exceedingly, nor could they
> Live, because the life of Man was too exceeding unbounded
> His joy became terrible to them, they trembled & wept
> Crying with one voice. Give us a habitation & a place
> In which we may be hidden under the shadow of wings
> For if we who are but for a time, & who pass away in winter
> Behold these wonders of Eternity we shall consume
> But you O our Fathers & Brothers, remain in Eternity
> But grant us a Temporal Habitation. do you speak
> To us; we will obey your words as you obey Jesus
> The Eternal who is blessed for ever & ever. Amen
>
> (30:21-31)

The emanations' request portrays the realization that in order for there to be beings at all and not just process or flux, there must be some mitigation of this pure process of Eternity, some semblance of endurance in a particular place ("a habitation and a place") and time ("a Temporal Habitation"). It is this logical necessity for a degree of presence which occasions the appearance of Beulah, the illusion of pure presence, unmitigated fullness: "So spake the lovely Emanations; & there appeared a pleasant / Mild Shadow above; beneath: & on all sides round" (30:32-3). This shadow, an epiphenomenon and adumbration of infinity (Eternity), provides respite for beings which are not strong enough, as it were, to endure constant transformation:

> Into this pleasant Shadow all the weak & weary
> Like Women & Children were taken away as on wings
> Of dovelike softness, & shadowy habitations prepared for them.
>
> (31:1-3)

Those individuals which lack an intrinsic dynamic identity take on derivative, shadowy, static identities—hypostatizations of process. Like women and children whose identities are functions, respectively, of their husbands and parents, these individuals are unable to forge their own being as a union or continuity of difference, and as a result they take up residence in a static identity.

The strong individuals, however — the truly human who exist in an ecstatic mode, continually becoming more (i.e., other, in some degree) than they are — remain in the transformations of Eternity, actively embracing and promoting change and development:

> But every Man returnd & went still going forward thro'
> The Bosom of the Father in Eternity on Eternity
> Neither did any lack or fall into Error without
> A Shadow to repose in all the Days of happy Eternity.
>
> (31:4-7)

In embracing the process of Eternity, the strong individuals dwell in "the Bosom of the Father" — i.e., at the heart of the originary, most basic power, the progenitor of all things. When these individuals "lack or fall into Error," however — i.e., when they fail to be truly human — they assume, like those in Beulah, a derivative, insubstantial identity, a static identity of mere presence, becoming just a shadow of their true, dynamic being. More significant, however, is the more subtle point which Blake makes in these lines: the very notion and occurrence of "lack," "fall," and "Error," are made possible only by the "Shadow to repose in" — i.e., by the Beulahic ideals of presence.

Ololon and Beulah:
The Search For Fulfillment in Presence

Since Beulah is the realm of presence and stasis, where beings endure in fullness without the tension and flux caused by deficiency of any kind, the descent of Ololon, or lamentation, from Eternity into Beulah expresses the transition of the search for infinity from a region of tension and process to a realm of presence. This descent is perceived by the inhabitants of Beulah, those who locate their identity in presence rather than process, as the advent of ultimate fulfillment:

> Into this pleasant Shadow Beulah, all Ololon descended
> And when the Daughters of Beulah heard the lamentation
> All Beulah wept, for they saw the Lord coming in the Clouds.
>
> (31:8-10)

The identification of being with presence, then, results in the relocation of full being from a region of process to a realm of permanence — which can only be an unreal, illusory realm. But the descent of the urge for infinity does not stop here. In locating full being in Beulah, Ololon/lamentation creates the urge to *actualize* the Beulahic world of presence and permanence and achieve immediate fulfillment and full presence in actuality. The establishment of pure presence as an ideal thus arouses desire for full actualization, as well as a desire to bypass the struggle necessary to achieve greater actualization. This desire afflicts entire nations, which yearn to achieve effortlessly the fulfillment which other nations have achieved only through revolution:

> And all Nations wept in affliction Family by Family
> Germany wept towards France & Italy: England wept & trembled
> Towards America: India rose up from his golden bed:
> As one awakend in the night: they saw the Lord coming
> In the Clouds of Ololon with Power & Great Glory!
>
> (31:12-16)

The nations have given up the labor which brings true fulfillment through transformation and development and instead they yearn for immediate fulfillment. Immediate satisfaction, however, is the opposite of true fulfillment, for it puts an end to the process of actualization which constitutes the individual's real being.

The entire natural world also manifests this fixation on immediacy, yearning for actuality to embody the complete presence of Beulah: "all the living Creatures of the Four Elements," we are told, "wail'd / With bitter wailing" (31:17-18), and these natural beings that are fixated on immediacy, we are told, "in the aggregate are named Satan / And Rahab" (31:18-19). They are the immediate, present actuality which offers false fulfillment (Rahab) and usurps the intrinsic being of individuals by presenting itself as the only reality (Satan). These powers of immediacy "know not of Regeneration, but only of Generation" (31:19): beings immersed in immediacy are aware only of birth and death, not of growth and transformation. For them, individuals do not conserve their identity through change; they merely come into existence and pass out of existence, and their being is coterminous with their existence—i.e., with their immediacy. The idea that an individual can perish and become something other, while still retaining its intrinsic being or unique identity, is inconceivable to the view for which being is constituted by presence. Beings with such a view are merely natural beings, creatures without the capacity even to incorporate the non-actual into their own immediacy—much less to constitute their immediacy out of non-actuality. They have the same view of identity that the Elect have: "unforgiving and unalterable: these cannot be Regenerated / But must be Created, for they know only of Generation" (31:21-2).

This vision is expressed in the figures of "the Fairies, Nymphs, Gnomes & Genii of the Four Elements" (31:20), which are the fundamental building blocks of nature. They present themselves as being unalterable; it seems that they have no points of intersection with each other—that one cannot pass into another or arise from another. They do not develop (they are "unalterable") or change their stance with regard to other beings (they are "unforgiving"), but are rigid and unyielding, manifesting themselves only through the categories of being or not being, and having nothing to do with becoming and transformation. These elementary powers are mysterious, autonomous forces that appear absolutely independent and unalterable. They are the powers of immediacy, both cause and effect of the orientation exclusively toward presence and thus also of the opposition and destruction which prevails in existence:

> These are the Gods of the Kingdoms of Earth: in contrarious
> And cruel opposition: Element against Element, opposed in War
> Not Mental, as the Wars of Eternity, but a Corporeal Strife.
> (31:23-5)

The Wars of Eternity serve to actualize the individual by allowing it the confrontation with otherness that is necessary to define, refine, and transform it into a less limited form. The Corporeal Strife of existence, on the other hand, destroys individuals and allows their being to be devoured by other individuals.

Nonetheless, this corporeal strife has a necessary function, for it is the destruction necessary for the process of actualization: it takes place "in Los's Halls continual labouring in the Furnaces of Golgonooza" (31:26). The necessity of corporeal strife derives from the fundamental lack at the heart of existence, which manifests itself everywhere: "Orc howls on the Atlantic: Enitharmon trembles: All Beulah weeps" (31:27). And this lack is the ground and origin of Ololon/lamentation.

Deficiency, Self-Difference, and Ecstasis

Explicit Ecstasis

This lack at the heart of existence does not manifest itself only as the "cruel opposition" of "Corporeal Strife," however; it is also the origin of all the pleasant, joyful, tender, and loving relations among individuals. In fact, all particular, concrete instances of novelty and beginning, of striving and growing, of perceiving and expressing, are manifestations of the lamentations of Beulah—the attempt to fill the lack, to make the non-present present. Blake makes this point in a wonderful lyrical passage that begins with a direct address to the reader—"Thou hearest the Nightingale begin the Song of Spring" (31:28)—and ends with the declaration: "This is a Vision of the lamentation of Beulah over Ololon!" (31:45). Through this passage we are led to recognize that normal events which we are likely to ignore as insignificant are of ultimate importance, and are instances of the ecstatic unity-in-diversity which is at the heart of Being.

The first revelation we are given is that there is nothing of greater value or being than a single nightingale or lark, every aspect of which manifests the ecstatic or self-overflowing movement:

> The Lark sitting upon his earthy bed: just as the morn
> Appears; listens silent; then springing from the waving
>   Corn-field! loud
> He leads the Choir of Day! trill, trill, trill,
> Mounting upon the wings of light into the great Expanse:
> Reecchoing against the lovely blue & shining heavenly Shell.
>
> (31:29-33)

The fact that the lark listens silent at first and then sings indicates a change in the bird—a process which cannot be explained by the static, hypostatized being of the Four Elements. The lark embodies ecstasis, the process of individuality reaching out beyond its immediate actuality and embracing otherness. Its silent listening, taking account of otherness, is an instance of such ecstasis, as are its springing up and its singing. The spring and the morn attest to the regeneration present here which the Four Elements know nothing of. Virtually all the images in the passage, in fact, exhibit ecstasis: the waving Cornfield, the Choir of Day, the flight on the wings of light, the Great Expanse. There is a hint of frustration in the image of the "shining heavenly Shell," which places a limit on the ecstatic expansion, but this limit is little more than the (provisional) delineation and definition of the lark's identity—that against which its own being can reflect or re-echo back into itself, or the present actuality encapsulating the embryo of the future. The lark's "wings of light" indicate that this ecstatic, self-exceeding urge is intrinsic, part of the lark's individual being, a point which is reinforced by the description of the lark's singing: "His little throat labours with inspiration;

every feather / On throat & breast & wings vibrates with the effluence
Divine" (31:34-5). The laboring and vibrating exhibit the energy inherent in
the lark, while the "effluence Divine" of its song attests to the fact that the
bird's self-differing being is ultimate, an intrinsic source of value and being
rather than a mere repository of extrinsic being. This ontological stature is
further indicated by the fact that "all Nature listens silent to him" (31:36).
Even the Sun, normally seen as the source of all light and thus a symbol for
the central source of Being, defers to the lark as a source in its own right: "the
awful Sun / Stands still upon the Mountain looking on this little Bird /
With eyes of soft humility, & wonder love & awe" (31:36-8).

As ecstasis, the inherent being of the lark includes an intrinsic relatedness
to otherness—to possibility (its own inherent otherness) and also to other
actual individuals. The relatedness to other individuals is evident when the
lark listens to the nightingale and when the sun together with all of nature
listens silently to the lark. Through this taking account of others, the individual expands its own being, assimilating part of the being of the other
without depriving the other of that being—such is the reality of inspiration
and influence. When the lark hears singing, it becomes in-spired—it literally
takes in being from otherness. In turn, when the lark sings, it ex-presses an
"effluence Divine" that inspires others and evokes a beginning, or growth—
i.e., a similar pouring forth—in them: "Then loud from their green covert all
the Birds begin their Song" (31:39). These birds, in turn, awake and inspire
other beings, until all is one grand harmony of individuals engaged in mutual
inspiration—i.e., mutual enhancement and nourishment:

> The Thrush, the Linnet & the Gold finch, Robin & the Wren
> Awake the Sun from his sweet reverie upon the Mountain:
> The Nightingale again assays his song, & thro the day,
> And thro the night warbles luxuriant; every Bird of Song
> Attending his loud harmony with admiration & love.
>
> (31:40-44)

Whether caused by a fullness of one's own being or by an emptiness, this
singing epitomizes the ecstatic urge, the movement beyond one's actual identity, for both fullness (joy) and emptiness (pain, lamentation) constitute a
lack, a need for (i.e., a need to become) otherness. Thus "this is a Vision of the
lamentation of Beulah over Ololon" (31:45)—a manifestation of the intrinsic
need of individuals to move beyond their so-called actual identity, even in
instances of apparently immediate satisfaction.

Implicit Ecstasis

This intrinsic ecstatic movement beyond immediacy also occurs in botanic life, although in less explicit manner. Blake now states this point quite expressly:

Thou percievest the Flowers put forth their precious Odours!
And none can tell how from so small a center comes such sweets
Forgetting that within that Center Eternity expands
Its ever during doors, that Og & Anak fiercely guard.

(31:46-9)

The ecstatic, effluent movement bears witness to the irrepressible and inexhaustible being that lies within an individual—i.e., within a finite physical area or quantity. Being is not a function of presence, but of effectiveness, or differing activity: changing, growing, expanding—in a word, becoming. The ebullient becoming which is the center of each individual links the individual to otherness—the otherness which it yearns to become (which is partially embodied in other individuals), and the otherness which it yearns to give itself to. As the manifestation of a fundamental need or lack, the ecstasis is thus at bottom the same as sorrow and lamentation, and joy easily turns into tears: "First eer the morning breaks joy opens in the flowery bosoms / Joy even to tears, which the Sun rising dries" (31:50-51).

The ecstatic movement is the expansion of Eternity—the myriad of possibilities—into actuality, the becoming in existence what the individual is intrinsically, i.e., in possibility or essence. This actualization of essence is expressed in images of waking, opening, and bursting forth:

...first the Wild Thyme
And Meadow-sweet downy & soft waving among the reeds.
Light springing on the air lead the sweet Dance: they wake
The Honeysuckle sleeping on the Oak: the flaunting beauty
Revels along upon the wind; the White-thorn lovely May
Opens her many lovely eyes: listening the Rose still sleeps
None dare to wake her. soon she bursts her crimson curtaind bed
And comes forth in the majesty of Beauty; every Flower:
The Pink, the Jessamine, the Wall-flower, the Carnation
The Jonquil, the mild Lilly opes her heavens! every Tree,
And Flower & Herb soon fill the air with an innumerable Dance
Yet all in order sweet & lovely, Men are sick with Love!
Such is a Vision of the lamentation of Beulah over Ololon.

(31:51-63)

The fact that actualization is expressed through images of opening indicates that growth or actualization entails an admission of otherness, through a breach in an individual's present actuality. This openness to otherness is evident first of all in the merely implicit mode of possible togetherness or proximity: the Wild Thyme waves *among* the reeds and springs *on* the air; the Honeysuckle sleeps *on* the Oak; and the beauty revels *upon* the wind. The openness is present too in the silent listening of the Rose, and in the waking of the Honeysuckle and the Whitethorn. Each individual is open to other individuals in fundamental ways, such that each individual moves only in coordination with other individuals, in "an innumerable Dance / ...all in order sweet and lovely." The intrinsic being of an individual, while completely its own, is nonetheless tied to other beings in an essential way, thus making their being its and its theirs, in mediated fashion.

Through the description of the rose Blake is able to strike a delicate balance between openness and self-directedness, ensuring that openness and influence are not perceived as subjection. In the first place, nothing wakes the rose; her waking is the result of intrinsic movement, spontaneous transformation. In addition, all further development—even destruction—is self-induced. And all development entails a degree of destruction: the very blossoming of the rose bursts the bud in which the rose lay dormant. Change, the loss of (the immediate) identity, is part of (the greater) identity; actualization involves the destruction of the actual.

The opening to otherness, the ecstatic self-differing urge, the destruction, or supersession, or transcendence of the immediate, present actuality—these are all ways of expressing the ultimate process of Being which is the core of individuality. It is love, at an ontological level, and love is sickness, a disruption of the status quo, of equilibrium. To be sick is to be in a state that does not adequately embody one's intrinsic being. There is a gap between one's essence and one's (present state of) existence, and this gap causes the ecstatic movement of actualization which is "a Vision of the lamentation of Beulah over Ololon." The ecstatic, self-exceeding movement of actualization, that is, manifests the fundamental quest for presence and fullness—the ascendance of the ideal of presence (Beulah), and its consequent constitution of lamentation as the quest for full presence.

CHAPTER XI

States and Individuals: The Actuality
Versus the Being of Individuality

Milton's Vision

Having presented two series of brilliant and concrete instances demonstrating the ecstatic self-differing of individual being, Blake has prepared us for a declaration by the Seven Angels of the Presence concerning the ultimate nature of individual being. The focus now returns to "Milton [who] oft sat up on the Couch of Death & oft conversed / In a vision & dream beatific with the Seven Angels of the Presence" (31:1-2). As we have seen, although Milton is dead, his being remains, part of it as his posthumous presence in the realm of existence, and another part in the realm of possibility, which, we have seen, has been evicted from eternity and is now an aspect of actuality. This latter aspect of Milton's being, we have said, constitutes his essential individuality, which has never been fully actualized, directly or indirectly. Yet this individuality retains its being—as the open-ended possibilities inherent in the effects which Milton's posthumous presence has on immediately actual (living) individuals. More specifically, through his works, his memory, or even more indirectly, Milton's posthumous presence influences living individuals to take fuller account of Being itself. This effect often takes the form of a beatific dream or a vision, in which the individual receives access to being which lies beyond his or her previous powers to apprehend. In such instances, Milton is in a sense "convers[ing] . . . with the Seven Angels of the Presence," interacting with those powers (largely the belief in immortality) which, as we have seen, preserve the unactualized being of the dead by virtue of the new possibilities it engenders in the living. Every effect which Milton's posthumous presence has on the living is both a result of and a contribution to the power of the Seven Angels of the Presence.

The vision which Milton communicates is the distinction between true being and fulfillment, on the one hand, and its false counterpart, on the other.

"I have turned my back upon these Heavens builded on cruelty" (32:30), Milton declares, renouncing the feudalistic, *quid pro quo* metaphysics, and the quest for fulfillment at the expense of other individuals. One aspect of Milton's being, however, continues to strive for fulfillment in immediacy: "My Spectre still wandering thro' them [the 'Heavens builded on cruelty'] follows my Emanation / He hunts her footsteps thro' the snow & the wintry hail & rain" (32:4-5). The hunting indicates the cruel, predatory aspect of the quest for immediacy, which views the emanation—i.e., the objective counterpart of one's desire, the otherness in conjunction with which one's being attains completion—as an actually existing piece of reality that has to be tracked down and possessed, rather than as a product or construct of one's own process of actualization. The snow and hail and rain point to the desolation of the world in which such a hunt takes place: a world of annoying and oppressive homogeneity, completely unattractive, offering no productive relation with otherness.

Milton's vision ends with an account of the relation between the authentic and inauthentic aspects of individuality. "The idiot reasoner," he says, "laughs at the Man of Imagination / And from laughter proceeds to murder by undervaluing calumny" (32:6-7). The idiot Reasoner is the Spectre—the positivist ego which is attuned only to actuality, or immediate presence. The Man of Imagination, on the other hand, directs himself toward the non-actual, the possible, the potential. This orientation is seen as foolhardy by the positivist reasoner, who laughs at the attribution of being to the non-present. The calumny of this scoffing—denying the reality of the non-present—murders individuals, destroying their true being by denigrating the non-actuality into which their actuality is continuously being transformed.

Compelled Combination
versus Free Brotherhood

The characterization of these opposite aspects of individual being continues as each aspect describes itself. The first four lines of the speech that follows seem to be spoken by Hillel in response to Milton, and the rest of the speech seems to be given by the Seven Angels, who also address their words to Milton.[1] The first four lines are spoken by one who was compelled by Satan to combine with other individuals, while the speakers of the remaining lines were combined freely in brotherhood. "Hillel who is Lucifer" describes extrinsic, Satanic unity, a form of unity in which the unique being of individuals is not preserved:

> We are not Individuals but States: Combinations of Individuals
> We were Angels of the Divine Presence: & were Druids in
>   Annandale
> Compelld to combine into Form by Satan, the Spectre of Albion,
> Who made himself a God &, destroyed the Human Form Divine.
>
> (32:10–13)

The spectrous unities of individuals—the immediate unities of homogeneity—are not true individuals at all; rather, they are states or nations, mere aggregated immediacies with no intrinsic being. States or
nations are combinations of individuals, the contingent constellations which
result from accidental convergence of a plurality of individuals. The individuals who constitute such states are descended from "Angels of the Divine
Presence" and "Druids in Annandale," those prototypical deifiers of the totality at the expense of the individual. Their creation of feudalistic unities that
reduce individuals to a homogeneous substance is the result of the
homogenizing activity of "Satan, the Spectre of Albion, / Who made himself a God &, destroyed the Human Form Divine."

In contrast to these spectrous states of individuality is the true form of
individuality, the Human Form described by the Seven Angels. "But the
Divine Humanity & Mercy gave us a Human Form," the angels reveal,
"Because we were combined in Freedom & holy Brotherhood" (32:14–15).
The Seven Angels are the unperverted orientation toward presence, the co-
presence of all individuals through intrinsic relatedness in mediation. The
true, Human form of individuality is its combination with other individuals,
through time, on the basis of their intrinsic relatedness to each other. The
false, spectrous aspect of individuality, on the other hand, unites individuals
on the basis of co-presence—of extrinsic, merely accidental relations, which
are often relations of opposition and destruction. Such beings, "those combined by Satans Tyranny first in the blood of War / A Sacrifice &, next, in
chains of imprisonment: are Shapeless Rocks / Retaining only Satans
Mathematic Holiness, Length: Bredth & Highth" (32:16–18). These aspects
of individuals have no intrinsic being or definite, unique identity; they are
mere masses of immediacy, globs of actuality with exterior manifestations
(dimensions) but no intrinsic being or inner direction. This false form of
individuality arises because of Satan's tyranny, the reasoning that deprives the
individuality of intrinsic being by reducing Being to presence. The spectrous orientation to presence destroys true individuality, as we have seen, by

"calling the Human Imagination: which is the Divine Vision & Fruition /
In which Man liveth eternally: madness & blasphemy" (32:19-20).

The Human Imagination, the self-differing orientation to otherness, to
possibility, is Being itself, the essence and consummation of individuality. It
is in this openness and movement into otherness that individuals live
eternally—i.e., that their being achieves actualization beyond their mere
immediate presence in time and space. This eternal life is achieved through
the imagination in two ways—first, in the individual's own orientation
beyond its immediate identity, opening itself to other individuals, and second, in the orientations of other individuals to this individual, assimilating it
into their being and thus allowing it to preserve and develop itself in
mediated actuality. Thus, for example, when Blake's imagination embraces
Milton's posthumous presence, both Milton and Blake move beyond their
immediate, circumscribed actuality toward eternal life.

Such transcendence toward eternity, however, is hampered by "those com-
bind in Satans Tyranny," who say that Imagination is "blasphemy, against /
Its own [Satanic] Qualities" (32:21). For these reasoners, imagination speaks
falsehoods because the realities it expresses are not immediately actual. These
reasoners take their own qualities to be ultimate being—their orientation to
immediacy and their reduction and abstracting of individuality to extrinsic
form. In truth, however, these qualities "are Servants of Humanity, not Gods
or Lords" (32:21). The qualities of reason are subservient to those of imagination, rather than vice versa: true being consists in orientation to otherness and
the non-actual, and attention to one's own immediate actuality and to
immediacy in general is only an adjunctive activity. For as we have already
seen, presence is a construct: immediacy is a product of mediation.

States, Individuals, and Immortality

Having described to Milton the natures of these true and false aspects of
individuality, the Seven Angels advise him: "Distinguish therefore States
from Individuals, in those States. / States Change: but Individual identities
never change nor cease" (32:22-3). A state is the individual's immediacy, its
particular status or state of affairs at any time. The individual, however, is not
identical with its immediate actuality, and thus while its actuality changes,
the individual's true identity remains, unalterable and indestructible. This
distinction is crucial, because it is on the basis of such a distinction that one
can affirm immortality in the face of literal, eternal death. For if an individual's being is not constituted by its actuality, the individual's being is not

annihilated when the individual perishes. As the Seven Angels tell Milton, "You cannot go to Eternal Death in that which can never Die" (32:24). For as Los explained earlier, "not one Moment / Of Time is lost, nor one Event of Space unpermanent. / But all remain" (22:18-20). Only the individual's immediacy changes and passes away, not the individual's being, which is preserved through indirect actualization in other individuals. Organized religion, however, has ignored the true nature of individuality and focused instead on two of its states, creating a destructive feudalistic metaphysics as a result: "Satan & Adam," the Angels say, "are States Created into Twenty-seven Churches" (32:25). Satan, as the "opake," is the state in which the intrinsic being of an individual is invisible, while Adam, the "solid," is the minimally subsisting "atomic" individuality, reduced by Satanic opacity to the verge of non-being. These states of affairs have been absolutized, raised to ultimate principles, by organized religion, which sees the individual as having total ontological dependence on an extrinsic centralized source of being (in the form of a supreme being).

The way to counter these negative states is through the creation of positive states. Such, in fact, is the purpose of this very poem, which creates the positive state named Milton, in which desire for infinity is fulfilled through the embrace of finitude. Thus the Angels tell Milton that he is "a State about to be Created / Called Eternal Annihilation that none but the living shall / Dare to enter" (32:26-8). Milton's incipient annihilation constitutes a state of immediacy and not the ontological status of Milton's being, which is a dynamic power—that which makes Milton's immediacy grow and develop and become other, and which can never die, only enter into ever different states. The Angels' declaration that "none but the Living shall / Dare to enter" this state of annihilation emphasizes that only individuals who have identified themselves with their intrinsic ecstatic, self-differing process rather than with their self-present state will dare to lose all immediacy. These individuals, in giving up all immediacy and entering a state of non-existence, "shall enter triumphant over Death / And Hell & the Grave: States that are not, but ah! Seem to be" (32:28-9). Such voluntary entry into annihilation is a triumph over death because it derives from the realization that death is not ultimately real, that it is not really the destruction of one's being that it seems to be. Death and hell and the grave only seem to be states of immediate actuality, for they are in truth the end or overcoming of all states. Their only power over individuals is through delusion, in which individuals see death as the destruction of their being and thus lose their true being by ignoring it and fixating on immediacy and avoidance of death.

The ethical ramifications of this vision of individual being are clearly expressed in the Seven Angels' final exhortation to Milton, which is also an address from Blake to the reader: "Judge then of thy Own Self: thy Eternal Lineaments explore / What is Eternal & what Changeable? & what Annihilable!" (32:30-31). This exhortation, coming after the lyrical account of ecstasis and the analyses of the authentic and inauthentic aspects of individuality, reveals the purpose of all the previous metaphysical inquiry: to know what one's being consists in, so that one can achieve true fulfillment. An individual's true being, the Angels imply, lies in that aspect which is permanent and unchanging. This permanence, however, is not mere presence — static, persisting immediacy — but rather the endurance of a process which produces change and which is itself continually changing.

The Angels make this point when they remind Milton that "the Imagination is not a State: it is the Human Existence itself" (32:32). Imagination is the principle and process of movement beyond the immediate, of surpassing the immediate present by drawing new actuality from the realm of possibility — i.e., the realm of the individual's otherness. This orientation and striving toward the possible, the non-actual, the other, is the essence of human being, the culmination of individuality, and not a mere state, or faculty. Mere orientation to otherness, however, is not necessarily Imagination, for if such orientation is tyrannical and reductive rather than admiring and expansive, it ceases to be authentic individuality. Thus, "affection or Love becomes a State, when divided from Imagination" (32:33): when love is not a movement of expansion, of growth, of becoming other, it is a mere actuality or fact, not the essence of human being. In such instances the other which is the object of attraction is seen just as a means for one to consolidate one's own immediate actual identity, rather than as a goal to which one can ascend, as an otherness which can and should supersede one's own immediate actuality.

The inauthentic attempt to perpetuate the immediate is also a function of memory. "The Memory is a State always," the Angels say, "& the Reason is a State / Created to be Annihilated & a new Ratio Created" (32:34-5). The faculties of memory and reason attempt to preserve and fix being in immediacy, not content to let it flow in and out of presence. The static scheme of relations which reason establishes among individuals is invalid the moment after it is formulated and must therefore be annihilated as soon as it is created and a new ratio or schema of relations established to reflect the present order of things. This new order must in turn be superseded, and so on *ad infinitum*. As fixation on immediacy, these faculties are contingent attributes of individuality and not part of its essence. The essential enduring nature of individuality, in fact, is not something that is ever present or immediate per se, for "whatever can be Created can be Annihilated" (32:36). Rather, the essence lies, as we have said, in the process or form (never graspable or quantifiable) that underlies the immediate, perceptible actuality of an individual. For while everything immediate can be, and is, created and annihilated, "forms cannot / The Oak is cut down by the Ax, the Lamb falls by the Knife / But their Forms Eternal Exist, Forever" (32:36-8).[2] The forms (the particular powers of being — the essences or strategies of being) cannot be destroyed, and it is these forces, which bring all immediacy into existence, that constitute the true being of individuals. Just as the species endures while individuals perish, so an individual's intrinsic identity remains as its immediate moments pass and perish.

Moreover, even after the individual itself perishes, it continues to be, as we have seen in the case of Milton. This principle of posthumous presence is embodied in the Seven Angels, the principles and powers that guard Milton's being even though he is dead: "Thus they converse with the Dead watching round the Couch of Death" (32:39). Because of these powers or aspects of Being, ultimate Being remains with the dead:

> For God himself enters Death's Door always with those that enter
> And lays down in the Grave with them, in Visions of Eternity
> Till they awake & see Jesus & the Linen Clothes lying
> That the Females had Woven for them, & the Gates of their Fathers
> House.
>
> (32:40-43)

God, or Being itself, remains with the dead, "in Visions of Eternity": by virtue of the visions which surviving individuals have of eternity, imagining the dead as continuing to be. By means of the survivors' visions, the dead transcend their immediacy of annihilation (the "Linen Clothes") and see Jesus "& the Gates of their Fathers House" — i.e., apprehend true being (as opposed to actuality) and enter eternity through indirect actualization. In order to arise in this way, however, one must see with Blake's vision and not that of Christian orthodoxy. If one is caught in the vision of orthodoxy, such eternal life remains invisible — as, indeed, does the message of this very passage, which, apart from the context of the poem, can very easily be read as a straightforward account of the orthodox doctrine of the resurrection of the body.

Consequences of Failing to Distinguish
States from Individuals

We are now presented with a concrete instance of the distinction between an individual's authentic and inauthentic aspects, and we are shown the consequences of failing to "distinguish...States from individuals in those States":

> And the Divine Voice was heard in the Songs of Beulah Saying
> When I first Married you, I gave you all my whole Soul
> I thought that you would love my loves & joy in my delights
> Seeking for pleasures in my pleasures O Daughter of Babylon
> Then thou wast lovely, mild & gentle. now thou art terrible
> In jealousy & unlovely in my sight, because thou has cruelly
> Cut off my loves in fury till I have no love left for thee.
>
> (33:1-7)

Here we see what happens when an individual's state is taken for its true being. This message of the Divine Voice comes to us, however, through "the Songs of Beulah": it is filtered through and distorted by the language of presence, which presents everything in terms of immediate feelings and experience—in this case, the experience of resented jealousy. Nonetheless, the Divine Voice can be heard in these expressions or Songs of Beulah, and its message is essentially as follows.

If individuals interact with each other on the basis of their true being, then one will love the other's loves—since the other's loves (i.e., relations with others) constitute its true being. In jealousy, however, the individual opposes the loves of its loved one, seeing the loved one as a commodity to be possessed rather than as a dynamic process whose essence is its acts of loving. Jealousy is thus a result of captivity in immediacy, and the jealous individual is thus a "Daughter of Babylon." Jealousy is love cut off from imagination, and hence is a state, and that which jealousy loves is also a state, merely the hypostatized husk of identity rather than the true identity itself, which is a dynamic system of relatedness to others.

In order truly to love an individual, we must love not its immediacy but its loves—i.e., its orientations to otherness—because such orientations constitute the identity of the individual. Thus the Divine Voice declares: "Thy love depends on him thou lovest & on his dear loves / Depend thy pleasures which thou hast cut off by jealousy" (33:8-9). Her loved one is constituted by his relatedness (love) to others—i.e., by his loves. Therefore, her love for him presupposes his love for others, for without his love of others he would not truly be, and her love would be deprived of its object. Thus by being jealous and denying him his relatedness to others, she has destroyed both him and herself: "Thou hast cruelly / Cut off my loves in fury till I have no love left for thee," he tells her, and "therefore I shew my Jealousy & set before you Death" (33:6-10). The cruelty of jealousy derives from lack of imagination — i.e., from antipathy to otherness, failure to recognize otherness as having intrinsic value and as being ultimately part of one's (self-differing) self. And when she opposes him with jealousy, he no longer sees her as part of himself and thus he likewise becomes jealous and cruel to her. The Divine Voice continues its explanation:

> Behold Milton descended to Redeem the Female Shade
> From Death Eternal; such your lot, to be continually Redeem'd
> By death & misery of those you love & by Annihilation.
>
> (33:11-13)

Here, distorted by Beulah, the Divine Voice articulates Milton's redemption of his emanation (the otherness in relation to which he is truly himself) in terms of a *quid pro quo* act of ransom. Such, the Divine Voice says, is the fate of its own other: to find fulfillment only in an act which destroys that which brings fulfillment. When the females (the particular instances or aspects of this emanation) see this consequence, the Divine Voice predicts, they will renounce jealousy:

> When the Sixfold Female percieves that Milton annihilates
> Himself: that seeing all his loves by her cut off: he leaves
> Her also: intirely abstracting himself from Female loves
> She shall relent in fear of death: She shall begin to give
> Her maidens to her husband: delighting in his delight
> And then & then alone begins the happy Female joy
> As it is done in Beulah, & thou O Virgin Babylon Mother of
>   Whoredoms
> Shalt bring Jerusalem in thine arms in the night watches; and
> No longer turning her a wandering Harlot in the streets
> Shalt give her into the arms of God your Lord & Husband.
>
> (33:14-23)

"Such are the Songs of Beulah in the Lamentations of Ololon" (33:24), we are told. This declaration reiterates the fact that the preceding lines embody a distorted vision: what is taken as the Divine Voice is "heard in the Songs of Beulah" (33:1), which are themselves mediated through the Lamentations of Ololon. When we learn in the next lines, at the beginning of the following plate, that "all the Songs of Beulah sounded comfortable notes / To comfort Ololons lamentation" (34:1-2), we have further external evidence that the ethic of free love enunciated by the Divine Voice is itself tainted with the fixation on immediacy which it purports to oppose. Ololon, we remember, is lamenting Milton's descent because it sees loss of self-presence as loss of being, and Beulah consists of the weak who could not endure the wars of Eternity. The words of the Divine Voice, then, are the somewhat distorted expression of the way to fulfillment, conceiving of fulfillment, "as it is done in Beulah" (33:20), as immediate presence and gratification, and refusing to acknowledge and accept the limitations inherent in existence—limitations which can be overcome only through valorizing mediation and renouncing pure presence. Thus the Voice identifies the debilitating effects of jealousy not as the restricting, quantitative vision which jealousy implies but rather as a reciprocation of jealousy on the part of the beloved.

This distortion aside, however, the Divine Voice does present a valid account of the perversion of individuality in jealousy and of fulfillment of individuals through imaginative, generous love. It also reveals that the sexual jealousy of human nature is a manifestation of a deeper, ontological jealousy—immediacy's jealousy of possibility or mediated being, expressed here as Babylon's jealousy of Jerusalem. The "Virgin Babylon Mother of Whoredoms" is unproductive, unfulfilling immediacy which enslaves individuals in false fulfillment and rejects Jerusalem, the possibility of authentic fulfillment, as false and unworthy of individuals' attention. Babylon is the embodiment of the assumption that Being is limited to the actual present, an assumption which devalues possibility and mediation of all kinds.

Such fixation on immediacy, however, is not inevitable, and the Divine Voice offers hope that the power of immediacy and the opposition to otherness can be overcome. Beulah itself finds a similar hope in Ololon's decision to descend after Milton:

> Are you the Fiery Circle that late drove in fury & fire
> The Eight Immortal Starry-Ones down into Ulro dark
> Rending the Heavens of Beulah with your thunders & lightnings
> And can you thus lament & can you pity & forgive?
> Is terror changd to pity O wonder of Eternity!
>
> (34:3-7)

As a result of Ololon's descent, Beulah, the realm of ideals, itself begins to take into account alternatives to pure presence. Beulah sees the descent of Ololon/lamentation as an indication that devotion to pure presence may be abandoned in favor of the "thunders & lightnings" of Eternal energy and transformation. The realm of ideals is beginning to recognize that the flux, deficiency, and destruction which it has always found terrifying might actually be redemptive: "Is terror changed to pity?" Beulah asks. "O wonder of Eternity!" This, as we shall see, is indeed the case, for by descending into immediate actuality in search of the Beulahic ideal of pure presence and permanence, lamentation comes to realize that the terrors of Eternal flux are actually "the mercy of Eternity," and thus prepares the way for overcoming the ideal of presence and the *quid pro quo* metaphysics of homogeneity which it fosters.

CHAPTER XII

The Discovery of Ecstatic Finitude
in the Search for Immediate Infinity

Immediacy and the
Process of Actualization

Four Degrees of Immersion in Immediacy

Although Ololon's descent will ultimately result in an overcoming of
enslavement to presence, before this can occur, Ololon/lamentation must
first experience the inadequacy of immediacy in its various forms. Thus as
they descend,

> ...the Four States of Humanity in its Repose,
> Were shewed them. First Beulah a most pleasant Sleep
> On Couches soft, with mild music, tended by Flowers of Beulah
> Sweet Female forms, winged or floating in the air spontaneous
> The Second State is Alla & the third Al-Ulro;
> But the Fourth State is dreadful; it is named Or-Ulro.
>
> (34:8-13)

These are the "states of Humanity in its Repose"—states in which human
being is in various degrees passive, subordinate to extrinsic forces. In these
states of dormancy and lack of growth and transformation, the intrinsic
uniqueness of individuals—which results in dynamic interaction, the Wars of
Eternity—is vitiated. Beulah, the first stage of repose from the Wars of
Eternity, is a benign dormancy. This "first State is in the Head" (34:14), we
are told; it is the intellectual passivity in which "Contrarieties are equally
True" (30:1). It is a flight from the intellectual warfare in which one struggles
to form one's being and establish its place in the entire scheme of things;
instead, it accepts pre-established categories for the various forms of Being,
such as the ideal forms of Platonism. The second state, Alla, is homophonous
with Allah; individuals who repose in Allah have abdicated all intrinsic being

and submitted to ontological degradation. Alla also suggests Allamanda, where (we have seen) there is complete overcoming of individual distinctness altogether. Alla is located in the heart (34:14), the seat of the indefinite and obscure, unifying and homogenizing emotions, which constitute immediate reaction—response to what is present—rather than circumspect and imaginative action, response to what is not present. The third state of repose, Al-Ulro, is located in the loins (34:15), and its name suggests an association with the sleeping Albion, as well as with Alla/Allah. Al-Ulro is the realm of the instincts, and an individual who resides at this level has even further abdicated its intrinsic being and active control of its own life, existing only according to the modes established by the collective memory of the species. Finally there is the dreadful fourth state, named Or-Ulro and located in the "Stomach & Intestines terrible, deadly, unutterable" (34:16). This is the ultimate passivity, in which the only action is mere self-perpetuation through involuntary bodily functions. This state, moreover, involves immediate destruction of otherness, motivated by the fiery desire of Orc.

These, then, are the successive stages of dormancy—i.e., inauthenticity and abdication of sovereignty—into which individuality can fall; they constitute varying degrees of withdrawal from possibility and capitulation to (past and present) actuality. In their proper subordinate roles, these varying functions are valuable and necessary components of individuality, "and he whose gates are opend in those Regions of his Body / Can from those Gates view all these wondrous Imaginations" (34:17-18)—i.e., these various modes of openness and voluntary submission to otherness. By themselves, however, without the active guidance and control of the individual's intrinsic, self-transforming identity, these functions become counterproductive and destructive, constituting abdication of the sovereignty of identity.

Ololon's Descent into Immediacy

As we saw earlier, when the urge for infinity—Ololon/lamentation—locates being in the realm of presence rather than process (i.e., when Ololon descends to Beulah), the first step has been taken on a path that leads from Eternity/infinity to mere immediate actuality. Now Blake shows us that Ololon's descent goes beyond Beulah and ends in Or-Ulro, the realm of virtually pure immediacy, where one actuality has to be destroyed to make room for another:

> ...Ololon sought the Or-Ulro & its fiery Gates
> And the Couches of the Martyrs: & many Daughters of Beulah

> Accompany them down to the Ulro with soft melodious tears
> A long journey & dark thro Chaos in the track of Miltons course
> To where the Contraries of Beulah War beneath Negations Banner.
>   (34:19-23)

Here the ramifications of the Beulahic valorization of presence are felt in full force: the contraries, which in Beulah were "equally true," are here mutually destructive, each questing for full immediate actuality, which can be achieved only at the expense of the other. The fact that Ulro appears to Ololon as "a vast Polypus / Of living fibres down into the Sea of Time & Space growing / A self-devouring monstrous Human Death Twenty-seven fold" (34:24-6) indicates that Ulro is the mere immediacy of existence, the collectivity of merely natural existents that enroots itself in time and space and is constantly feeding on itself, life living on death and destroying the ecstatic, mediated and mediating human aspect of existence. The fact that existence takes the form of this self-devouring polypus is the result of the seductive power that lies at the heart of immediacy—the power that elicits acquisitive behavior. This aspect of immediacy is expressed as the six females who produce the polypus:

> Within [the polypus] sit Five Females & the nameless Shadowy
>   Mother
> Spinning it from their bowels with songs of amorous delight
> And melting cadences that lure the Sleepers of Beulah down
> The River Storge (which is Arnon) into the Dead Sea.
>   (34:27-30)

The females are the powers which produce the natural beings that nature holds out as lures to desire. The numerous tentacles and fibers of desire which these objects evoke from individuals form the polypus, the world of Ulro, of writhing and grasping desires demanding immediate gratification. The "songs of amorous delight"—the promises of fulfillment offered by natural objects—"lure the Sleepers of Beulah down / The River Storge (which is Arnon) into the Dead Sea": i.e., they lure those who are immersed in Beulahic ideals of presence into a lifeless, homogeneous, self-enclosed world with no exit, no element leading beyond the limits of its immediacy. To repose in the presence and permanence of absolute, pre-established ideals (Beulah), that is, is to be already engaged in the quest for immediate gratification that can never be achieved. But, as we shall see, through this frustrated quest for immediacy, Ololon/lamentation is able to realize the futility of the entire valorization of presence.

Entelechy versus Immediacy

At this point Blake pauses in his account of the journey of Ololon/ lamentation to explain the authentic function which ideals have for human existence. Ideals, we are shown, have the legitimate function of protecting and fostering unborn reality. "Around this Polypus" of desire, we are told, "Los continual builds the Mundane Shell" (34:31). In building the Mundane Shell — the metaphysical realm — Los limits the polypus of desire by establishing a realm beyond immediate actuality. By thus constituting a transcendent realm, the Mundane Shell transforms the vast system of desires from a massive self-perpetuating urge into an embryonic form of something other: desires can now be seen as inadequate and perverted but nonetheless valid attempts to overthrow and transcend the merely immediate, actual state of identity. The Mundane Shell or metaphysical realm created by Los is the mediator, that is, between the brute immediacy of the actual world and the vague, indefinite realms of Being that lie beyond that immediacy:

> Four Universes round the Universe of Los remain Chaotic
> Four intersecting Globes, & the Egg form'd World of Los
> In midst; stretching from Zenith to Nadir, in midst of Chaos[.]
> One of these Ruind Universes is to the North named Urthona
> One to the South this was the glorious world of Urizen
> One to the East, of Luvah: One to the West; of Tharmas.
> But when Luvah assumed the World of Urizen in the South
> All fell towards the Center sinking downward in dire Ruin.
>
> (34:32-9)

"The Egg form'd World of Los / In midst" is the aspect of Being that is constituted by the process of actualization, where mere actuality is connected with possibility and mere possibility is gathered into actuality. And the Mundane Shell, as we have seen, is a metaphysical system formed by the extrapolation and projection of various aspects of present actuality. Shells are made to be broken, however, and any metaphysics is only a provisional system made to protect the embryonic actuality until it bursts the shell, at which point a new shell (metaphysics) is created — because the actuality which has hatched is itself an embryo for another actuality which will supersede it, and so on, *ad infinitum*.

The schematic drawing of the Mundane Shell and the Four Universes (on Plate 33, the previous plate) shows, like a Venn diagram, that the shell incorporates within itself — i.e., within embryonic actuality — portions of all the four realms of Being. In addition, each of these realms overlaps with two others—both within actuality and outside it—and achieves contact with its opposite (only within actuality). It is this connectedness of various aspects of Being which constitutes the transcendental ground of the intrinsic relatedness of individuals—a relatedness that is presupposed by the creative, destructive, and transforming process of actualization.

Presence and Negativity: Ololon's Encounter with Finitude

Ololon's Perspective on Mutual Destruction

These transcendental aspects of Being serve as an abode for Ololon, the seeker for infinity: "Here in these Chaoses the Sons of Ololon took their abode / In Chasms of the Mundane Shell which open on all sides round!" (34:40-41). These fundamental regions of Being are chasms—openings or gaps in actuality as it is constituted by the present metaphysics. Ololon takes up abode in these gaps in order "to watch the time, pitying and gentle to awaken Urizen" (34:43). Lamentation, that is, dwells in the gaps in actuality—i.e., dwells in the non-present or non-immediate which permeates immediacy—hoping that somehow desire can be satisfied and existence renovated by some element of Being which is not actualized. And since the most obvious chasm or gap in actuality—i.e., the most obvious instance in which actuality is deficient—is in the phenomenon of perishing or death, it is here that Ololon seeks fulfillment of its quest:

> They stood in a dark land of death of fiery corroding waters
> Where lie in evil death the Four Immortals pale and cold
> And the Eternal Man, even Albion, upon the Rock of Ages[.]
> Seeing Miltons Shadow, some Daughters of Beulah trembling
> Returnd, but Ololon remain before the Gates of the Dead.
>
> (34:44-8)

The perseverance and integrity of Ololon/lamentation is signalled by the fact that it does not, like other offspring of static ideals, abjure the destructiveness of immediacy and take refuge in the passivity and accord offered by the ideal realm of Beulah; while "some Daughters of Beulah trembling / Retur[n]" to the pure presence of the realm of ideals, "Ololon remain[s] before the Gates of the Dead," refusing to ignore the brute fact of destruction, hoping instead to find a solution to the problem of finitude.

The picture is bleak, however, and when Ololon/lamentation attends more closely to the ultimate nature of immediacy (i.e., to "the Heavens of Ulro"), the prospects of finding infinity in immediacy appear non-existent:

> And Ololon looked down into the Heavens of Ulro in fear
> They said. How are the Wars of man which in Great Eternity
> Appear around, in the External Spheres of Visionary Life
> Here renderd Deadly within the Life & Interior Vision
> How are the Beasts & Birds & Fishes, & Plants & Minerals
> Here fixd into frozen bulk subject to decay & death[?]
>
> (34:50-55)

Ololon/lamentation has hoped to find fulfillment in immediacy but finds only frustration and destruction. Ololon sees first that the essential differentiation and opposition among individuals leads to destruction in actuality. Individuals themselves are, in their immediacy, mere rigid masses—"frozen bulk" with no intrinsic being. Moreover, whereas knowledge and metaphysical speculation are inherently stimulating and expansive, the knowledge and metaphysics of immediacy—i.e., positivism and materialism—are terrifyingly restrictive: "Those Visions of Human Life & Shadows of Wisdom & Knowledge / Are here frozen to unexpansive deadly destroying terrors" (34:55-35:1). The metaphysics of immediacy, that is, reduces the being of individuals, rather than expanding that being by making individuals aware of possibility and otherness and thus allowing them to be more than their immediate actuality.

Even the dynamic process of actualization, in which individuals delineate, transform, and achieve themselves through struggle with other individuals, is, in the realm of mere immediacy, destructive rather than productive: "War & Hunting: the Two Fountains of the River of Life / Are become Fountains of bitter Death & of corroding Hell" (35:2-3). War is ultimately based on the necessary and legitimate impulse of self-preservation, self-definition, and self-enhancement; hunting, too, derives from the legitimate effort to establish, preserve, and enhance one's being. As such, these impulses constitute the very "Fountains" of life. But when these impulses are enacted immediately rather than through mediation—i.e., indirectly (e.g., through empathy or sympathy) or through deferral—they become counterproductive, resulting in greater destruction than enhancement.

Ololon/lamentation sees that such destructive immersion in immediacy also destroys the authentic bond among individuals, changing "Brotherhood...into a Curse & a Flattery / By differences between Ideas, that Ideas themselves, (Which are / The Divine Members) may be slain in offerings for sin" (35:4-6). To one immersed in immediacy—that is, to one who assumes that being and actuality are identical—connection with other individuals is either a restricting burden (i.e., "a curse") or an unwarranted attribute of approbation ("a flattery"): it is no longer the mutually enhancing intrinsic relatedness which is its authentic nature. This perversion of Brotherhood, moreover, is caused by "Difference between Ideas"—i.e., by ideological disputes. Ideas, as "Divine Members," are the elements constituting Being itself: that is, they are pure possibilities. And as possibilities, they are inherently other than the actuality of individuals, and thus constitute a threat to the actuality of an individual. Consequently, as we have seen, the individual that takes its immediate actuality as its true being will oppose those ideas or possibilities that would lead to essential alteration or transformation of its immediate actual state. And it will attempt to "slay" those ideas or ideals by destroying those other individuals which embody or espouse them, denying all Brotherhood or sameness with these others in doing so. Ololon's vision thus reveals that the denial and perversion of Brotherhood among individuals is motivated by an attempt to destroy possibilities which threaten to cause changes in oneself—changes which are epitomized by those seen to constitute "sin," the destruction of one's self-righteousness or self-sameness—one's present identity. Destruction of individuals, then, is a destruction of threatening possibilities, and is thus an "offerin[g] for sin"—an attempt to avoid the destruction, by definition "sinful," of rigid, self-same identity.

Identification of Being with presence, then, and the consequent devotion to immediacy, is what denies the ultimate togetherness or sameness of individuals and renders difference *merely* destructive rather than productively destructive. This is the vision of Ololon/lamentation, the desire for infinity. In this vision, the very fabric of existence is constituted by mere death, unredemptive destruction. Ololon thus exclaims:

> O dreadful Loom of Death! O piteous Female forms compelld
> To weave the Woof of Death, On Camberwell Tirzahs Courts
> Malahs on Blackheath, Rahab & Noah. dwell on Windsors heights
> Where once the Cherubs of Jerusalem spread to Lambeths Vale
> Milcahs Pillars shine from Harrow to Hampstead where Hoglah
> On Highgates heights magnificent Weaves over trembling Thames
> To Shooters Hill and thence to Blackheath the dark Woof! Loud
> Loud roll the Weights & Spindles over the whole Earth let down
> On all sides round to the Four Quarters of the World, eastward on

> Europe to Euphrates & Hindu, to Nile & back in Clouds
> Of Death across the Atlantic to America North & South.
>
> (35:7-17)

The Female or reproductive forms become in the realm of mere immediacy agents of generation rather than regeneration. Reproduction, or the arising of new individuals out of old, is in immediacy merely the emergence of another entity (soon to be destroyed) rather than the transformation and therefore the mediated existence of a previous individual being. The females are here devouring and productive, not re-productive, for mere immediacy manifests no carryover from the being that is destroyed to the one that is produced. Existence thus falls under the control of the self-aggrandizing powers represented by Zelophehad's daughters (Malah, Rahab, Noah, Milcah, and Hoglah), and the whole earth becomes a giant Loom of Death. Such is the vision of Ololon at this point: immediate actuality is merely the scene of the continuous arising and perishing of entities.

The Limitation of Ololon's Perspective

Immersed in the realm of immediacy, however, Ololon is oblivious to the very process of actualization which produces the immediacy of actuality:

> . . . they
> Could not behold Golgonooza without passing the Polypus
> A wondrous journey not passable by Immortal feet, & none
> But the Divine Saviour can pass it without annihilation.
> For Golgonooza cannot be seen till having passd the Polypus
> It is viewed on all sides round by a Four-fold Vision
> Or till you become Mortal & Vegetable in Sexuality
> Then you behold its mighty Spires & Domes of ivory & gold.
>
> (35:18-25)

As desire for fulfillment or infinity, Ololon/lamentation is caught up in the Polypus of self-aggrandizing desire, and no one in this position can apprehend the actualizing process, or Golgonooza, the essence of which is to enhance through negating and destroying. This process is totally unseen from a perspective for which Being is identical with pure presence or immediacy. For Golgonooza is that dimension of Being the very occurrence of which demonstrates that mere presence is not ultimate or primary—that presence is itself based on a destructive/productive making-present. But to apprehend this dimension of Being, one must get beyond the equation of

Being with presence, and this means, in practical terms, ceasing to identify one's own being with one's immediate self-presence, the desiring ego-consciousness (the polypus). To completely give up this attachment to one's own self-presence, however, is impossible except in death: "the Polypus," Blake says, is "not passable by Immortal feet, & none / But the Divine Saviour can pass it without annihilation." Only through mortality, annihilation, can one completely overcome all one's self-perpetuating desires and move beyond presence to the non-present destructive/productive ground of presence. It is possible, however, to gain a distant glimpse of this region—to view from afar Golgonooza's "mighty Spires & Domes of ivory & gold"—without dying. This glimpse can occur, Blake says, in sexual intercourse, when "you become Mortal and Vegetable in Sexuality," giving the self over to otherness—"becom[ing] Mortal" ("dying" in the sexual sense)—in the immediate moment (becoming "Vegetable"). This experience of yielding up one's immediate actuality, Blake says, is the closest we can come, apart from literally dying, to overcoming our self-presence and actually *experiencing* the non-present—and hence ultimately non-experienceable—destructive/productive ground of presence.

Ololon's Descent:
Desire for Infinity Enters the Finite

Ololon, then, in its present form as devotion to presence, is oblivious to this non-present actualizing ground. But in confronting the negativity of death, Ololon/lamentation has taken a step toward relinquishing its hold on presence. Now, in examining death more closely, Ololon discovers that death or annihilation does not mean absolute negation:

> ...Ololon examined all the Couches of the Dead.
> Even of Los & Enitharmon & all the Sons of Albion
> And his Four Zoas terrified & on the verge of Death
> In midst of these was Miltons Couch, & when they saw Eight
> Immortal Starry-Ones, guarding the Couch in flaming fires
> They thunderous uttered all a universal groan falling down
> Prostrate before the Starry Eight asking with tears forgiveness
> Confessing their crime with humiliation and sorrow.
>
> (35:26-33)

In examining Death, Ololon encounters the remains of the dead, expressed here as "Couches [reposing places] of the Dead." Ololon is thus forced to recognize that the perishing of an individual entity or the passing away of a principle does not mean that everything is as though the thing had never existed. For although the thing is no longer actually present, traces, remnants, and effects (the "Couches" or graves) of the thing still remain, and those traces and effects constitute the mediated presence of the thing's unique being, which is incontrovertible evidence that in a fundamental and ultimate sense the thing which has perished continues to be. Thus when Ololon/ lamentation encounters Milton's remains, it is forced to acknowledge the being of the non-present, and hence also the being of some preserving principles, for it is only by virtue of such transcendental powers or principles of mediation that any remnant of Milton's unique identity can be encountered. If it were not for such powers of Being—the "Eight / Immortal Starry-Ones, guarding the Couch in flaming fires"—there could not even be memory of Milton: all would be as though Milton had never existed. Ololon's recognition of such powers of posthumous presence is pivotal, for it undermines the devotion to presence, which Ololon then renounces—a renunciation expressed as repentance for evicting these principles from Eternity, and as submission to the Starry Eight, the principles of posthumous presence.

This recognition by Ololon of the being of mediation or non-presence paves the way for interaction between Eternity and existence, the infinite and the finite aspects of Being. No longer is the realm of ultimate Being divorced from the realm of finite existence:

> O how the Starry Eight rejoic'd to see Ololon descended!
> And now that a wide road was open to Eternity,
> By Ololons descent thro Beulah to Los & Enitharmon.
>
> (35:34-6)

Ololon's descent thus marks the transfer of lamentation, the desire for infinity, from the immediately infinite to the finite aspect of Being—i.e., from Eternity to existence. Fulfillment is now to be sought through the mediated presence constructed by the actualizing process rather than in the pure presence of the Beulahic vision of Eternity. And in such a seeking of fulfillment in the realm of the finite, the finitude of existence is itself overcome, for the mediated presence of an individual can continue indefinitely. The acknowledgement of the being of mediation, then, opens up "a wide road" from the finite to the infinite, from existence "to Eternity."

When lamentation, the regret for what is not, thus accepts the being of the non-existent, the implications are tremendous,

> For mighty were the multitudes of Ololon, vast the extent
> Of their great sway, reaching from Ulro to Eternity
> Surrounding the Mundane Shell outside in its Caverns.
>
> (35:37-9)

The multitudes of Ololon include everything that laments—i.e., everything that experiences deficiency of some sort—which means that aspects of all individual beings are found in Ololon. The reorientation of Ololon toward the mediated presence of the actualizing process thus has fundamental repercussions for all of existence, transforming the way individuals deal with their deficiencies or finitude and making real fulfillment possible for the first time. Thus the descent of Ololon has affinities with the Second Coming, which also promises ultimate fulfillment: "and all silent forebore to contend / With Ololon for they saw the Lord in the Clouds of Ololon" (35:40-41). Blake leaves the degree and even the validity of this identification vague, however, for the identity holds only if one understands the Second Coming in a particular way—namely, as ascendence of mediation over presence, an ascendancy manifested as voluntary self-sacrifice and determined patience.

Lamentation and the
Infinity of the Finite

Change and the Infinity of the Moment

Blake now pursues the ramifications of Ololon's recognition of mediation by analyzing the moment in which the recognition occurs. This analysis constitutes a further meditation on the nature of time and a presentation of the condition for the possibility of the mediation which Ololon's descent both recognizes and partakes of. To begin with, we are told that

> There is a Moment in each Day that Satan cannot find
> Nor can his Watch Fiends find it, but the Industrious find
> This moment & it multiply. & when it once is found
> It renovates every Moment of the Day if rightly placed[.]
> In this Moment Ololon descended to Los & Enitharmon
> Unseen beyond the Mundane Shell Southward in Miltons track.
>
> (35:42-7)

The moment here described is the moment presented earlier (28:44-29:3) from which "all the Great / Events of Time start forth & are concievd" (29:1-2). It is the instant of novelty, of transformation—the point at which otherness or difference emerges. This originary, creative moment is the cornerstone of actuality; as we saw earlier, all the larger dimensions of time are constructed upon this primal instant. The originary nature of this moment makes it absolutely irreducible and inviolable: "Satan cannot find / Nor can his Watch Fiends find it." The instant of origination or emergence of otherness is impervious to the reductively destructive power of Satan, for it is by its very nature not a self-present element locatable in the world of homogeneous time and space. In addition, as a point of origin, it is by definition unique: it is other, unlike anything else, and its very occurrence is constituted by this ecstasis of otherness; thus the homogenizing force of Satan is powerless against it.

Because the originary moment is in this sense absolute, it constitutes the foundation for the intrinsic uniqueness of all beings. Thus "when it is once found / It renovates every Moment of the Day if rightly placed": it forms the ground for the uniqueness of all other moments, for these moments derive their unique intrinsic being from the uniqueness of their relationship to the originary moment. The non-originary moments, that is, derive their unique being from their function in transmitting previous originary moments and preparing the way for succeeding originary moments.

The movement of the urge to fulfillment (Ololon) from the immediately infinite to the finite aspect of Being is an originary occurrence of this type: it is "in this [originary] moment," we are told, that "Ololon descended to Los & Enitharmon." The very occurrence of Ololon's transformation is thus evidence for the truth of the recognition which occasioned the transformation in the first place: namely, the acknowledgement of the infinity of the finite, the recognition that Being resides in change and transformation as much as in (illusory) presence or self-presence. For the infinity of the finite individual, we have said, consists in its ecstasis and consequent mediated presence in other individuals. Blake now presents the condition for the possibility of such mediation, through an analysis of the way in which a temporal moment reaches beyond itself.

Ecstasis and Transcendence

The originary moment, Blake says, has an intrinsic ecstasis, or movement beyond itself:

> Just in this Moment when the morning odours rise abroad
> And first from the Wild Thyme, stands a Fountain in a rock
> Of crystal flowing into two Streams, one flows through Golgonooza
> And thro Beulah to Eden beneath Los's western Wall
> The other flows thro the Aerial Void & all the Churches
> Meeting again in Golgonooza beyond Satans Seat.
>
> (35:48-53)

The rock of crystal portrays the definite and determinate actuality of the moment, while the fountain embodies the moment's ecstatic aspect. The fact that the ecstatic apsect arises out of the self-enclosed, impervious aspect indicates that integrity and invulnerability, on the one hand, and ecstasis, on the other, are not mutually exclusive, but rather are, in fact, mutually implicit. For ecstasis presupposes a definite, determinate actuality which is to be surpassed, and definite actuality occurs, as we have seen, only by virtue of *activity*, which is in its very nature an ecstatic or self-differing movement beyond the status quo.[1] This dialectic is an instance of the dialectic noted earlier between Beulah and Eternity, or presence and process.

This mutual implication of ecstasis and determinateness is developed further in the image of the two streams, which portray the ways in which the ecstatic aspect of a moment moves beyond the moment's immediacy. One stream, we are told, "flows thro Golgonooza / And thro Beulah to Eden beneath Los's western Wall." This stream expresses the fact that ecstasis leads to an indefinite, transcendent union with all that is. Passing beneath the western wall of Los's realm, this stream enters the chaotic realm of Tharmas, or non-differentiation, moves from this homogeneity to Beulah, "where Contrarieties are equally True" (30:1), and finally comes to rest in Eden, the original paradise which represents the oneness or infinity of all things. The very fact of ecstasis, in other words, leads ineluctably to a vision of a primordial and ultimate sameness of all things: for without some such sameness, no ecstasis—no contact with otherness—would be possible. Thus the fact of ecstasis leads logically, first of all, to a realm in which individual uniquenesses are blurred; this is the watry realm of Tharmas, which, as the western realm, is also the realm of perishing, the supreme instance of the blurring of individual distinctions. Furthermore, if such blurring of individual uniqueness, or mutual habitation of the same area of being, is possible, there must be a sense in which distinct entities are not mutually exclusive— i.e., there must be a realm "where Contrarieties are equally True." This is the realm of Beulah, the transcendent realm of permanent, ideal forms in which all individuals participate (although that participation by no means constitues the entire being of the individual). And finally, as the condition of the possibility for contrarieties being equally true, there must be an aspect of individuality, more fundamental than the contrarieties, which pre-empts all distinctions whatsoever. This means that there must be a sense in which all things participate in (without being reducible to) a primal unity or sameness, for only a fundamental sameness of all things could pre-empt contrarieties. Ecstasis thus ultimately manifests, as a condition for the possibility of its own occurrence, a fundamental sameness of all things.

Blake pursues his analysis of this aspect of ecstasis by means of a meditation on wild thyme:

> The Wild Thyme is Los's Messenger to Eden, a mighty Demon
> Terrible deadly & poisonous his presence in Ulro dark
> Therefore he appears only a small Root creeping in Grass
> Covering over the Rock of Odours his bright purple mantle
> Beside the Fount above the Larks nest in Golgonooza
> Luvah slept here in death & here is Luvahs empty Tomb
> Ololon sat beside this Fountain on the Rock of Odours.
>
> (35:54-60)

The wild thyme—which punningly signifies "wild time," as well—embodies the aspect of ecstasis which links Los, or the actualizing process, with Eden, the primal Oneness or sameness of all things. In immediate actuality (i.e., "in Ulro dark") the wild thyme "appears only a small Root creeping in Grass." But when we see beyond the wild thyme's mere immediate actuality, we see how it embodies ecstatic union with all things. This ecstatic aspect is constituted by the thyme's odor, its "essence" which diffuses outward indefinitely from the immediate, finite presence of the thyme.[2] It is this diffusion throughout all the rest of actuality which embodies Los's message to Eden—i.e., which constitutes the connection of the actualizing process of Los/entelechy with the common ground or sameness of all things. For entelechy, as the movement of becoming other, manifests in this movement the implicit (partial) sameness of all things, by virtue of the implicit identity between the present individual and what it becomes. And the essence of the process of entelechy—i.e., its centrifugal, self-differing movement—is most readily grasped in phenomena such as odors, which manifest their sameness by their ability to infiltrate and permeate everything. For this reason the wild thyme is said to be Los's messenger to Eden.

This aspect of ecstasis is part of the actualizing process and is closely associated with temporal ecstasis, with the second aspect of ecstasis (yet to be discussed), with the principle of connectedness among individuals (Luvah), and with the new Ololon; for the wild thyme and the Rock of Odours are located

> Beside the Fount above the Larks nest in Golgonooza
> Luvah slept here in death & here is Luvahs empty Tomb
> Ololon sat beside this Fountain on the Rock of Odours.
>
> (35:58-60)

The sameness embodied by ecstasis is thus the protector of the principle of connexity, Luvah; it is the aspect of Being which preserves connexity in a latent state when it is not actual, and the ground whence connexity once again becomes active. This sameness is also the basis for Ololon's repose in the realm of the actual and finite, for it constitutes the implicit infinity-by-transcendence in each actuality.

Ecstasis and Mediated Actuality

There is also another mode of infinity in ecstasis: that mode is infinity through mediated actuality, and it is portrayed by the route of the second stream. This stream "flows thro the Aerial Void & all the Churches / Meeting again in Golgonooza beyond Satans Seat" (35:52-3). This is the route that an actuality takes when it perishes, passing through nothingness ("the Aerial Void") and all attempts to deny and mitigate nothingness ("all the Churches"), re-entering the process of actualization in mediated form, which is invulnerable to the reductiveness of Satan. That is, in passing away, an actuality, while in one sense passing into nothingness, in another sense moves beyond that nothingness and re-enters actuality as posthumous presence. The Churches constitute a bridge between nothingness and actuality; they enhance posthumous presence by allowing people to believe in a resurrection of the dead (in whatever vulgarized or perverted form). For posthumous presence occurs to the degree that surviving individuals make present what has passed away by taking account of it—i.e., by maintaining (consciously or unconsciously) that it still *is*, in some form.

This infinity provided by ecstasis through mediation or posthumous presence is analyzed further through the image of the lark:

> Just at the place to where the Lark mounts, is a Crystal Gate
> It is the enterance of the First Heaven named Luther; for
> The Lark is Los's Messenger thro the Twenty-seven Churches
> That the Seven Eyes of God who walk even to Satans Seat
> Thro all the Twenty-seven Heavens may not slumber nor sleep.
> (35:61-5)

The lark manifests the aspect of Los/entelechy which is embodied in the Churches. The lark is the transitive property, or transmitting aspect, of actualization—the principle by which the past is transmitted to the future, and a predecessor united with its successor. It is this aspect of actualization which activates the powers that guarantee posthumous presence—i.e., the Seven Eyes of God. This transitive property occurs through ecstasis, expressed as the lark's mounting movement, which is responsible for actuality's passing into otherness. Here, "at the place to where the Lark mounts, is a Crystal Gate," which signifies the threshold between actuality and the otherness into which it passes. The Crystal Gate reminds us, through its similarity to the rock of crystal from which the fountain flows, that passing into otherness is largely identical with the ecstatic process itself, for the gate opens into the posthumous perpetuation of actuality: it "is the enterance of the First Heaven named Luther."

The passing into otherness which underlies posthumous presence must be repeated indefinitely, with each actuality transmitting and thus preserving the being that is entrusted to it. This process is expressed as the meeting of the larks:

> But the Larks Nest is at the Gate of Los, at the eastern
> Gate of wide Golgonooza & the Lark is Los's Messenger
> When on the highest lift of his light pinions he arrives
> At that bright Gate, another Lark meets him & back to back
> They touch their pinions tip tip: and each descend
> To their respective Earths & there all night consult with Angels
> Of Providence & with the Eyes of God all night in slumbers
> Inspired; & at the dawn of the day send out another Lark
> Into another Heaven to carry news upon his wings
> Thus are the Messengers dispatchd till they reach the Earth again
> In the East Gate of Golgonooza....

(35:66–36:9)

The lark arises from its origin in the process of actualization (Golgonooza) to a "Heaven to carry news": i.e., it transmits the novelty of its actualizing process to another actuality, which constitutes a "heaven," or realm of ultimacy and immortality for this novelty, preserving it in posthumous presence. The meeting of the larks and the touching of their wings expresses the mutual ecstasis of an actuality and its successor: each reaches beyond its own immediacy and into the immediacy of the other—the predecessor into the future, the successor into the past. Each instance of ecstasis arises from and returns to its immediacy of actualization: after the larks touch, they "descend / To their respective Earths." But this apparently dormant period of ecstasis does not signal its inactivity, for "all night [the larks] consult with Angels / Of Providence & with the Eyes of God all night in slumbers inspired." The apparent dormancy of ecstasis is thus actually the period of its interaction with transcendent powers, receiving an influx of new possibilities from them and thus actualizing them, apparently, so "that the Seven Eyes of God . . . / May not slumber nor sleep." Ecstasis thus mediates between the transcendent realm of pure possibilities and the actuality of the future, by receiving abstract possibilities from the transcendental realm and transmitting concrete possibilities (in the form of posthumous presences) to the future. Ecstasis thus has both a receptive and a projective function, and the two combine to effect the continual transmission of finite actuality beyond itself into a new instance of actuality. This continual transmission preserves and develops the original actuality in mediated form, and thus constitutes its immortality or infinity.

The Individual and the Transcendent: Blake's Role

Such, then, is the second mode of infinity which ecstasis effects in finitude, and it is this mode which accompanies the descent of Ololon. For Blake declares that

> . . . the Twenty-eighth bright
> Lark. met the Female Ololon descending into my Garden
> Thus it appears to Mortal eyes & those of the Ulro Heavens
> But not thus to Immortals, the Lark is a mighty Angel.
>
> (36:9-12)

The previous twenty-seven larks were the instances of ecstasis which transmitted posthumous presence to the twenty-seven heavens or institutionalized systems of preservation and sanctification (which are named on the following plate). The present meeting of the lark with Ololon thus signals the creation of a new mode of such preservation, this mode constituted by the recognition of the significance of posthumous presence.

The fact that this meeting occurs as Ololon is descending into Blake's garden indicates that both Blake and the garden are in some way implicated in the meeting. The garden, it seems, might easily provide the occasion for the vision of Being which Blake expresses in *Milton*. For a garden is that aspect of the phenomenal world which manifests most explicitly the nature of the ecstatic actualizing process, which constitutes all entities. The transformations of arising, growing, and perishing are all readily observable here in great variety, as are the various embodiments of ecstasis (i.e., the various plants and birds) which Blake employs in the poem.

The question then becomes: how is Blake's vision of Being as ecstasis

related to the descent of Ololon, and why is Ololon portrayed as descending
into Blake's garden? We can infer the answer from the following description
of Ololon's appearance to Blake:

> . . . Ololon step'd into the Polypus within the Mundane Shell
> They could not step into Vegetable Worlds without becoming
> The enemies of Humanity except in a Female Form
> And as One Female, Ololon and all its mighty Hosts
> Appear'd: a Virgin of Twelve years nor time nor space was
> To the perception of the Virgin Ololon but as the
> Flash of lightning but more quick the Virgin in my Garden
> Before my Cottage stood, for the Satanic Space is delusion.
>
> (36:14-20)

Ololon's entrance into the world of immediate experience ("Vegetable
Worlds")—i.e., the world of grasping desire ("the Polypus") and restrictive
conceptualization ("the Mundane Shell")—occurs "in a Female Form,"
because if it were present in this realm in another (presumably the male)
form, it would be opposed to the ecstatic transcendence of mere immediacy
which constitutes humanity. For lamentation or the quest for infinity to be
present in female form thus means that it occurs in a receptive and productive
form rather than an assertive and acquisitive form: i.e., it occurs as the *object*
of thought rather than as its *subject*. Were this lamentation to occur as subject
(i.e., in male form), it would be the enemy of Humanity, for as the quest for
presence it is opposed to the powers of mediation and deferral which constitute Humanity. However, in occurring as an object of thought (i.e., in
female form), it does not pose such a threat, but rather provides a ground for
development.

But to occur as an object of thought means that it must have a subject to
think it, and this is precisely Blake's role in the descent of Ololon: Blake is the
subject who has the intuition that *is* the descent of Ololon. Ololon's appearance "as the / Flash of lightning but more quick . . . in [Blake's] garden"
expresses the flash of enlightenment in which the very principle of lamentation appeared to Blake—as an object for his reflection rather than as a mood
or desire (i.e., a subjectivity) that possesses him. In this instant Blake intuits
the principle or power underlying all the numberless instances—"all [the]
mighty Hosts"—of lamentation. Blake's vision of Ololon is closely interrelated with his vision of ecstasis, which, as we have seen, is a constitutive
factor of the moment in which Ololon descends. It is Blake's vision of ecstasis
which discovered the infinity within finitude, an infinity which makes it

possible for the quest for fulfillment or infinity to pursue its aims in the finitude of existence—makes it possible, that is, for Ololon to descend. Moreover, ecstasis itself has been found identical, ultimately, with lamentation: both phenomena are movements beyond an insufficient actuality toward completion or fulfillment in otherness or non-immediacy. This identity of the two principles was expressed in the two visions of ecstasis involving the birds and the flowers, where we are told that each is "a Vision of the lamentation of Beulah over Ololon" (31:45,63). Ololon's appearance, then—the manifestation of the quest for ultimate fulfillment or infinity—is made possible by Blake's vision of the principle that causes things to move beyond their own immediate actuality.

Our present account of these events is seriously deficient, however, if we assume from it that the descent of Ololon is merely a figurative way of expressing a philosophical insight that Blake achieved. For Ololon is not an imaginary figure that Blake has created, or an idea that he has conceived, or an abstraction that he has produced through induction; rather, Ololon is a fundamental aspect or dimension of Being. This is not to say that Ololon is totally independent of Blake; on the contrary, Ololon/lamentation requires Blake's unique being in order to become manifest in its truth and to descend into finitude. For as we have observed before, transcendental principles and powers rely on the unique being of individuals to achieve actualization. Indeed, the very process of actualization itself achieves its transcendent goals only through the activity of unique individuals. Blake now explicitly recalls this fact, and reminds us that his writing of this very poem is the result of a directive from the entelechic power itself:

> For when Los joind with me he took me in his firy whirlwind
> My vegetated portion was hurried from Lambeths shades
> He set me down in Felphams Vale & prepard a beautiful
> Cottage for me that in three years I might Write all these Visions
> To display Natures cruel holiness: the deceits of Natural Religion
>
> (36:21-5)

Blake's visions and his articulation and communication of them are thus seen to be an accomplishment of entelechy itself, which relies on Blake's unique individual being in order to attain its goal. Yet despite Los's reliance on Blake, it is clear that Los retains his intrinsic power and autonomy, for it is Los who initiates the actions and Blake who responds. This relationship makes it clear that Blake sees Los as an autonomous principle with intrinsic power, and not a mere figment or conception of Blake's mind. And it is also clear that Blake is a unique, autonomous individual with intrinsic being, and not a mere epiphenomenon or puppet of a transcendental power. Thus while both the individual and the transcendental principle have intrinsic being, each relies upon the other in order to be itself.

That this is also the relationship between Blake and Ololon is evident from Blake's response to her presence:

> Walking in my Cottage Garden, suddenly I beheld
> The Virgin Ololon & address'd her as a Daughter of Beulah
> Virgin of Providence fear not to enter into my Cottage
> What is thy message to thy friend? What am I now to do
> Is it again to plunge into deeper affliction? behold me
> Ready to obey, but pity thou my Shadow of Delight
> Enter my Cottage, comfort her, for she is sick with fatigue.
>
> (36:26-32)

The fact that Ololon appears as a virgin indicates that she is unconsummated and unproductive. Blake sees his role as being a messenger between Ololon and Milton, so that the consummation can take place, this consummation constituting the reconciliation and union of the quest for infinity (Ololon) with the acceptance of finitude (Milton as the justifier of the ways of God to men). But although this consummation is thus dependent upon Blake's action, it is not for this reason the product of his activity. Blake serves as the facilitating agent rather than the sole cause of this union; prior causes include the unique being of Ololon the principle and of Milton the individual. It is from this unique being that Blake takes his directive, asking Ololon, "What am I now to do?" It is thus the principle of lamentation itself which directs Blake's actions and it is the authentic function of his unique individual being to attend and respond to the expressions or manifestations of this principle.

Blake's posture is not one of total disinterest and self-abnegation, however. He assures Ololon that he is "ready to obey" her directives, "but," he requests, "pity thou my Shadow of Delight / Enter my Cottage, comfort her, for she is sick with fatigue." This Shadow of Delight, which is often taken to be Blake's wife, is also that aspect of Blake which requires "delight" or immediate pleasure or gratification of some sort—that aspect which is unable to labor toward a goal indefinitely without the respite of reaping benefit from labor. This aspect includes Blake's physical being (the "Shadow" or insubstantial presence of his greater being—a projection which is devoted to and yields "Delight" or pleasure) and perhaps also his affective or emotional side. It is that aspect which is reluctant "to plunge into deeper affliction"—that part which laments the deficiency of actuality and desires completion. Blake is thus appealing to lamentation to satisfy his own lamenting aspect, hoping that by ministering to the principle of lamentation (Ololon) and helping it to actualize its true being, he will ameliorate the situation of his own lamenting aspect. And as we shall see, Blake will achieve this result, for by facilitating the union of the desire for infinity with the acceptance of finitude, he will allow lamentation to find comfort with finitude.

PART FIVE

Beyond Presence:
Ololon, Milton, and the
Reconciliation of Desire with Finitude

CHAPTER XIII

Overcoming Satan, the Reductive
Destruction of Individuals

The directive which Ololon/lamentation gives to Blake is clear: "Knowest thou of Milton who descended / Driven from Eternity," she says. "Him I seek!" (37:1-2). Lamentation—the desire for infinity—is now drawn toward Milton, whose unactualized essence it dismissed from Eternity in apparently denying infinite being to unactualized particulars. But having realized, through its confrontation with death, that being and presence are not coterminous, Ololon now declares to Blake: "Terrified at my Act / In great Eternity which thou knowest! I come him to seek" (37:2-3). We were told earlier that Ololon dismissed from Eternity Milton's (unactualized) essence and that the Seven Eyes of God which preserve posthumous presence also descended as a result. Ololon did not recognize that embracing the ultimate finitude of Eternal Death could lead to infinity. Now, however, lamentation is drawn toward Milton, feeling that he may indeed satisfy its quest.

In more conventional terms we might say that Ololon's search for Milton expresses Blake's own gradual recognition that his own lamentation—i.e., his own experience of deficiency and his corresponding desire to overcome that deficiency or finitude and achieve infinity—can be satisfied by embracing that very finitude. Once again, however, it is important to remind ourselves that this way of speaking, while phenomenally accurate, is ontologically misleading, for lamentation and the embrace of finitude are not merely actions or attributes of Blake but also fundamental existential principles and powers that call to Blake and are responded to by him. Blake's own involvement in the rapprochement of Ololon and Milton, or desire and finitude, is thus one of observing and responding to their overtures.

Blake's Vision of Milton

The Epiphany of Milton

This rapprochement of Ololon and Milton effects a purification (by means of clarification) of each power, a process in which the Satanic or reductively

destructive element of each is overcome. Milton, or the embrace of death, is
the first to be clarified and purified. The clarification occurs through Blake's
vision of Milton's various elements, a vision which is occasioned by lamentation's request to meet the justifier of finitude:

> So Ololon utterd in words distinct the anxious thought
> Mild was the voice, but more distinct than any earthly
> That Miltons Shadow heard & condensing all his Fibres
> Into a strength impregnable of majesty & beauty infinite
> I saw he was the Covering Cherub & within him Satan
> And Raha[b], in an outside which is fallacious! within
> Beyond the outline of Identity, in the Selfhood deadly
> And he appeard the Wicker Man of Scandinavia in whom
> Jerusalems children consume in flames among the Stars
> Descending down into my Garden, a Human Wonder of God
> Reaching from heaven to earth a Cloud & Human Form
> I beheld Milton with astonishment & in him beheld
> The Monstrous Churches of Beulah, the Gods of Ulro dark
> Twelve monstrous dishumanized terrors Synagogues of Satan.
> A Double Twelve & Thrice Nine: such their divisions.
>
> (37:4–18)

Lamentation thus evokes "Miltons Shadow," the posthumous presence of
Milton's unique being. Blake is now able to observe that despite its "majesty
& beauty infinite," Milton's being contains destructive and perverting
powers: this being serves as "the Covering Cherub," the power guarding the
feudalistic Yahweh and thus containing the destructive principles of Satan
(homogenization) and Rahab (false fulfillment). Blake realizes that despite
the majesty of Milton's attempt to justify and accept human finitude, Milton's
attempt—and his entire being—are flawed by his feudalistic metaphysics,
which deprives individuals of intrinsic being, all of which is attributed to a
supreme being, or God. Thus Milton's attempt to justify human suffering
and finitude by attributing all being to God but holding individuals account-
able for a universal "sin" is Satanic, reducing individuals to empty,
homogeneous entities. And since it offers the false fulfillment of perpetual
immediacy in a hereafter, Milton's attempt also contains Rahab, the principle
of false fulfillment through immediacy. In this respect Milton is like "the
Wicker Man of Scandanavia," sacrificing independent individuals (the
children of Jerusalem) to Yahweh, just as the Wicker Man imprisoned children
within itself for sacrifice to deities of another feudalistic, *quid pro quo*
metaphysics. Thus while Blake recognizes that Milton is "a Human Wonder

of God," he also realizes that part of Milton's being is an obfuscation ("a Cloud") of this "Human Form." He proceeds to delineate further the destructive aspects by identifying them with various other historical manifestations of the same principle.

Milton as Satan: The Gods of Ulro

First Blake lists the twelve "Gods of Ulro" (37:16), which "are the Twelve Spectre Sons of the Druid Albion" (37:34). As "Spectre Sons of the Druid Albion" these gods constitute false or perverted principles generated by a materialist vision of the unity of individuals (the Druid Albion), a vision which is itself based on a Satanic metaphysics of homogeneity. These false principles are gods which demand that the being possessed by individuals be sacrificed to the gods as rightfully theirs: Baal, Ashtaroth, Chemosh, Molech, Belial, and "Saturn Jove & Rhea" (37:20-33). Each of these gods is a central figure in a feudalistic metaphysics in which all being belongs to the gods, and individuals have no intrinsic being and thus no ultimately unique identity. Many of the deities are vegetation or fertility gods, which in a strict *quid pro quo* system demand sacrifice (often of humans) before they will yield being to humans in the form of productive crops. Many are also storm gods or gods of war, which preside over a *quid pro quo* cosmos whose ultimate reality consists of strife and mutual destruction. Milton's religion, as manifested in *Paradise Lost* (his attempt to justify the ways of God to men), is thus seen by Blake to be based upon the same *quid pro quo* feudalistic metaphysics which gives rise to these pagan deities and therefore to be ontologically as destructive as they were. Like Milton's religion, the beliefs and ceremonies surrounding these pagan deities were attempts to overcome finitude, and both are ultimately more destructive than redemptive, being at heart Satanically destructive of the ontological status of individual being.

Milton as Rahab: The Churches of Beulah

If the pagan religions embody the overt Satanic destructiveness of Milton's feudalistic *quid pro quo* metaphysics, various patriarchs of the Judaeo-Christian tradition exemplify the more subtle and insidious destructiveness and delusion perpetrated by this metaphysics. Blake divides "the Twenty-seven Heavens & their Churches" (37:35) into three groups. The first is composed of "Giants mighty Hermaphroditic" (37:37) and includes the antediluvian patriarchs from Adam to Lamech, listed in Genesis 5. The giant and hermaphroditic form of these figures expresses their supposed self-sufficiency (many of them lived over eight hundred years). They embody an existence of brutal self-aggrandizement in a world in which humans must wrest their being from a cruel deity. This mode of existence culminates in Lamech, the father of Noah, whose lust for vengeance (Genesis 4:23-4) and vision of a cruel God (Genesis 5:29) epitomize the *quid pro quo* vision of being.

The second group of "Heavens and their Churches" is comprised of the patriarchs from Noah to Terah, listed in Genesis 11. "These are the Female-Males," Blake says, "a Male within a Female hid as in an Ark & Curtains" (37:39-40). Here the self-assertive urge (the Male) is disguised by a submissive exterior (the female) in which humans yield their being up to a higher being in exchange for protection and prosperity. This new attitude of humans toward their being was inaugurated by Noah, who was saved from destruction because he was submissive to God (Genesis 6:7-9). Because of Noah's submissiveness God made a covenant with him, first by warning him of the flood and instructing him to build an ark (Genesis 6:18, 7:1), and then—in response to Noah's sacrifice—by promising never again to destroy all creatures (Genesis 8:20, 9:17). In this *quid pro quo* system God gives Noah prosperity because Noah has given everything to God, and he declares to Noah: "For your lifeblood I will surely require a reckoning; of every beast I will require it of man; of every man's brother I will require the life of Man. Whoever sheds the blood of man, by man shall his blood be shed" (Genesis 9:5-6). Here the being of individuals is completely interchangeable and homogeneous, because it is not intrinsic to the individuals but merely lent to them by the omnipotent lord of this feudalistic system. Noah's submissive actions of sacrifice are thus based on the same ontological assumptions as the violent self-assertion of Lamech *et al.*, with the only difference being that Noah utilizes the more subtle techniques of slave morality, pursuing his goals under the guise of doing the will of a more powerful being. This submissiveness was embodied in later generations in the curtained ark ("an Ark & Curtains") which contained the books of the Law, the decrees of God to man.[1]

The third group of Heavens and Churches is composed of "Abraham, Moses, Solomon, Paul, Constantine, Charlemaine, [and] Luther" (37:41-2). "These seven," Blake says, "are the Male-Females, the Dragon Forms / Religion hid in War, a Dragon red & hidden Harlot" (37:42-3). These figures constitute imperialistic religion, religion as masculine and militant, openly self-aggrandizing like a devouring Dragon. But despite this overt self-assertion, there lies at the heart of this militance the same ontological submissiveness (the female aspect) that Noah embodied. And this ontological submissiveness implicit in militant religion, moreover, is like that of a harlot, pretending to give itself to another only in order to acquire personal gain. This form of religion incorporates within itself the previous submissiveness, just as Noah's submissiveness incorporated Lamech's aggressiveness. Imperialistic religion thus represents the culmination of the dialectic of aggressive and submissive self-aggrandizement: overt self-aggrandizement is shown to be at heart ontologically submissive, and this submissiveness is shown to be implicitly and intrinsically an attempt at self-aggrandizement. Here, as in the previous two forms of religion, individuals are in competition for a limited amount of homogeneous being which is at the disposal of one central source. Thus, whether this feudalistic metaphysics results in overt aggression, in covert aggression masked by righteousness and submissiveness, or in aggression hidden within a submission which is itself masked by assertiveness—no matter what the outward form, the feudalistic metaphysics of presence is destructive of individual being.

Milton's Satanic Vision of Being

In Blake's vision, all these forms of ontological destructiveness are present in Milton's religion:

> All these are seen in Miltons Shadow who is the Covering Cherub
> The Spectre of Albion in which the Spectre of Luvah inhabits
> In the Newtonian Voids between the Substances of Creation.
>
> (37:44-6)

These various forms of destructiveness are grounded in spurious metaphysical assumptions, two of which are the false vision of communal being ("the Spectre of Albion") and the false form of relatedness or connexity ("the Spectre of Luvah"), which lies at the heart of the false form of communal being. The Spectre of Albion is the (false) form of community in which individuals lack intrinsic being and are unified through external rather than intrinsic relatedness. This view of community is found "in the Newtonian Voids between the Substances of Creation": i.e., it is found where individual entities are seen as self-enclosed, predetermined substances, and where between individuals is found nothing at all. In this vision, moreover, while nothingness reigns outside individual entities, it also reigns within them; entities are composed of bounded chaos, and these boundaries, which constitute the outlines of their identities, simply divide the homogeneous chaos of all being into external and internal:

> For the Chaotic Voids outside of the Stars are measured by
> The Stars, which are the boundaries of Kingdoms, Provinces
> And Empires of Chaos invisible to the Vegetable Man.
>
> (37:47-9)

Even the stars themselves, which seem to be mighty entities with tremendous positive being, are from the perspective of Milton's feudalistic metaphysics mere conglomerates of chaos. For if there is no such thing as intrinsic being or intrinsic relatedness, there can be no legitimate order of any kind either among entities or within an individual entity: nothing can be differentiated from anything else, and as a result all is chaos, with entities being merely arbitrary boundaries within the chaos of homogeneous being.

In fact, if there is no such thing as unique intrinsic being, all complex or conglomerate identities are mere delusions projected upon homogeneous, undifferentiated chaos. All unity and identity must thus be spurious and delusory, according to the fundamental tenets of this system. The stars, which are thus themselves "Empires of Chaos" (the chaos being "invisible to the Vegetable Man," who projects a gestalt upon it), are taken as elements of still larger unities such as the constellations of Orion and Ophiucus. But these constellations, whose unified identity is a delusion (the result of blindness to all the other stars in the region), are no more illusory than other complex identities, such as the kingdoms of Og and Sihon, which were devoured by the Hebrew conquest. If the Israelites could legitimately possess these kingdoms, then these kingdoms and their rulers and peoples must have had no intrinsic rights or being. But without such intrinsic being, the kingdoms have no identity or being whatsoever: they are ultimately totally indistinguishable from everything else, which is also chaos. Thus the kingdoms of Og and Sihon, whose lands and rulers the Israelites thought to be unique (Og was thought to be descended from giants; the land of Sihon was judged rich and fertile), are, according to the tenets of Satanic metaphysics, Blake reveals, merely portions of the cosmic chaos: "The Kingdom of Og. is in Orion: Sihon is in Ophiucus / Og has Twenty-seven Districts; Sihons Districts Twenty-one" (37:50-51). One cannot have it both ways: either individual being is intrinsic and unique and thus not expropriatable by others, or it is extrinsic and homogeneous and thus nothing at all.

The feudalistic metaphysics of homogeneous being thus entails a universe in which all unities, from the individual to the most complex conglomerate, are illusory projections onto an undifferentiated chaos. The entire cosmological or metaphysical system itself is merely an illusory order constructed from the supposed substances ("Mountains") and the voids ("Valleys") between them (a distinction which, we have seen, is itself spurious):

> From Star to Star, Mountains & Valleys, terrible dimension
> Stretchd out, compose the Mundane Shell, a mighty Incrustation
> Of Forty-eight deformed Human wonders of the Almighty
> With Caverns whose remotest bottoms meet again beyond
> The Mundane Shell in Golgonooza....
>
> (37:52-6)

The "Forty-eight deformed Human Wonders of the Almighty" are composed of Og's twenty-seven districts and Sihon's twenty-one. A few lines later, at the beginning of the next plate, we are told that

> Forty-eight Starry Regions are Cities of the Levites
> The Heads of the Great Polypus, Four-fold twelve enormity
> In mighty & mysterious commingling enemy with enemy
> Woven by Urizen into Sexes from his mantle of years[.]
>
> (38:1-4)

These "Forty-eight Starry Regions" are called "deformed Human Wonders of the Almighty" because their true unique intrinsic being (their "Human" aspect) has been deformed by the metaphysics of homogeneity. The homogeneity of these regions is reinforced by the equation of these forty-eight regions with the forty-eight cities of the Levites, which were taken from other tribes and given to the Levites as if they were mere homogeneous, interchangeable commodities (see Numbers 35 and Joshua 21). In addition, as the home of the Levites, these cities make a further contribution to the feudalistic metaphysics of homogeneity, for the Levites were declared by the feudalistic Yahweh to belong to him (Numbers 3:11-13) and were servants of the tabernacle in which Yahweh was worshipped (Numbers 4). As such, the cities of the Levites constitute "the Heads of the Great Polypus"—the organizing centers of the amorphous, self-devouring monster that the world becomes in a metaphysics of homogeneity. In such a system all individuals are enemies which, nonetheless, are somehow mysteriously the same, since in the very act of devouring each other they produce a "commingling [of] enemy with enemy."

Blake reminds us that this system of mutual destruction is ultimately the product of Urizen, the principle of individuation and self-consolidation: the system is "woven by Urizen into Sexes from his mantle of years." The meaning of this passage is obscure: how can somthing be woven *from* a mantle? The passage would make sense if the prepositions "into" and "from" were transposed, giving the statement: "...woven by Urizen *from* Sexes *into* his mantle of years." In this case the two Sexes would constitute the warp and the woof which are woven together to form Urizen's mantle. Or, more abstractly, aggressiveness (the male) and submissiveness (the female) would be combined by Urizen in his forming mutual destruction, the external manifestation of temporal existence ("his mantle of years"). This figurative reading of the hypothetically emended passage, however, makes it possible to make sense of the passage as it stands in Blake's text. For temporal existence (the "mantle of years") is the substance that is woven into aggression and submission (the "Sexes"), each of which is constituted only in the process of being united (in conflict) with its opposite—i.e., in the "commingling [of] enemy with enemy."

The Manifest Inadequacy of this System

This self-devouring world of existence produced (both epistemologically and literally) by the feudalistic metaphysics of homogeneity has gaps or unexplained elements, however, which if pursued, lead to a vision of the actualizing activity of Los, and through this activity to Eternity or infinity:

> ...the Mundane Shell, a mighty Incrustation
> Of Forty-eight deformed Human Wonders of the Almighty
> [Has] Caverns whose remotest bottoms meet again beyond
> The Mundane Shell in Golgonooza, but the Fires of Los, rage
> In the remotest bottoms of the Caves, that none can pass
> Into Eternity that way, but all descend to Los
> To Bowlahoola & Allamanda & to Entuthon Benython.
>
> (37:53-9)

The Mundane Shell, although composed of mighty collectivities of a multiplicity of beings, nonetheless does not give a total and complete account of things—as Ololon had realized earlier. For beyond all entities, conglomerates of entities, and generalities there lies the actualizing process which creates and destroys entities. In metaphysics—the Mundane Shell—this process manifests itself as caverns, or empty spaces, i.e., places where a thing is not, either because it has ceased to exist or because it has not yet arisen. Although such absence, non-presence, or nothingness occurs in metaphysics in a plurality of forms, all forms of non-presence are ultimately grounded in and lead to the actualizing process, named Golgonooza, in which beings arise and perish. It is through this productive destruction, as we have seen, that beings can move beyond the finite, atomistic existence which they are accorded in the Mundane Shell (metaphysics) and achieve the infinity of mediated actuality. Blake emphasizes, however, "that none can pass / Into Eternity that way [i.e., via non-actuality (the Caves)], but [i.e., unless they] all descend to Los / To Bowlahoola & Allamanda & to Entuthon Benython." To achieve the infinity of mediated presence, that is, one must perish and one's unique individual being must then be incorporated once again—through the distinguishing and synthesizing functions of Bowlahoola and Allamanda—into the external, sublunar world of existence (Entuthon Benython). Such is the vision to which one is led if one enters into the Caverns of the Mundane Shell.

Overcoming Satan: Milton's Descent

The Separation of Humanity from Spectre

This vision of the inauthentic aspect of Milton resulting from the deficiencies of his metaphysics constitutes Milton's consolidation of his powers and his descent to Blake, as Blake now indicates:

> And Milton collecting all his fibres into impregnable strength
> Descended down a Paved work of all kinds of precious stones
> Out from the eastern sky; descending down into my Cottage
> Garden: clothed in black, severe & silent he descended.
>
> (38:5-8)

And when Milton thus descends to Blake, his Spectre Satan—i.e., his inauthentic aspect, constituted by his *quid pro quo* metaphysics—manifests itself as separate and opposed to Milton:

> The Spectre of Satan stood upon the roaring sea & beheld
> Milton within his sleeping Humanity! trembling & shuddring
> He stood upon the waves a Twenty-seven-fold mighty Demon
> Gorgeous & beautiful: loud roll his thunders against Milton
> Loud Satan thunderd, loud & dark upon mild Felpham shore
> Not daring to touch one fibre he howld round upon the Sea.
>
> (38:9-14)

Milton's true being, his "Humanity," is still dormant ("sleeping"); it is not yet actualized. Yet Milton's posthumous presence within Blake is so formidable that Satan does not dare to assault Milton's being.

Blake's Vision of Satan

Blake's vision of Milton's Satanic aspect includes insight into the authentic, intrinsic being of Satan. "I also stood in Satans bosom," Blake says, "&

beheld its desolations! / A ruind Man: a ruind building of God not made
with hands" (38:15-16). The reductive destruction which is Satan's being is
not the product of human action: Satan is "not made with hands." Rather,
Satan is a structure of being which was originally in the service of Being itself
("God"), but is now "ruind." The appearance of Satan's reductive destructiveness in all its forms and disguises is thus not merely a product of human
will, having no basis in the ultimate nature of things. Rather, Satan is a power
with its own intrinsic being (a "Man") which has been "ruind" or perverted,
having assumed an inauthentic actualization. The necessary and redemptive
reduction of being to homogeneity which is a prerequisite for construction
has, through becoming an end in itself (as we saw in the Bard's Song),
produced mere destruction and reduction with no renovating qualities.

Blake envisions this perverted, destructive being of Satan's as a landscape,

> Its plains of burning sand, its mountains of marble terrible:
> Its pits & declivities flowing with molten ore & fountains
> Of pitch & nitre: its ruind palaces & cities & mighty works;
> Its furnaces of affliction in which his Angels & Emanations
> Labour with blackend visages among its stupendous ruins
> Arches & pyramids & porches colonades & domes.
>
> (38:17-22)

Satan's actual being consists of all instances of desolation, destructive energy,
ruination, affliction, and oppression that are found in existence — i.e., Satan's
actuality is constituted by all instances in which the unique being of entities is
thwarted, stymied, and perverted in its attempt to actualize itself. Satan's
appearance here as a passive landscape reiterates the fact that this evil destructiveness of individual being is not simply an action or the product of an action
but is rather a region or aspect of actuality itself.

It is this aspect of actuality, Blake realizes, which gives rise to false visions
of individual being and of fulfillment. It is these "furnaces of affliction,"
Blake declares,

> In which dwells Mystery Babylon, here is her secret place
> From hence she comes forth on the Churches in delight
> Here is her Cup filld with its poisons, in these horrid vales
> And here her scarlet Veil woven in pestilence & war:
> Here is Jerusalem bound in chains, in the Dens of Babylon.
>
> (38:23-7)

False fulfillment, in the form of redemption through *quid pro quo* self-
aggrandizement (expressed here as "Mystery Babylon" with "her Cup filld

with its poisons"—i.e., the Eucharist), is grounded in the Satanic aspect of reality, whose universal suppression and destruction of entities seems to demonstrate that fulfillment is first and foremost a matter of self-preservation through self-assertion. It is this equation of fulfillment with self-perpetuation through dominion over others that makes the Christian image of redemption possible, and which psychologically precludes the scrutiny to which the mysterious nature of such redemption would normally be subjected. It is thus also this destructive, Satanic aspect of reality which renders inactive the true image of fulfillment—Jerusalem, the community of all individuals—which falls victim to the false image, Babylon.

Overcoming Satan through Accepting Finitude

Blake's realization that it is perishing, or ultimate finitude, which lies at the heart of Satan's power evokes a challenge of the ultimacy of perishing itself. This challenge is issued by the unique being of Milton, which Blake has incorporated and whose essence it is to find a way of accepting finitude:

> In the Eastern porch of Satans Universe Milton stood & said
> Satan! my Spectre! I know my power thee to annihilate
> And be a greater in thy place, & be thy Tabernacle
> A covering for thee to do thy will, till one greater comes
> And smites me as I smote thee & becomes my covering.
> Such are the Laws of thy false Heavns! but Laws of Eternity
> Are not such: know thou: I come to Self Annihilation
> Such are the Laws of Eternity that each shall mutually
> Annihilate himself for others good, as I for thee.
>
> (38:28-36)

At first glance Milton seems simply to be advocating a radical altruism in opposition to Satanic egoism—and such, indeed, is part of the meaning of this passage. The real nature and significance of Milton's action, however, is more subtle and profound. For in opposing Satan's ethic and offering to sacrifice himself to Satan, Milton is not simply opposing (in an altruistic manner) another person or identity: he is opposing part of himself, the egoistic self that destroys otherness by reducing it ontologically to a homogeneous substance to be devoured by the self. Paradoxically, the way in which Milton opposes this aspect of himself—and this constitutes the subtlety and profundity of his action—is by refusing to master it, thus refusing in effect to oppose it at all. Milton's refusal to suppress and master his own self-aggrandizing, egoistic aspect results from his realization that the attempt to overcome one's egoism by an act of will is itself based on a more fundamental egoism: for the attempt to overcome one's egoism is motivated by the same desire for self-aggrandizement that is behind egoism itself. The only difference is that for the suppressor of egoism, self-aggrandizement takes the form of self-righteousnes—i.e., of storing up riches in heaven—while simple egoism understands self-aggrandizement in more immediately tangible terms.

In deliberately annihilating his own egoism, then, Milton would actually be constituting a more subtle form of egoism, which would then itself become a target for an even more subtle and insidious egoism. The primary role of Milton's unique being, however, is to expose and overcome this insidious self-aggrandizement in all its forms. Thus he declares:

> I come to discover before Heavn & Hell the Self righteousness
> In all its Hypocritic turpitude, opening to every eye
> These wonders of Satans holiness shewing to the Earth
> The Idol Virtues of the Natural Heart, & Satans Seat
> Explore in all its Selfish Natural Virtue & put off
> In Self annihilation all that is not of God alone:
> To put off Self & all I have ever & ever Amen.

(38:43-9)

The self-annihilation that Milton speaks of here and in the beginning of his speech (quoted above) thus means getting rid of all elements of self, even the self that wants to get rid of self. And this self-annihilation can be achieved, paradoxically, only if one's own selfhood is not opposed. Such radical self-annihilation is achieved only when one locates one's true identity beyond the self-presence of all desiring, and then, residing in this true identity, dispassionately observes one's passions as they take their course (in a manner similar to that extolled by Zen Buddhism). This is what Milton means by putting off "all that is not of God alone."

The crucial point in this process of overcoming the Spectre or ego is the locating of one's true being beyond all self-aggrandizing urges. Such an identification is possible, as we saw earlier, only if one rejects the Satanic metaphysics of presence and sees Being as a matter of process and mediation. For if one equates Being with presence, then one is forced to be egoistic and self-aggrandizing if one wants to continue to be at all. This is the Satanic view. Milton, however, knows that one's being is not limited to one's immediately present actuality (i.e., one's life)—indeed, Blake has made Milton's very presence in this poem evidence of this fact. Thus Milton is able to give up his immediate actuality—i.e., to die—without fear, for he knows that death does not destroy his being, although it does destroy his immediate presence or actual existence. As he tells Satan,

> Thy purpose & the purpose of thy Priests & of thy Churches
> Is to impress on men the fear of death; to teach
> Trembling & fear, terror, constriction; abject selfishness
> Mine is to teach Men to despise death & to go on
> In fearless majesty annihilating Self, laughing to scorn
> Thy Laws & terrors, shaking down thy Synagogues as webs.
> (38:37-42)

This vision of death is one more reason why Milton is able to allow his own Spectre or ego to continue unsubdued. For if death does not destroy one's own being, neither does it annihilate the being of those one destroys. Therefore, just as Milton willingly annihilates himself for others, so will he allow others to be annihilated (by his Spectre) for himself. To refuse to allow others to be destroyed while one is oneself seeking Eternal Death would be a paternalistic, egoistic act of self-righteousness in which one sets oneself up as holy. One overcomes Satan, or self-aggrandizing destructiveness, not by destroying it—which would be to employ the very self-aggrandizing Satanic destructiveness one is trying to escape—but rather by realizing that it neither constitutes nor destroys true identity.

The Epiphany of Satan

Milton's assertion of the nature of authentic individual identity also constitutes a clarification of the nature of the more habitual identity—the Spectre of Satan. Blake now pursues this analysis of the destructive aspect of individual being by having Satan himself appear and declare his creed:

> Satan heard! Coming in a cloud, with trumpets & flaming fire,
> Saying I am God the judge of all, the living & the dead
> Fall therefore down & worship me. submit thy supreme
> Dictate, to my eternal Will & to my dictate bow
> I hold the Balances of Right & Just & mine the Sword
> Seven Angels bear my Name & in those Seven I appear
> But I alone am God & I alone in Heavn & Earth
> Of all that live dare utter this, others tremble & bow.
> Till All things become One Great Satan, in Holiness
> Oppos'd to Mercy, and the Divine Delusion Jesus be no more.
> (38:50-39:2)

In this outburst Satan manifests the various ways in which opposition to otherness, deriving from a metaphysics of presence, appears in existence. This opposition to otherness is actually a fundamental oblivion to the fact that others have their own unique, intrinsic being. Ignoring the uniqueness and intrinsicness of individual being, Satan asserts that he is "God the judge of all" and that he "hold[s] the Balances of Right & Just." Here Satan assumes that all things are ultimately constituted by a homogeneous substance, for only on the basis of such an assumption can one thing presume to establish laws for another.

It would seem that what we have said so far about Satan might be said about Milton as well. For Milton, too, assumes a fundamental homogeneity among individuals, that homogeneity by virtue of which his posthumous presence is preserved. Indeed, we have seen that the entire actualizing process of Los/ entelechy presupposes such a homogeneity. The difference between Satan and Milton, then, is not in the assumption of homogeneity per se, but rather in the type of homogeneity or sameness that is assumed. In a word, Satan's homogeneity is immediate, Milton's is mediated. Satan, that is, assumes a homogeneity of substance, which is actualized only as the total immediate co-incidence of two or more individuals—i.e., as the total obliteration of all difference, such as when a wax grape and a wax apple are melted into one lump. The authentic homogeneity of individuals, however (i.e., that man-ifested by Milton and Los), is not an immediate, observable phenomenon that occurs as obliteration of differences. Rather, authentic homogeneity is the ground of sameness by virtue of which differences are able to come to stand and maintain themselves *vis-a-vis* each other. The authentic ho-mogeneity of all things is that by virtue of which it is possible for a stamp to leave its mark upon wax, or for the human imagination to leave its mark upon the stamp (by forming it), or for Milton to leave his mark upon Blake. This is the homogeneity which a cause has with its effect, or which the past has with the present, or the present with the future. It is a homogeneity of mediation rather than immediacy or presence.

The two opposing views of homogeneity are thus grounded in two oppos-ing ontologies, two fundamentally different assumptions about the meaning of being. Satanic homogeneity is based on an ontology which equates being with presence, and which easily leads to a positivism for which only the immediately actual truly has being. Miltonic sameness, in contrast, is grounded in a vision in which Being is a productive/destructive mediating process, with presence and non-presence, the immediate and the mediated, and sameness and difference being interconstitutional.

Satan, the principle of reductive homogenization, thus occurs where Being is seen as a vague, indefinite, amorphous substance which is nonetheless manifest in immediate presence. Blake thus describes Satan as "coming in a cloud [Being as an amorphous substance], with trumpets & flaming fire" (Being as immediacy, power in action). And Blake also has Satan indirectly claim that he is the power of Presence itself, by declaring that the "Seven Angels [of the Presence] bear [his] Name." Milton, on the other hand, as the principle of self-annihilation or the acceptance of finitude, occurs where Being manifests itself in definite, particular actualities which are constantly transforming themselves by embracing otherness.

Blake/Milton's Vision of Being and its Renovating Results

Blake expresses this dialectical context of Milton's vision in the passage immediately following Satan's speech:

> Suddenly around Milton on my Path, the Starry Seven
> Burnd terrible! my Path became a solid fire, as bright
> As the clear Sun & Milton silent came down on my Path.
> And there went forth from the Starry limbs of the Seven: Forms
> Human; with Trumpets innumerable, sounding inarticulate
> As the Seven spake; and they stood in a mighty Column of Fire
> Surrounding Felphams Vale, reaching to the Mundane Shell.
>
> (39:3-9)

It is significant that Blake uses similar imagery to describe the epiphanies of Milton and Satan: fire, trumpets, and the Seven Angels. This similarity indicates that the principles of Milton and Satan—i.e., self-annihilation versus self-aggrandizement, or acceptance of otherness versus denial of otherness—occur in the same region, vying for the same ontological territory, so to speak. It is the differences in the two descriptions, however— particularly in the appearance of the fire, the trumpets, and the Seven Angels—which are of greatest significance. First, while in the description of Satan these three elements appear (ironically) without interconnection, in the epiphany of Milton they are interconstitutional: the Starry Seven form a column of fire, and as they speak, the trumpets sound. In addition, each element in Milton's epiphany, while closely interrelated with the others, nonetheless retains a distinct form of its own: the fire forms a column, and is "a solid fire, as bright / As the clear Sun;" the trumpets sound "articulate," and the Seven Angels have distinct limbs and are autonomous, whereas for

Satan they were merely avatars of his being. Moreover, in Milton's case the Starry Seven surround Milton, turn Blake's path into "a solid fire," and give forth "Forms Human," functioning in each instance as a mediating power. In surrounding Milton they manifest the fact that they are, as we have seen earlier, the powers that make posthumous presence possible. As such powers, they are also the powers which constitute one's path—i.e., one's route to the future, which consists of the open-ended possibilities bequeathed by the unique being of one's predecessors (a bequest expressed in this case as the meeting of Blake and Milton). In addition, as the powers (underlying the human visions of immortality) that make present that which is no longer immediate, the Seven Angels of the Presence produce forms of existence which are uniquely Human, for Humanity consists, as we have seen, in the actual and explicit orientation to the non-immediate or non-actual. And finally, as a huge "Column of Fire [that] / Surround[s] Felphams Vale [and] reach[es] to the Mundane Shell," these powers of making present encompass all of immediate actuality ("Felphams Vale") and constitute the connection between the immediate and the transcendent realms and thus the support of (i.e., the condition for the possibility of) the abstract and general principles which make up this metaphysical system which is the Mundane Shell. For without the mediated presence of that which is not immediately present, the metaphysical generalities of the Mundane Shell could never have been constructed.

The nature of this mediating power of the Starry Seven is epitomized by the image of "solid fire," an oxymoron which suggests a substance which is insubstantial, or a process which is solid and static. The image thus expresses the fact that the making-present of the Starry Seven is the very sub-stance of actuality itself: it is the destructive/productive process that stands beneath and constitutes the immediacy of actuality.

As this self-differing substance or substantial process the Starry Seven coincide with Los, the very principle of actualization. This identity is made explicit in the following passage, as the Seven speak, saying,

> Awake Albion awake! reclaim thy Reasoning Spectre. Subdue
> Him to the Divine Mercy, Cast him down into the Lake
> Of Los, that ever burneth with fire, ever & ever Amen!
> Let the Four Zoa's awake from Slumbers of Six Thousand Years
> Then loud the Furnaces of Los were heard! & seen as Seven
>   Heavens
> Stretching from south to north over the mountains of Albion.
>   (39:10-15)

The Seven powers (systems of belief) that make present that which has perished are the furnaces of Los which, in their function of transforming and purifying, transform actuality into mediated actuality and thus appear "as Seven Heavens" or regions of immortality, or posthumous presence. The call for Albion to awake and reclaim his inauthentic, reasoning aspect—i.e., that positivist notion of unity which attends only to the immediate and views individuals as homogeneous entities related to each other externally and quantitatively—issues from these mediating powers themselves: their very occurrence constitutes a refutation of the metaphysics of presence and a call to individuals—and to the collective (Albion), as well—to abandon such a vision. The mere act, that is, of taking account of the dead constitutes a form of being for the dead, the non-present. As a call to Albion, these powers appear to the true form of community (which is the mutual interrelatedness of unique, sovereign individuals) to arise from its dormancy as mere potential and achieve actualization. As an appeal to this mediated unity of all individuals, the powers of making-present also constitute an appeal to the dormant non-actual dimensions of Being—the Four Zoas, whose fall to the center (19:21) constituted the demotion of non-actual dimensions of Being to mere aspects of presence—for the actualization of mediated unity among individuals also inherently activates these non-actual dimensions of Being.

Milton's espousal of self-annihilation thus occurs within the context of an appeal from the powers of making-present to the fundamental dimensions of Being itself. This incipient fundamental alteration in the dispensation of Being occurs as a response to the Starry Seven, who themselves become explicitly manifest only in Milton's assertion of the being of the non-actual (the assertion embodied in his embrace of Eternal Death). And since Milton's response, we recall, is a response to Blake the Bard's appeal, and becomes fully actualized only in subsequently being responded to by Blake, it thus becomes evident that Blake's grappling (in the Bard's Song) with the question of human finitude has precipitated a chain of events which may lead ultimately to an alteration in the dispensation of Being itself. As the notion of Being is thought through and reformulated, Being itself assumes a new form.

The Subsequent Status of Satan

The first actual manifestation of this alteration is found in the emergence of the Satanic principle into its true form as the power which devours otherness:

> Satan heard; trembling round his Body, he incircled it
> He trembled with exceeding great trembling & astonishment

Howling in his spectre round his Body hungring to devour
But fearing for the pain for if he touches a Vital,
His torment is unendurable: therefore he cannot devour:
But howls round it as a lion round his prey continually.

(39:16-21)

At the same time, however, that Satan becomes manifest as the urge to devour which he truly is (in his Spectrous form), he is prevented from actually devouring anything by the pain which such action would cause for himself. And the reason that such devouring causes him pain is because in devouring others he is ultimately devouring himself. What has happened is as follows. Milton's embrace of Eternal Death has increased the power of the forces of mediation. With the activation of the Starry Seven and their appeal to Albion, it is no longer possible naively to equate one's identity with one's immediate actuality. And it is therefore also impossible for one to assert an identity that does not include an intrinsic relatedness to otherness. This impossibility is one manifestation of the appeal of the Starry Seven for Albion to awake. This appeal is also heard by Satan, the self-aggrandizing aspect of individuals — that aspect which denies and destroys otherness, assimilating it into one's immediacy. And when this self-aggrandizing aspect is confronted with the fact that identity is a matter of mediation and mutuality, it is at an impasse, for since others are a part of itself, it cannot harm them without harming itself. Thus the pain Satan feels "if he touches a Vital" of another.

In other words, as the intrinsic unity of all individuals becomes more explicit, one's self-conscious, spectrous identity itself begins to expand, including as aspects of itself what was once regarded as other. Blake expresses this growing ambiguity regarding self and other through several ambiguous pronoun references: in this new state Satan is said to be "trembling round *his* Body" and "howling in *his* Spectre round *his* Body" (emphasis added). Syntactically, both the Body and the Spectre are Satan's own. But they also belong to Albion, who has just been mentioned by the Starry Seven, and who, several lines later, arises and "sees his embodied Spectre / Trembling before him" (39:46-7). And both the Body and the Spectre also refer to Milton, whom Satan confronts on the previous plate (38:9-14). Thus Satan, who is himself the "Reasoning Spectre" (39:10) of Albion, the Spectre of Milton (38:29), and the Spectrous form of a metaphysical principle (i.e., of the Miller of Eternity), yearns in each of these forms to devour a Body which is simultaneously his own being, the being of Albion, and that of Milton. The agent in each instance always turns out ultimately to be a perverted form of the patient.

This unity also expresses the fact that each instance of the devouring of others is an act in which both the agent and patient are at once an individual (Milton), the principle of the union of individuals (Albion), and a fundamental, metaphysical power (Satan, the power of homogenization). The urge to devour otherness is thus seen to be the Spectrous or insubstantial form of a fundamental principle of Being. As such, however, it is not truly an authentic power in its own right, but merely an epiphenomenon or by-product of this fundamental principle of homogenization. Despite this epiphenomenality, however, it is necessary, Blake says, to conceive of Satan as a power in its own right. Blake explains:

> Loud Satan thunderd, loud & dark upon mild Felphams Shore
> Coming in a Cloud with Trumpets & with Fiery Flame
> An awful Form eastward from midst of a bright Paved-work
> Of precious stones by Cherubim surrounded: so permitted
> (Lest he should fall apart in his Eternal Death) to imitate
> The Eternal Great Humanity Divine surrounded by
> His Cherubim & Seraphim in ever happy Eternity.
>
> (39:22-8)

Satan appears in his Spectrous form as a mighty power in his own right rather than as the derivative and perverted form or epiphenomenon of another power. This appearance as a power commensurate with the ultimate power which constitutes Human being itself ("The Eternal Great Humanity Divine") is permitted by Blake, Milton, and the ultimate powers themselves so that Satan does not fragment (i.e., "fall apart in his Eternal Death") into a multiplicity of particular and apparently unrelated powers of reduction whose Satanic essence would thereby be less obvious and thus more insidious. Allowing Satan to appear as (i.e., to be conceived as) a power in his own right thus serves to define the insidious reductive destruction of otherness that pervades existence and to locate this destructiveness in relation to other dimensions of existence. Thus it is revealed that

> Beneath [Satan] sat Chaos: Sin on his right hand Death on his left
> And Ancient Night spread over all the heavn his Mantle of Laws
> He trembled with exceeding great trembling & astonishment.
>
> (39:29-31)

Satan, the reductive destruction of otherness and the producer of sameness, thus appears as the nexus of Chaos, Sin, Death, and Ancient Night, just as Los, the constructive production of otherness, functions as the nexus of the Four Zoas, or non-actual dimensions of Being. While Los actualizes otherness by drawing together the non-actual dimensions of Being, Satan de-actualizes otherness by drawing together in conflict the various dimensions of mere immediacy—i.e., by actualizing non-differentiation (Chaos), proscription of otherness (Sin), inertia (Death), and absolute oblivion of otherness (Ancient Night), which is constituted by obscuring otherness with the homogeneity of abstractions and generalities (Laws). The non-differentiation of Chaos constitutes the primordial ground and the primal, cosmic manifestation of Satanic homogenization, and the Mantle of Laws embodies the cultural manifestation of this homogenization. At Satan's right hand, Sin (the concept, not the act) is the ultimate form of positive (i.e., deliberate, voluntary) denial of otherness (through refusing to actualize otherness by committing certain acts), and Death, on Satan's left hand, is the final homogenization of whatever is not already inert homogeneity.

The appearance of Satan as a positive form which, in de-actualizing otherness by actualizing various dimensions of mere immediacy or non-being, is inverse and complementary to Los's activity, constitutes both a limitation of Satan and a mitigation of his denial of otherness, for the very assumption of form is the inauguration of otherness. As such, it is also the subordination of Satan to Los, the giver of form, or inaugurator of otherness. Satan is further subordinated to Los by his assumption of an identity and function which mirrors that of Los: as the destroyer of otherness, or the great homogenizer, Satan once more assumes his station as the Miller of Eternity, performing that reductive destruction which is a necessary aspect of that constructive, productive process of actualization.

The Arising of Albion:
The Subsequent Status of Communal Being

The assumption of this form by Satan and his subordination to Los constitute Albion's response to the admonition issued by the Starry Seven: "Reclaim thy Reasoning Spectre. Subdue / Him to the Divine Mercy, Cast Him down into the Lake / Of Los" (39:10-12). The subjugation of Satan is thus also the arising of Albion—the resumption by communal being of its true form as the mediated unity of one individual with another:

> Then Albion rose up in the Night of Beulah on his Couch
> Of dread repose seen by the visionary eye; his face is toward
> The east, toward Jerusalems Gates: groaning he sat above
> His rocks.
>
> (39:32-5)

The true form of togetherness arises from its dormancy, and, looking toward the image of its fulfillment (Jerusalem), struggles to actualize itself. This process involves collectives of individuals, which Blake expresses as support which various cities and regions of Britain provide for Albion and his throne (39:35-45).

This incipient actualization of the true form of communal being is not consummated, however: "[Albion] strove to rise to walk into the Deep. but strength failing / Forbad & down with dreadful groans he sunk upon his Couch / In moony Beulah" (39:50-52). The true form of togetherness is not yet able to actualize itself by entering the abyss of finitude ("the Deep"), for it requires tremendous spiritual strength to conduct oneself in response to mediated presence rather than in reaction to immediate actuality. Although a few spiritual giants may have succeeded in living in this way (e.g., Milton), most individuals remain "in moony Beulah," reposing in the delusion of a substantial, unchanging identity whose finitude is largely obscured or repressed.

The Fainting of Urizen:
The Subsequent Status of Identity

The inability of Albion to enter the Deep as Milton did embodies Blake's acknowledgement that his (Blake's) vision of Being is by no means in and of itself the solution to the frustration and torment plaguing existence. This admission, however, does not mean that the vision is totally inconsequential for existence, and Blake reminds us once again of the transformation which the vision of infinity as attainable in finitude —expressed as Milton's going to Eternal Death —effects in the very principle of individual existence:

> Urizen faints in terror striving among the Brooks of Arnon
> With Miltons Spirit: as the Plowman or Artificer or Shepherd
> While in the labours of his Calling sends his Thought abroad
> To labour in the ocean or in the starry heaven. So Milton
> Labourd in Chasms of the Mundane Shell. . . .
>
> (39:53-7)

Milton's spirit, in embracing Eternal Death and thus valorizing mediated presence over pure presence and immediate actuality, has succeeded in rendering powerless (i.e., causing to faint) Urizen, the principle of individuation, separation, or self-subsistence. Milton's victory over Urizen is simply another aspect of his victory over Satan (and vice versa), for as we have seen, "Satan is Urizen / Drawn down by Orc & the Shadowy Female into Generation" (10:1-2). This overcoming of Urizenic limitation—of the finitude constituted by individuation itself—is accomplished through Milton's "labou[r] in Chasms of the Mundane Shell," which chasms, we have seen, are the gaps in immediate actuality (as constituted by metaphysics) which lead ineluctably to a vision of the mediating activity of Los, the principle of actualization. The fainting of Urizen, which in positivist language would be expressed as an event occuring in Blake's imagination, is in truth the product of a complex mediation involving Milton's posthumous presence. Milton's posthumous presence is itself, as we have seen, with Blake— "here before / My Cottage," Blake says in the present passage. This posthumous presence of Milton with Blake constitutes the first mediation. But even this mediated presence of Milton is not totally immediately present: it is also present in mediated form in the Chasms of the Mundane Shell, struggling with Urizen. This doubly mediated presence occurs when "Blake's" thought, the ultimate agent of which is not Blake but Milton in his posthumous presence, projects itself to be with that which is not immediately present—just "as the Plowman or Artificer or Shepherd / While in the labours of his Calling sends his Thoughts abroad / To labour in the ocean or in the starry heaven." And finally, this doubly mediated presence of Milton labors in a region constituted by absence, or non-presence: the Chasms of the Mundane Shell. Thus the power of mediation, although not universally active in all individuals to the extent necessary for their assumption of infinite form, is nonetheless powerfully actualized in certain instances, and is present to a degree in all individuals who send their thoughts abroad—i.e., who direct their attention to the non-immediate or non-present. These two facts—that attunement to mediated presence is inherent in all individuals and that it is actually predominant in some (like Blake and Milton)—constitute strong evidence that the awakening of Albion is possible and that Ololon can find solace in finitude by actualizing the power of mediated presence: that the true form of society can be actualized and that the desire for infinity can be satisfied within finitude. Blake is now prepared to examine the latter of these possibilities, embodied in

> ...the Virgin Ololon [who]
> Stood trembling in the Porch: loud Satan thunder'd on the stormy Sea
> Circling Albions Cliffs in which the Four-fold World resides
> Tho seen in fallacy outside: a fallacy of Satans Churches.
>   (39:58-61)

Ololon's trembling is a reflection of the fact that Satan is still active. And one of the primary results of Satanic activity is found in the false perception of the Four-fold World which resides in Albion's Cliffs—i.e., the four dimensions of Being—which are reduced to mere aspects of presence by the feudalistic metaphysics of orthodox Christianity. Such fallacy, we will now see, is a product of Ololon herself—i.e., of lamention, or the desire for infinity.

CHAPTER XIV

Milton and Ololon United:
Desire for Infinity Embraces Finitude

Toward Self-Conscious Lamentation:
Uncovering the Grounds

In the preceding account of Satan, Blake has summarized his critique of the fundamental distortions of vision that result in ontological and literal destruction of individual being. Blake now pursues this critique, focusing on the specific epistemological distortions which must be overcome before the desire for infinity can find fulfillment within finitude. Blake pursues this analysis through a dialectical confrontation between Milton and Ololon. "Before Ololon," Blake says, "Milton stood & percievd the Eternal Form / Of that mild Vision; wondrous were their acts by me unknown / Except remotely" (40:1-3). The encounter of the attitude of acceptance of finitude with the desire for infinity results in "wondrous" interactions between them—a dialectic of such profundity, sublimity, and subtlety that its details can be only dimly apprehended. Blake's presentation of this dialectical interchange, he is implying, is to be taken as an approximation—a necessarily incomplete and obscure account—a probing and groping attempt to grasp something which is ultimately not totally graspable. The dialectic occurs in several stages.

Other Dimensions of the Struggle with Finitude

Just as Milton is said to perceive Ololon's essence or "Eternal Form," so now Ololon is seen to have a partial vision of Milton's essential nature, the struggle to accept finitude:

> I see thee strive upon the Brooks of Arnon. there a dread
> And awful Man I see, oercoverd with the mantle of years.
> I behold Los & Urizen. I behold Orc & Tharmas;

257

> The Four Zoa's of Albion & thy Spirit with them striving
> In Self annihilation giving thy life to thy enemies.
>
> (40:3-7)

The mutual perception by the two powers indicates that they have begun to take account of each other. Ololon's awareness of Milton's struggle with the finitude of individual identity—i.e., with Urizen—indicates that lamentation (the desire for infinity) is aware of the opposition which the finitude of existence represents to fulfillment, for lamentation is itself the reaction against this same finitude. Only now, however, does lamentation take express account of the struggle between the urge to overcome finitude and the principle of acceptance of finitude. Now, too, the quest for infinity becomes aware of the involvement of the Four Zoas, the fundamental principles or regions of Being, in the struggle with finitude: all struggle with finitude is also a struggle with the fundamental structures of Being which underlie existence. And finally, Ololon here comes to an awareness that perishing is somehow integrally involved in this struggle, although the necessity and inevitability of this perishing is not yet completely clear. This growing awareness of Ololon constitutes lamentation's movement beyond its own immediacy and into explicit relatedness with other dimensions of Being as a whole. At this stage, however, lamentation does not yet see its own involvement in this larger arena: it merely stands at a distance and "beholds" these principles as powers that are separate from itself. It does not see its own implication in Milton's struggle with Urizen.

The Implicit Dimension

This supposed separation between desire for infinity and the dispensation of Being as a whole is narrowed, however, in Ololon's next flash of insight. Ololon asks:

> Are those who contemn Religion & seek to annihilate it
> Become in their Femin[in]e portions the causes & promoters
> Of these Religions, how is this thing? this Newtonian Phantasm
> This Voltaire & Rousseau: this Hume & Gibbon & Bolingbroke
> This Natural Religion! this impossible absurdity?
>
> (40:9-13)

Here Ololon realizes the counterproductiveness of attempts by skeptics and Deists to overcome the ontological finitude imposed upon individuals by the feudalistic metaphysics of orthodox Christianity. In trying to overcome this tyranny, Voltaire, Rousseau, Hume, Gibbon, and Bolingbroke posited a rational universe in which all events occur as a result of a series of natural causes, and thus derive ultimately from a First Cause, or Prime Mover—the God of Deism. This system of natural religion purports to free the individual from suppression by liberating the individual from the tyranny of the capricious gods of other religions. In actuality, however, Deism merely exchanges an overt tyranny for a covert, more insidious suppression. For in making the being of individuals subordinate to the First Cause, it is reducing them to epiphenomena of another being and depriving them of their unique intrinsic being. Thus while these skeptics act to overcome the subordination of individual beings to another being (i.e., to overcome religion), the objectified, or "feminine" aspect of this attempt—i.e., the system (thoughts) which this attempt (act of thinking) produces—actually promotes this very subordination. Moreover, this system is ultimately an "impossible absurdity," for there can be no such thing as a first cause of individual being: there must either be an infinitely receding series of causes, or no extrinsic, natural causes at all for individual beings. For if one individual is caused by another, it is necessary to ask what caused the first individual. It is thus impossible for the ground of all beings to be just another being. One individual simply cannot be reduced to an effect of other individuals, no matter what significant influences one individual may receive from others.

Self-Conscious Lamentation

These realizations constitute a significant advance for Ololon, for she now begins to take account of the implicit dimension of things, becoming aware of the fact that actions have widespread ramifications and that ultimate results can be contrary to intentions. Although she does not fully comprehend this dimension—"How is this thing?" she asks—Ololon immediately applies the principle to herself: "Is Ololon the cause of this?" she inquires (40:14). Lamentation is here confronted with the fact that the impossible absurdity of Natural Religion, and all other religions as well, is caused by that very desire for infinity that lamentation *is*. This realization constitutes the inauguration of self-conscious lamentation—a desire for infinity that takes account of itself and of the ramifications of its actions in the context of the totality of Being.

Confronted with its own implication in promoting that very finitude which it is trying to overcome, lamentation reacts with shame and sadness: "O where shall I hide my face / These tears fall for the little-ones: the Children of Jerusalem / Lest they be annihilated in thy annihilation"

(40:14–16). The desire for infinity here seems about to capitulate in resignation to finitude, assuming that all must be in vain if actions undermine themselves. Specifically, Ololon weeps over the possibility that Milton's annihilation might also constitute the annihilation of "the Children of Jerusalem"—i.e., of individuals seeking fulfillment. This fear, however, that if Milton embraces self-annihilation all hope to achieve infinity will be destroyed, is based on Ololon's failure to grasp the reality of mediated presence.

The Alternative to the Quest for Immediate Infinity

As soon as the desire for infinity begins to doubt the worth of its own effort, the false fulfillment of immediate pleasure appears, constituting the alternative to the quest for infinity:

> No sooner she had spoke but Rahab Babylon appeard
> Eastward upon the Paved work across Europe & Asia
> Glorious as the midday Sun in Satans bosom glowing
> A Female hidden in a Male, Religion hidden in War
> Namd Moral Virtue; cruel two-fold Monster shining bright
> A Dragon red & hidden Harlot which John in Patmos saw.
>
> (40:17-22)

As soon as the desire for infinity begins to capitulate to finitude, various forms of immediate, or finite, gratification and self-aggrandizement appear, in various combinations of submission and aggression. These modes of existence, as we have seen before, are thoroughly Satanic, residing "in Satans bosom," whence they issue to destroy the unique intrinsic being of individuals.

The historical instances of the predominance of this Satanic vision also appear:

> And all beneath the Nations innumerable of Ulro
> Appeard, the Seven Kingdoms of Canaan & Five Baalim
> Of Philistea. into Twelve divided, calld after the Names
> Of Israel: as they are in Eden. Mountain. River & Plain
> City & sandy Desart intermingled beyond mortal ken.
>
> (40:23-7)

These twelve kingdoms, which worshipped feudalistic deities in a *quid pro quo* system, embody the capitulation to finitude—i.e., to immediacy. They have their ultimate form in the twelve tribes of Israel, which each desired autonomy and ascendancy over all other nations, and over each other as well. In such systems, as we have seen, everything is ultimately homogeneous: "Mountain. River & Plain / City & sandy Desart intermingled beyond mortal ken."

Milton's Epistemological Critique

Overturning the Metaphysics of Presence

Lamentation's turning against itself in despair thus leads ultimately to both ontological and literal desolation of individual being. The only way to prevent such an occurrence is to overcome finitude by accepting it and finding infinity within it. But before infinity can be found within finitude, the metaphysics of presence, which denies being to that which is not immediate, must be overthrown. This destruction is what Milton now proposes:

> But turning toward Ololon in terrible majesty Milton
> Replied. Obey thou the Words of the Inspired Man
> All that can be annihilated must be annihilated
> That the Children of Jerusalem may be saved from slavery.
> (40:28-31)

Autonomous individuals living in mutuality ("the Children of Jerusalem") must "be saved from slavery"—i.e., their being must not be limited to the immediate state of actuality. Therefore the actual must be annihilated, for it is only by virtue of such annihilation that growth, transformation, and progress can occur: the passing away of one state of affairs is necessary to make room for the next. In addition, universal annihilation of the immediate is necessary to demonstrate that what is immediate or actual is not ultimate. Annihilation thus frees individuals both literally and epistemologically from immediacy, or actuality, and allows the being of individuals to flourish instead of being restricted to the actual.

Rationalism

Milton now pursues the subject of epistemological liberation, attacking, in turn, rationalism, empiricism, aestheticism, and skepticism. He turns first to rationalism:

> There is a Negation, & there is a Contrary
> The Negation must be destroyd to redeem the Contraries
> The Negation is the Spectre; the Reasoning Power in Man

> This is a false Body: an Incrustation over my Immortal
> Spirit; a Selfhood, which must be put off & annihilated alway.
>
> (40:32-6)

As the Spectre, and the reasoning power in man, this negation is the Satanic reduction of individual being to an extrinsic homogeneity. In this negating action, rationalism would seem to enact that very annihilation which Milton advocates. In reality, however, this reasoning power merely negates the *form* of actuality, preserving the content in the generalizations which it derives from actuality. This reasoning power which reduces individuals to abstract aspects of their actuality is the act of negating, while the Spectre, as the insubstantial manifestation or form ("false Body") of an individual, constitutes the form or idea produced by the negating act. The converse is also true, however, for the Spectre is the inauthentic aspect of an individual that acts spectrously and produces and establishes abstract reason. This Satanic destruction of individual being must be eliminated so that contrariety, the legitimate, differentiating strife of individuation, can prevail, for such contrariety cannot occur where individual being is reduced to an extrinsic homogeneous substance. Nor can this purifying, tempering, defining contrariety occur where a generalization from the individual's immediate actuality is allowed to obscure its true being, or "Immortal Spirit."

Empiricism

One's own immediate actuality, then, must be destroyed in all its forms—including that of abstract generalization—so that it neither obscures (stymies epistemologically) nor obstructs (stymies literally) the movement into otherness which constitutes an individual's true being. Milton elaborates:

> To cleanse the Face of my Spirit by Self-examination.
> To bathe in the Waters of Life; to wash off the Not Human
> I come in Self-annihilation & the grandeur of Inspiration
> To cast off Rational Demonstration by Faith in the Saviour
> To cast off the rotten rags of Memory by Inspiration
> To cast off Bacon, Locke & Newton from Albions covering
> To take off his filthy garments, & clothe him with Imagination.
>
> (40:37-41:6)

To be authentic, an individual must constantly destroy and supersede all dimensions of its immediate state. The epistemological dimension of this supersession involves the repeated eschewing of what is immediately observable in favor of what is not present: the "Rational Demonstration" of empiricism must give way to "Faith." Likewise, what has been (including what is now, which always becomes a "has-been") must defer to what could be: Memory must be subordinated to Inspiration. Most important of all, these epistemological considerations must be reflexive, and apply not only to ordinary objects of knowledge but also to the power of knowing itself. The power of knowing, that is, should not be defined by what it knows or has known, but should rather be identified with what it might become. As Blake declared in *There is No Natural Religion*, "Reason [is] the ratio of all we have already known [and it] is not the same that it shall be when we know more."[1] Empiricist inquiries concerning the human understanding—such as those of Bacon, Locke, and Newton—must therefore be denied ultimacy of any kind, and Albion, the intrinsic relatedness of individuals which is the true ground of authentic knowledge, should be portrayed imaginatively rather than empirically: knowledge, and the primal connexity (Albion) which founds it, should be seen in terms of what it may become rather than in terms of what it has been.

Aestheticism

Blake/Milton's identification of authentic individual being with Life, Inspiration, Faith, and Imagination indicates conclusively that fulfillment of individual being consists in continuously moving beyond the immediate, destroying and overcoming the actualities which it is and which it knows, and becoming an other which is a less limited form of itself. Given this vision of individual being, poetry becomes an extremely important activity, for it embodies, perhaps more fully than any other endeavor, this movement away from the actual to the possible and the essential. Hence it is vital that this function of poetry be unimpeded by invalid conceptions of the poetic enterprise, and it is thus necessary, Milton says,

> To cast aside from Poetry, all that is not Inspiration
> That it no longer shall dare to mock with the aspersion of Madness
> Cast on the Inspired, by the tame high finisher of paltry Blots,
> Indefinite, or paltry Rhymes; or paltry Harmonies.
> Who creeps into State Government like a catterpiller to destroy.
> (41:7-11)

Poetry should embody the movement of becoming other that constitutes imagination and inspiration; and other purposes—such as producing aesthetic pleasure by decking out "in paltry Rhymes; or paltry Harmonies" what oft was thought but ne'er so well expressed—should not be tolerated, for they will ultimately corrupt the very vitals of the human enterprise ("creep[ing] into State Government like a catterpiller to destroy") by denying true poetry a voice.

Skepticism

Also crucial to authentic, fulfilled existence is the avoidance of skepticism, so popular in the eighteenth century. It is necessary, Milton declares,

> To cast off the idiot Questioner who is always questioning,
> But never capable of answering; who sits with a sly grin
> Silent plotting when to question, like a thief in a cave;
> Who publishes doubt & calls it knowledge; whose Science is
>   Despair,
> Whose pretence to knowledge is Envy, whose whole Science is
> To destroy the wisdom of ages to gratify ravenous Envy;
> That rages round him like a Wolf day & night without rest
> He smiles with condescension; he talks of Benevolence & Virtue
> And those who act with Benevolence & Virtue, they murder time
>   on time.
>
>   (41:12-20)

While skepticism might seem *prima facie* (like rationalism) to support authentic individuality by discounting its immediate actuality, it actually undermines this true being of the individual by demanding an even more radical immediacy: it refuses to acknowledge the true ontological status of actually existing things, because the things are present not in absolute immediacy but rather through the mediation of the senses. The primary effect of skepticism is to rob things of their inherent being, producing a Satanic destruction of individual being, the only outcome of which can be despair. The motivation of the skeptic is also Satanic: the skeptic questions in order "to gratify ravenous Envy"—i.e., in order to exalt his own being through a *quid pro quo* reduction of the being of another. This purpose is evident in the condescending tone of skepticism, which holds itself above both the things it doubts and those who fail to doubt. Thus although he extols benevolence and virtue, the skeptic, with his type of benevolence and virtue, constantly destroys the truly benevolent and virtuous: those who accept the being of another straightforwardly and with an open heart, never thinking to challenge the other's validity.

Overturning the Ground of Spurious Epistemologies

These various epistemological perversions—rationalism, empiricism, aestheticism, and skepticism—destroy the fulfilled state of autonomous individuals (Jerusalem) and the principle of authentic self-sacrifice, which is embodied in the image of Jesus:

> These are the destroyers of Jerusalem, these are the murderers
> Of Jesus, who deny the Faith & mock at Eternal Life!
> Who pretend to Poetry that they may destroy Imagination;
> By imitation of Natures Images drawn from Remembrance
> These are the Sexual Garments, the Abomination of Desolation
> Hiding the Human Lineaments as with an Ark & Curtains
> Which Jesus rent: & now shall wholly purge away with Fire
> Till Generation is swallowd up in Regeneration.
>
> (41:21-8)

These various epistemologies destroy the true being of individuality by denying being to the non-present. Faith—the orientation to that which is not present—is thus seen as invalid, and the idea of Eternal Life, or infinity beyond actuality, is seen as ridiculous. The reason for these denials is the assumption that what is not or has not been actual does not have being—a tacit assumption that manifests itself in the restriction of validity and reality to that which is identical to "Natures Images drawn from Remembrance" (without, ironically, attributing any mediation or distortion to remembrance). These epistemological distortions "are the Sexual Garments, the Abomination of Desolation / Hiding the Human Lineaments as with an Ark & Curtains." On the surface the epistemological assumptions appear to embody the true nature of individual being; in reality, however, they reflect only its superficial, immediately evident facade, i.e., its "Sexual Garments"—its state as a subject or object (i.e., male or female). This restriction of things to the categories of subject and object, or active and passive, constitutes the "Abomination of Desolation," the Babylon in which the true being of an individual—i.e., its unique, intrinsic identity, including its relatedness to other beings—is held captive. The captivity results from the fact that these epistemologies hide the true being ("Human Lineaments") of individuals, for this being does not occur in its truth if neither the individual itself nor other beings take account of it.

This concealment of the true being of things, however, was diminished by Jesus' self-sacrifice, which tacitly asserted, in the most radical way possible, that an individual's being is not coterminous with its immediate existence. By voluntarily going to Eternal Death, as Milton himself is now doing, Jesus challenged the metaphysics of presence by staking his life on a metaphysics of mediation, mutuality, and process. This act, Milton declares, provides the foundation for a complete overcoming of the metaphysics of presence and its concomitant epistemologies. Jesus, in his posthumous presence as the agent of this act, can now, through his mediated actualization in Milton/Blake, "wholly purge away with Fire" the obfuscating systems which destroy individual being. When this event occurs, "Generation [will be] swallowed up in Regeneration": the arising and perishing of individuals will be revealed as transformations in the mode of an individual's being, rather than transitions from nothingness to being, or vice versa. Arising will be seen to be transformation from possibility or implicitness to actuality or explicitness, and perishing will be acknowledged as a metamorphosis from immediate actuality to mediated presence. In this vision individual being will stand forth in its "Human Lineaments," as what it really is: a unique, intrinsic identity which is inherently and essentially interrelated multifariously with other individuals and thus mediately present in their being, and which is a devouring/productive process rather than a subject (male) or object (female).

CHAPTER XV

Infinity Within the Finite Individual: An Alternative Vision of Being

Ololon's Apocalypse

Ololon's union with Milton—that is, lamentation's adoption of Milton's perspective on the finite and the infinite—evokes the recognition that lamentation itself produces that very devotion to presence which Milton has just denounced. This devotion to presence is seen to constitute the "Feminine Portion" of lamentation—the objectified aspect (or world) which is tacitly posited (and thus in a sense produced) by the act of lamenting:

> Is this our Femin[in]e Portion the Six-fold Miltonic Female
> Terribly this Portion trembles before thee O awful Man
> Altho' our Human Power can sustain the severe contentions
> Of Friendship, our Sexual cannot: but flies into the Ulro.
> Hence arose all our terrors in Eternity! & now remembrance
> Returns upon us! are we Contraries O Milton, Thou & I
> O Immortal! how were we led to War the Wars of Death
> Is this the Void Outside of Existence, which if enter'd into
> Becomes a Womb? & is this the Death Couch of Albion
> Thou goest to Eternal Death & all must go with thee.
>
> (41:30-42:2)

The act of lamenting, Ololon realizes, produces a clinging to immediacy, a valorization of presence. For although lamenting actively opposes and tries to destroy the immediately actual (since it finds this actuality deficient), it desires primarily not the destruction of the actuality per se but rather the establishment of another actuality in its place—an actuality in which the lamenter's being is more fully present, more completely actualized in immediacy. Lamentation's ostensible opposition to immediacy, or presence, is thus not an opposition to immediacy or presence per se, but rather an opposition to the limitation of presence and a devotion to absolute presence.

Ololon also realizes that "this...Femin[in]e Portion [is] the Six-fold Miltonic Female"—i.e., that this devotion to unmediated presence constitutes an abdication of one's own unique being to otherness, as in the case of Milton's three wives and three daughters, who abdicated their being to Milton in hopes of thereby attaining the infinity which he seemed to possess. But such hope is merely another, more subtle and insidious instance of the assumption of a feudalistic metaphysics of presence, and Milton's diatribe against presence and his laudation of the mediating process of Regeneration have shown the futility of this aspiring to an absolute presence. As such opposition, Milton appears to lamentation as an "awful Man" who threatens lamentation by destroying the very illusion to which lamentation implicitly aspired—the illusion of pure, unmediated presence.

Although Ololon/lamentation has begun to separate itself from this untenable aspiration (by distinguishing itself from this "Feminine Portion"), it realizes that the mere recognition of the illusory nature of this aspiration is not sufficient to overcome it. Ololon realizes that although it is possible for one to affirm Milton's vision in mediation, or spiritually—i.e., with one's "Human Power"—one's immediate, actual identity (the "Sexual" power) cannot sustain that salutary strife of mutual contention that refines and purifies one's unique individual being by destroying one's immediate state. This immediate identity is always trying to preserve itself, and hence it can never give itself over into a mutual strife of which the very essence is to make this identity into something other; rather, this immediately self-present identity (the ego) "flies into the Ulro," the realm of overt self-aggrandizement where, ironically, it does not escape becoming-other but is actually subjected to involuntary, unredemptive becoming-other in being used and devoured by other beings.

It is this sexual power which caused Ololon's terrors in Eternity: the clinging to presence by immediate identity caused true lamentation's participation in infinity to be abandoned in the quest for presence. That is, the aspect of individual being which is immediate managed to impose its finite response to deficiency—i.e., grasping for a more intensive and extensive immediacy—on authentic lamentation's infinite response: ecstatic becoming-other into a more complex mediation. And this imposition occurred because of the metaphysics of presence, which values immediacy above mediation.

As Ololon/lamentation thus clarifies and purifies itself by recognizing its own perversion, it realizes that Milton is not the enemy of its quest for infinity, as it thought when it drove Milton from Eternity, but that they are rather mutually defining contraries: lamentation, as the desire for infinity, is the contrary of Milton, the desire to accept the finite (by justifying the ways of God to Men). As contraries, then, they are each implicit in the other, and thus Ololon/lamentation's realization of their contrariety is simultaneous with its recognition that entering finitude is the way to achieve infinity: it becomes aware of "the Void Outside of Existence, which if enter'd into / Becomes a Womb" (41:37-42:1). Lamentation has always recognized that in moving outside of existence—i.e., in dying—one enters a realm of nothing- ness, of non-presence. But it now achieves the further realization that this nothingness is not mere non-being but rather a negation of one's immediate actuality and self-presence, which, as such, allows one to be reborn or regen- erated in a new, less limiting form. Death is a negation of the original nega- tion constituted by individual finitude (to use Hegel's formulation). This recognition occurs only after Ololon/lamentation has given up her devotion to presence, for the regeneration attained through destruction is invisible from the perspective of a metaphysics of presence: to such a vision the mediated actuality of posthumous presence is nothing. Ololon/lamentation, however, has now recognized the being of that which is mediated, and it also sees that the failure to achieve such recognition is what incapacitates Albion, the authentic form of community: the "Void Outside of Existence" is "the Death Couch of Albion" (42:1) because Albion (society as a whole, in all its customs and institutions and forms of thought) has failed to acknowledge fully the regenerative function of perishing. Blake's Ololon/lamentation, on the other hand, has made this acknowledgement, and it now agrees with Milton that embracing Eternal Death is necessary and inevitable: "Thou goest to Eternal Death," Ololon declares, "& all must go with thee" (42:2).

The Virgin's Division:
Consummation of Lamentation

Even this acknowledgement, however, great as it is, does not constitute the attainment of infinity. Such attainment occurs only with actual immersion in finitude. Thus as soon as Ololon acknowledges the necessity of going to Eternal Death, she embraces finitude:

> So saying, the Virgin divided Six-fold & with a shriek
> Dolorous that ran thro all Creation a Double Six-fold Wonder!
> Away from Ololon she divided & fled into the depths
> Of Miltons Shadow as a Dove upon the stormy Sea.
> (42:3-6)

We are here reminded that the Ololon who has been speaking is a Virgin: lamentation has remained unconsummated because it has not yet been entered into by its contrary and become productive. Ololon/lamentation now loses this Virginity (the Virgin flees) and thus consummates its union with Milton: desire for infinity, that is, becomes one with acceptance of the finite. This consummation, however, is not a pleasant event. In the first place, Ololon/lamentation is not able to engage in this embrace of finitude whole-heartedly: part of it resists the embrace—i.e., the Virgin, that part of Ololon which, still devoted to immediacy and self-presence, values purity (self-sameness, self-presence) over mediation and interrelatedness. This Virgin is the Sexual Power and the Feminine Portion of lamentation, the aspects which desire immediacy and valorize presence, respectively. In refusing to embrace finitude, this aspect of lamentation becomes "Six-fold": it assumes the sub-missive form of Milton's three wives and three daughters, positing an other (an object counterpart) which is infinite and attempting to acquire this infin-ity by suppressing its own finite identity and assuming the identity of this other. The Virgin is thus "a Double Six-fold Wonder," ostensibly submis-sive, while ultimately self-aggrandizing. And as "a Double Six-fold" form, this aspect of lamentation is twelve-fold and thus allied with the Twelve Gods of Ulro, who are Satan (37:60). For by submitting to another, more powerful being, this aspect denies the unique, intrinsic being both of itself and of the other with which it attempts to identify—a denial which *is* Satan. The Vir-gin's flight "into the depths / Of Miltons Shadow" thus signifies the inau-thentic mode of immersion in otherness—that mode which reifies or idolizes the other's being as an unmediated presence that one can oneself assume through masochistic submissiveness, becoming as insignificant "as a Dove upon the stormy Sea." The fleeing into Milton's Shadow, or posthumous presence, means that this presence is itself seen as an immediate power—that it is reified as an immediate being that one can immerse oneself in, or an external will that one can submit to. Thus the aspect of lamentation that valorizes presence ignores Milton's true identity manifested in his Shadow—an identity which is constituted by opposition to this very valori-zation of presence—and takes refuge in the fact of its presence rather than in the fact of its mediated nature. This aspect of Ololon, we should recall, is the same aspect which earlier descended to Blake in his garden in search of Milton (36:10-37:3). It constitutes, moreover, that form of lamentation in which Blake, as "the loud voic'd Bard[,] terrify'd took refuge in Miltons bosom" (14:9), hoping to assume Milton's spiritual fortitude and thus be sustained in the terrible finitude which his vision had just revealed. Now, however, through a dialectic encounter with Milton as the acceptance of finitude, this aspect of lamentation has revealed itself to be unproductive and unfulfilling (a virgin).

Lamentation and the Crucifixion: Voluntary Death and Infinity

As soon as the unproductive form of lamentation, or the desire for infinity, has manifested itself, the true form of this desire becomes evident:

> Then as a Moony Ark Ololon descended to Felphams Vale
> In clouds of blood, in streams of gore, with dreadful thunderings
> Into the Fires of Intellect that rejoic'd in Felphams Vale
> Around the Starry Eight: with one accord the Starry Eight became
> One Man Jesus the Saviour. wonderful! round his limbs
> The Clouds of Ololon folded as a Garment dipped in blood
> Written within & without in woven letters: & the Writing
> Is the Divine Revelation in the Litteral expression:
> A Garment of War, I heard it namd the Woof of Six Thousand
>   Years.
>
> $\qquad\qquad\qquad\qquad\qquad\qquad\qquad$ (42:7-15)

Here Ololon/lamentation appears to Blake (i.e., "descend[s] to Felphams Vale") as a somewhat obscure, indefinite container of the Divine Presence, or Being. Blake, that is, dimly recognizes that lamentation (somewhat like Keats's melancholy) is in some way the abode or manifestation of Being itself. It is true that lamentation occurs within a context of, and as a response to, terrible suffering and destruction: it occurs "in clouds of blood, in streams of gore, with dreadful thunderings." However, when lamentation and its context of suffering and destruction appear not immediately but rather in mediation—i.e., in the context of their ultimate effects—they reveal themselves to be a manifestation of the ultimate nature of things (i.e., "the Divine Revelation"). This appearance of lamentation in mediated form occurs when it enters "the Fires of Intellect," the powers of spirit which purify a phenomenon of its mere immediacy by consuming that immediacy and allowing the greater being of the phenomenon to stand forth. These powers are themselves dependent upon the mediating powers which support posthumous presence ("the Starry Eight," the previous Seven Angels of the Presence plus Milton, who, as the power that embraces Eternal Death, constitutes a new addition to these powers). The Fires of Intellect, that is, presuppose, in their negation of the immediate, a mediated posthumous presence of that which is negated: otherwise the negation would result in mere nothingness rather than in a content for the intellect.

The terrible immediacy of lamentation, then, is destroyed by the Fires of Intellect, which rely on the powers of mediated presence. Then, when the immediacy of lamentation is negated, the powers supporting posthumous presence themselves become transformed, becoming "One Man Jesus the Saviour." It becomes evident, that is, that these powers of mediated presence achieve their fullest embodiment in the life and the voluntary suffering and death of Jesus. For Jesus, as we have observed before, established, by his voluntary embrace of death, the principle of posthumous presence, which is the ultimate instance of mediated presence. This fact becomes evident only when lamentation, together with its context of destruction, appears in its mediated or implicit form as the quest for infinity which it truly is. For only then can one see beyond the immediacy of Jesus' suffering and death and view its ultimate results: the activation of the principle of posthumous presence and the concomitant overthrow of the metaphysics of presence, releasing individual being from a destructive vision and opening the way to fulfillment within finitude.

The mediated appearance of lamentation and destruction thus also reveals that Jesus' bloody suffering and death is a manifestation of ultimate Being. For these "Clouds of Ololon," which now appear "as a Garment dipped in blood," are "written within & without in woven letters: & the Writing / Is the Divine Revelation in the Litteral expression." "The Litteral expression"—suffering and destruction—embodies implicitly the manifestation of ultimate Being itself. And that truth of Being which is embodied in suffering and destruction is the fact that Being is mutual strife and destruction. For the context of Jesus' death is "a Garment of War," and the message of suffering and destruction is woven into its very fabric: "written within & without in woven letters." Moreover, Blake declares, "I heard it namd the Woof of Six Thousand Years": the entire fabric of existence, since Creation itself, is composed of this strife and destruction.

Blake thus realizes that Jesus' suffering and death reveals the two sides of destruction: its external or immediate aspect as a terrible and abhorrent event, and its internal or implicit aspect as the regenerative process of Being itself. This vision has resulted from the dialectical encounter between Milton, the power of accepting finitude, and Ololon, the power that attempts to negate finitude. Through this encounter the attempt to negate finitude is purified of its devotion to presence and then manifests itself as the vessel of Being itself, that striving by virtue of which Being is the movement of continuous self-overcoming. And by giving way to the form of Jesus, the "moony Ark" of Ololon, or the indefinite form of lamentation, shows its ultimate, authentic form to be the voluntary alliance with this strife that constitutes Being—a voluntary alliance that occurs as the embrace of Eternal Death, the allowing oneself to become otherness, and in this very act of allowing, embodying (incarnating) the principle of Being itself.

Ramifications of Blake's Vision of Being

Cosmic Ramifications

As soon as Blake apprehends this truth of Being and perceives how infinity can be attained within finitude, he realizes the tremendous ramifications of this vision of being:

> And I beheld the Twenty-four Cities of Albion
> Arise upon their Thrones to Judge the Nations of the Earth
> And the Immortal Four in whom the Twenty-four appear Four-fold
> Arose around Albions body: Jesus wept & walked forth
> From Felphams Vale Clothed in Clouds of Blood, to enter into
> Albions Bosom the bosom of death & the Four surrounded him
> In the Column of Fire in Felphams Vale; then to their mouths the Four
> Applied their Four Trumpets & them sounded to the Four winds.
> (42:16-23)

"The Twenty-four Cities of Albion," as we have seen, are those collectives of individuals which support the true form of communal being (Albion) as the authentic, intrinsic relatedness among unique individuals, providing a unique role for each individual within an organic whole. The Nations, on the other hand, suggest mere conglomerates of individuals; as such, Nations easily deny the inherent being and unique relationships of individuals, making them all homogeneous citizens of one abstract unity. Given Blake's new vision of Being, the Cities now stand forth as the model of the authentic unity of individuals, the standard by which Nations must be judged. The Cities, that is, embody the true form of individual being as a unity with other individuals deriving from mutual responsiveness to individual uniquenesses.

Each instance of such responsiveness to uniqueness — i.e., to otherness — is an act of mediation and self-transformation whereby one allows one's own uniqueness to take up mediated residence in the other and receives the other's mediated presence into oneself. The Cities thus reflect and promote the occurrence of Being itself, which occurs, we have seen, as the continuous, mutual becoming-other of individual beings. The Nations, on the other hand, insofar as their organization does not acknowledge the uniqueness of individuals, oppose the occurrence of Being, for they reduce individuals to homogeneous beings, and place them in subordination to the abstraction of the state, thus espousing a feudalistic metaphysics of homogeneity in contradiction to the way Being actually occurs.

The Cities of Albion, in thus reflecting the truth of Being, reside in the four non-actual dimensions of Being, the "immortal Four." By virtue of Blake's vision of Being, these Four now assume positions around Albion's body, revealing themselves as the context or transcendental conditions for the possibility of the mutual interrelatedness which Albion is: mutuality, that is, presupposes something which is not immediately present, something by virtue of which an individual is able to reach out (spatially and temporally) beyond the enclosure of its own immediacy and self-presence.

Blake's vision of Being also results in the emergence of Jesus in his true form as the power of self-overcoming or becoming-other embodied in his voluntary death. No longer does Jesus appear as a mere quantity of being that functions (as in the doctrine of Atonement, expressed by the False Tongue) as a pawn in a *quid pro quo* metaphysical system. He takes his rightful place at the heart of true individual and communal being (i.e., in Albion's bosom), which is constituted by the dying or becoming-other which Jesus is. And in doing so, Jesus reveals himself as the unified manifestation of the non-actual dimensions of Being: his voluntary death, that is, now reveals itself to be the drawing together of the various non-actual dimensions of Being which constitute the ground and context of the actualizing process.

The fact that this epiphany is twice said to occur in "Felphams Vale" emphasizes that this transformation in the fundamental dispensation of Being arises, like all events, from unique, particular actualities. It is not a transcendent event that is superimposed upon the particular events of existence; rather it is itself an event of existence. Thus through their manifestation in the individual Jesus, which occurs by virtue of Blake's individual vision of Jesus, the Four non-actual dimensions of Being announce themselves in all directions, throughout all of existence: once their reality has been manifested in the paradigm of Jesus, they can be apprehended everywhere.

Personal Ramifications

As Blake apprehends the full significance of his vision, he is overcome. He declares:

> Terror struck in the Vale I stood at that immortal sound
> My bones trembled. I fell outstretchd upon the path
> A moment, & my soul returnd into its mortal state
> To Resurrection & Judgement in the Vegetable Body
> And my sweet Shadow of Delight stood trembling by my side.
>   (42:24-8)

The vision of Being which Blake has had is transforming and renovating, but it is also terrible and terrifying. For it reveals clearly that the path to infinity leads through the brutal reality of physical death. Confronted with this realization, Blake is momentarily immobilized on his path. This moment is the instant when his soul returns from the rapture of its vision of Being and re-enters—i.e., becomes aware of once more—the finitude of actual existence with all its suffering and death. The truth of Blake's vision survives this shock, however, for he realizes that this finitude—the "mortal state" of the "Vegetable Body"—is the locus of "Resurrection & Judgement." His vision of Being has revealed that infinity occurs as the self-destruction of the finite—i.e., in the very finitizing act of the finite—and not as a surmounting of the finite. He has recognized, as he was later to put it (*Jerusalem*, 55:64), that "the Infinite alone resides in Definite & Determinite Identity." Thus, despite the terrors of the way, Blake continues to affirm the value of the journey and the goal. Even his instinctive physical being—his "Shadow of Delight"—appears to have become reconciled to the terror.

Historical Ramifications

Blake's vision concludes with a revelation of the historical significance of this new formulation of Being and the new form of identity which it entails. In this final passage it becomes manifest that the new vision of Being inaugurates a new epoch in history and in Being itself:

> Immediately the Lark mounted with a loud trill from Felphams
>   Vale
> And the Wild Thyme from Wimbletons green & impurpled Hills
> And Los & Enitharmon rose over the Hills of Surrey
> Their clouds roll over London with a south Wind, soft Oothoon
> Pants in the Vales of Lambeth weeping oer her Human Harvest

> Los listens to the Cry of the Poor Man: his Cloud
> Over London in volume terrific, low bended in anger.
>
> (42:29-35)

From this particular event of Blake's vision (i.e., "from Felphams Vale") there issues "Los's Messenger" (see 35:61ff), the Lark, carrying news of the new Church and the new Heaven which Blake's vision constitutes—i.e., a new relation (the Church) between human existence and Being itself, and a new form of immortality or infinity (the Heaven). For the Lark which mounts at the instant of Blake's vision is "the Twenty-eighth bright / Lark, [which] met the Female Ololon descending into [Blake's] Garden" (36:9-10). And this lark moves beyond the twenty-seven Churches of the past, and beyond their respective Heavens, establishing at the zenith of its flight a new Heaven and a new Church. Blake's vision, that is, is immediately carried forth by the principle of mediation to all other individuals, where it becomes actualized to the level that the mediating power (the lark, Los's messenger) is able to raise it. Blake's vision is also carried forth by the type of ecstasis exemplified by the wild thyme—i.e., it has a direct effect (apart from its mediated presence in other individuals) on the unified ground of beings.

As a result of Blake's vision of Being, and in conjunction with its mediated dissemination throughout the world, the principle of actualization itself assumes a much more obvious role in presiding over events of the world: "Los & Enitharmon rose over the Hills of Surrey," we are told, and "their clouds roll over London with a south wind," the switch to present tense indicating that this new dispensation of the principle of actualization continues into the present. Moreover, in this new, more explicit relationship to the actual world of existence, this principle of actualization is seen to take account of and respond to the actions of individuals: "Los listens to the Cry of the Poor Man," and when he does so, "his Cloud / Over London in volume terrific, low bended in anger." Although this principle is only manifest in an indefinite, obscure form—i.e., as a cloud—its presence is nonetheless evident, as is its response to individual needs and desires. Blake's vision of Being thus results in a rapprochement between individual beings and the transcendental principles of Being, to the point where Being itself almost assumes the role of a providential deity.[1]

We are reminded, however, that this new dispensation of Being does not destroy pain and suffering. The process of actualization is based irremediably upon destruction, and it is thus inevitable that "soft Oothoon," the demand for individual delight, "pants in the Vales of Lambeth weeping oer her

Human Harvest." But although some suffering and destruction is inevitable, it is now possible, thanks to the new vision of Being, to mitigate and reduce the suffering and destruction. Specifically, it is now a real possibility that the suffering that results from cruelty and injustice might be eliminated. Such, at least, is the implication of the final lines of the poem:

> Rintrah & Palamabron view the Human Harvest beneath
> Their Wine-presses & Barns stand open; the Ovens are prepar'd
> The Wagons ready. terrific Lions & Tygers sport & play
> All animals upon the Earth, are prepared in all their strength
> To go forth to the Great Harvest & Vintage of the Nations.
>   (42:36-43:1)

The new vision of Being provides the ground for overcoming the bestial cruelty of rapacious individuals ("Lions & Tygers") and the callous injustice perpetuated by abstract conglomerates ("the Nations"). For the new vision of Being reveals the ontological irreducibility of individual being and thus constitutes the irrefragable basis for abolishing the destructive actions deriving from the assumption of the homogeneity of individuals. Thus as the new vision of Being supersedes the *quid pro quo* metaphysics of homogeneity, the lions and tigers of the world will cease their rapacious devouring of otherness, and the abstract, feudalistic conglomerates of individuals will yield themselves up to individuals, the only true beings.

But although such a scenario is possible, it is not inevitable: Blake views this harvest as imminent but not as actually occurring. Whether it occurs or not will ultimately be determined by the particular actions and interactions of individual beings. For as Blake has shown us again and again, it is the individual that constitutes Being itself: "God only Acts & Is, in existing beings or Men."[2]

NOTES

Preface

[1] Three books on *Milton* have appeared in the last decade: Susan Fox, *Poetic Form in Blake's Milton* (Princeton: Princeton University Press, 1976); John Howard, *Blake's Milton: A Study in the Selfhood* (Cranbury, N.J.: Associated University Presses, Inc., 1976); and David E. James, *Written Within and Without: A Study of Blake's Milton* (Las Vegas: Peter Lang, 1978). Fox focuses on the structure of *Milton*, Howard on the issue of Selfhood, and James on the theme of poetry. Of these three works, Howard's is closest to mine in its concerns.

[2] Hazard Adams, "Post-Essick Prophecy," *Studies in Romanticism* 21,iii:400-401.

[3] Morris Eaves, "Inside the Blake Industry: Past, Present, and Future," *Studies in Romanticism* 21,iii:389-90.

[4] Adams, 400.

[5] As Adams notes, "It is always interesting to observe what is simply skipped over in commentaries on the prophecies" (Ibid., 400).

[6] See, for example, James Rieger, " 'The Hem of their Garments': The Bard's Song in *Milton*," in Stuart Curran and Joseph Anthony Wittreich, Jr., eds., *Blake's Sublime Allegory: Essays on the Four Zoas, Milton, and Jerusalem* (Madison: The University of Wisconsin Press, 1973), pp. 259-80; John H. Sutherland, "Blake's *Milton*: The Bard's Song," *Colby Library Quarterly* 13,ii:142-57; and James, op. cit., pp. 1, 16, 38, and 90. Sutherland observes that there are at least three levels of meaning in *Milton*—the archetypal, the social/historical, and the psychological—but in his analysis he privileges the psychological. Rieger's analysis takes a similar tack. He begins by asserting the inadequacy not only of historical or aesthetic interpretations of the poem but also of psychological readings, at least in the Bard's Song: "The personages and events of Blake's myth can usually be translated into the 'corporeal' terms of history, aesthetics, and faculty psychology. But the pure sublimity of the Bard's Song forces us to abandon every level of traditional exegesis except anagogy. As the most strictly prophetic episode in all the so-called prophecies, it is aimed finally and singly at the 'Intellectual powers.'...Clearly, much more is involved [in the Bard's Song] than an artist's unpleasant working conditions, Parliament's pusillanimity before Cromwell, or, for that matter, Blake's practical aesthetics and his theory of psychological types" (pp. 259, 262). Almost immediately, however, Rieger goes on to embrace a psychological reading of the Bard's Song, equating Los with the imagination and identifying Rintrah, Palamabron, and Satan as wrath, love, and pity (pp. 262-3).

279

James, noting that the Bard's Song embodies, among other things, "conflict between ideologies" (p. 16), nonetheless identifies Los as "true poetry" and Palamabron and Satan as "different types of poets" (p. 16), and goes on to declare that "*Milton* is a poem primarily about poetry" (p. 1), and that all major events of the poem are "metaphors for poetry" (p. 90).

[7] The recent Freudian readings (Diana Hume George, *Blake and Freud* [Ithaca: Cornell University Press, 1980], and Brenda Webster, *Blake's Prophetic Psychology* [Athens, Ga.: University of Georgia Press, 1983]) and Jungian readings of Blake (Christine Gallant, *Blake and the Assimilation of Chaos* [Princeton: Princeton University Press, 1978]) are just the most obvious instances of this psychological bent: even more comprehensive or eclectic approaches, such as those of Damrosch and Mitchell, assume the primacy of the psychological aspect of Blake's myth. Damrosch asserts, for example, that "Blake's myth is above all else psychological. His cosmology, theology, and even epistemology are all transpositions of the central inquiry into the self" (*Symbol and Truth in Blake's Myth* [Princeton: Princeton University Press, 1980], p. 122). Mitchell makes a similar assumption, declaring, for instance, that "[Urizen] *is* reason, a particular mode of consciousness" (*Blake's Composite Art: A Study of the Illuminated Poetry* [Princeton: Princeton University Press, 1978], p. 117; emphasis is Mitchell's). Even such philosophical accounts of Blake's myth as those of Northrop Frye (*Fearful Symmetry: A Study of William Blake* [Princeton: Princeton University Press, 1947]); Peter Fisher (*The Valley of Vision: Blake as Prophet and Revolutionary*, ed. by Northrop Frye [Toronto: Toronto University Press, 1961]); Harold Bloom (*Blake's Apocalypse: A Study in Poetic Argument* [Ithaca: Cornell University Press, 1963]); and Thomas J.J. Altizer (*The New Apocalypse: The Radical Christian Vision of William Blake* [N.P.: Michigan State University Press, 1967]) assume, for the most part, that the Four Zoas and other characters are fundamentally psychological principles.

[8] J. Middleton Murry, *William Blake* (London: Jonathan Cape, 1933), p. 213.

[9] Ibid., 225.

Introduction

[1] Plate 19. All quotations of Blake's works are taken from *The Complete Poetry and Prose of William Blake*, ed. David V. Erdman, commentary by Harold Bloom (Berkeley: University of California Press, 1982).

[2] Thomas W. Herzig, "Book I of Blake's *Milton*: Natural Religion as an Optical Fallacy," *Blake Studies* 6,i:20.

[3] *The Book of Urizen* begins with the presentation of Eternity and Urizen, the simplest, most basic dimensions of Being. Eternity names the infinite reservoir of possibilities out of which particular actualities arise, while Urizen is the limiting power or principle, implicit in Eternity itself, by virtue of which certain possibilities are negated and others are allowed to flourish and thus constitute an actual individual

being. This individuating principle of existence (Urizen) itself presupposes another principle—entelechy, or Los, who guards and guides an entity by selecting only certain possibilities to be actualized. Since this principle is implicit in the principle of individuation, Blake presents it as emerging from Urizen/individuation. In a similar manner, entelechy itself presupposes and depends upon the movement of an entity beyond its own immediate actuality into otherness. This movement beyond itself—or ec-stasis—manifests itself as pity and as reproduction, and Blake presents this principle, which he names Enitharmon, as emerging from Los. Proceeding in this manner, Blake reveals that entelechy and ecstasis (Los and Enitharmon) presuppose an even more fundamental principle: the implicit union or identity of an entity with otherness. For the otherness into which entelechy is continuously transforming an individual is ultimately in some sense the same as the original individual, and the movement of ecstasis in pity or reproduction presupposes a fundamental sameness between pitier and pitied, or reproducer and reproduced. This implicit sameness of an individual and a specific other Blake names Orc, who is presented as the child of Los and Enitharmon. Orc is the principle of eros, the simultaneous having and not having, as Plato observed, of an other which is perceived as intrinsic to one's own being. As such, Orc embodies in incipient form the principle of mediated presence which becomes central in *Milton*. In *Urizen* Blake presents the successive emergence of each of these principles as a new strategy for overcoming the finitude of existence without capitulating to the non-differentiation of the infinite possibilities which constitute Eternity. The principle of entelechy thus emerges when the inadequacy of mere differentiation has been demonstrated; likewise, ecstasis (pity/reproduction) manifests itself when the transformations produced by entelechy have proved incapable of overcoming finitude; and eros occurs only when the self-othering of ecstasis in pity and reproduction results in the homogenization of individuals—the assumption that if one individual can become another, then all individuals must be the same, i.e., interchangeable. Eros, too, however, is unable to overcome finitude, although as the principle of mediated presence it seems to have the innate capability of doing so. For eros is restricted to immediacy or imminence by the direction which entelechy has taken. Eros, that is, under the control of entelechy, emerges as desire, the urge for immediate, actual self-aggrandizement, rather than mediated enhancement, achieved through the enhancement of an other with whom one identifies. The true nature of eros—the assertion of its individual uniqueness through its response to the mediated presence of other specific, unique individuals—is suppressed by the Urizenic principle (also operating in Los), which is always present as the literal, immediate separation and opposition among individuals.

[4] *Complete Poetry*, p. 625.

[5] Ibid.

[6] Howard, pp. 143-4.

[7] Daniel Stempel, "Blake's Monadology: The Universe of Perspectives," *Mosaic* 8,ii:91.

[8] Donald D. Ault, *Visionary Physics: Blake's Response to Newton* (Chicago: University of Chicago Press, 1974), pp. 72-3.

[9] *Complete Poetry*, p. 705.

[10] *Complete Poetry*, p. 592.

[11] Murry, p. 213.

[12] Howard, p. 52. But although Howard thus acknowledges that Los is more than just the human imagination, he does not draw out the full implications of this fact in his analysis of the poem. James makes a similar point about the identification of artistic creation and creation in the natural world, and finds an analogue for this idea in Milton's invocations to his muse in *Paradise Lost*: "The implication is that the power at work in the process of artistic creation is the same as the *primum mobile* which created the universe and set it in motion.... For Milton each act of poetic creation is an *analogue* [my emphasis] to the creation of the universe" (p. 67). But this is not Blake's view: for Blake, imaginative creation is not just an analogue to, but rather a further step in, the creation/redemption of the universe.

[13] Fox, p. 191.

[14] Peter Fisher (p. 248) suggests that "Ololon" derives from the Greek *ololuzein*, which denotes lamentation to the gods.

[15] James, p. 1.

[16] In contrast to structuralist and post-structuralist thought, however, Blake does not make this principle absolute: he adamantly maintains the intrinsicness and sovereignty of the being of the individual identity.

[17] James, pp. 48-9.

[18] The illuminations, as Mitchell observes, "by going from a highly sophisticated style, with overtones of commercial engraving, to a crude unfinished style," perform much the same function, "enact[ing] the transition from a false heaven of self-righteous security to an earth of vital, but as yet unrealized potential" ("Style and Iconography in the Illustrations of Blake's *Milton*," *Blake Studies* 6,i:53-4.)

[19] See Joseph Anthony Wittreich, Jr. " 'Sublime Allegory': Blake's Epic Manifesto and the Milton Tradition," *Blake Studies* 4,ii:15-44, for a discussion of the way in which Spenser and Milton also abandoned linear narrative in order to rouse the reader's faculties to act.

[20] As Brian Wilkie observes ("Epic Irony in *Milton*," in *Blake's Visionary Forms Dramatic*, ed. by David V. Erdman and John E. Grant [Princeton: Princeton University Press, 1970], p. 361), "Better than either [*Jerusalem* or *The Four Zoas*] *Milton* exhibits the dynamics of the relationship between literally human beings and the figures of Blake's mythology." Wilkie describes this feature as the union of the epic mode, and its focus on unique, particular events, with the mythic mode and its concern for the universal.

Chapter I

[1] As W.J.T. Mitchell notes ("Blake's Radical Comedy: Dramatic Structure as Meaning in *Milton*," in *Blake's Sublime Allegory*, ed. by Stuart Curran and Joseph Anthony Wittreich, Jr. [Madison: University of Wisconsin Press, 1973], p.289), "At least four possible relationships between creation (the making of three classes) and destruction (the slaying of Albion) can be seen in this summary of the action: (1) three classes were created to restore the order which was lost when Albion was slain; (2) the creation of three classes was an oppressive, divisive act which caused Albion's death, his 'fall into Division'...; (3) the creation of three classes and the death of Albion are two ways of describing the same event; (4) the creation and death are two events which occurred simultaneously, but the first seems to be still going on, while the latter happened in the past."

[2] Jolande Jacobi, ed., *Paracelsus: Selected Writings*, trans. Norbert Guterman, Bollingen Series XXVIII (New York: Pantheon Books, 1951), p. 215. Los's attempt to overcome the deficiencies of human existence is not, however, an attempt to escape form—i.e., finitude—altogether. In fact, Los's activity entails precisely the opposite, for it consists of opposing indefiniteness and non-differentiation, expressed here as "indefinite druid rocks & snows of doubt & reasoning":

> Urizen lay in darkness & solitude, in chains of the mind lock'd up
> Los siezd his Hammer & Tongs; he labourd at his resolute Anvil
> Among indefinite druid rocks & snows of doubt & reasoning.
>
> (3:6-8)

The indefiniteness of doubt and reasoning designates Urizen, the "Creator of Men" (*Visions of the Daughters of Albion* 5:3), or the principle of individuation apart from its entelechic aspect; for apart from entelechy, individual existence is inert and undirected—the amorphous matter which Urizen becomes in *The Book of Urizen* (III.10-13) when separated from Los. Entelechy is intrinsically opposed to doubt, which is the adamant refusal to acknowledge what is not immediately actual ("rocks"), and to reason, which covers over individual uniqueness with the homogeneousness of its generalities ("snows").

[3] Bloom observes, "Rintrah's prophetic wrath plows up nature, making possible a new planting of more human life. Palamabron's civilizing pity (of a kind that need not divide the soul) levels the plowed land, breaking up the resistant clods of reluctant nature, completing the work of the prophet. But to be harrowed is to be tormented or distressed, and this darker aspect of the word will be relevant to Palamabron. Satan grinds down created life; his mills must be made subservient to the apocalyptic Harvest, for they seek their own reductive and meaningless ends" (p.312).

[4] For an enlightening discussion of the issue of atonement, see Florence Sandler, "The Iconoclastic Enterprise: Blake's Critique of Milton's Religion," *Blake Studies*, 5:13-57.

[5] See James, p. 19.

[6] See Fox, p. 115, and Howard, p. 170.

Chapter II

[1] I develop these points more fully in "The Metaphysical Grounds of Oppression in Blake's *Visions of the Daughters of Albion*," *Colby Library Quarterly* 20,iii:164–76.

[2] For an explanation of "Thullough's" significance, see the discussion of Chancellor Thurlow in David V. Erdman, *Blake: Prophet Against Empire*, third ed., (Princeton: Princeton University Press, 1977), pp. 214–18.

[3] The effectiveness of weeping as a technique of aggression and self-preservation is immediately revealed once again, for when

> Enitharmon saw his tears
> . . . .
> She wept: she trembled! she kissed Satan; she wept over Michael
> She form'd a Space for Satan & Michael & for the poor infected[.]
> Trembling she wept over the Space, & clos'd it with a tender Moon.
>
> (8:40-44)

The purpose and significance of Enitharmon's action will become clearer when we have more information about her and about the nature of space; the point here is that Satan's weeping has provided a haven for him, demonstrating the efficacy of his facade of mildness.

[4] The precise nature of this Satanic transformation of reality is made more explicit by the fact that "... Los hide[s] Enitharmon from the sight of all these things, / Upon the Thames whose lulling harmony repos'd her soul..." (11:1-2). The continuous change—like the flowing of the Thames—wrought by the entelechic power makes these occurrences invisible from the standpoint of mere actuality or presence (Enitharmon). For the Satanic triumph occurs not in the realm of immediate actualities, but in the time between those actualities. Enitharmon, actuality, perceives only the immediate, actual configurations of this process—i.e., the "lulling harmony," or co-presence of musical elements, rather than the melody, or the temporal gestalt of the whole entelechic process. Thus the very natures of Los (process, entelechy) and Enitharmon (actuality, presence) preclude the Satanic victory from ever becoming perceivable, graspable, or confrontable as an immediate phenomenon. This fact stymies opposition to Satan, and allows him tremendous power, letting him become, as we have seen, an absolute principle to which is sacrificed the intrinsic unique being of individuals.

Chapter III

[1] As Frye suggests ("Notes for a Commentary on *Milton*," in *The Divine Vision: Studies in the Poetry and Art of William Blake*, ed. by Vivian de Sola Pinto [London: Victor Gollancz Ltd., 1957], p. 131), "her particular sin is...the associating of love with possession...."

[2] The fact that Leutha is repelled by Elynittria's arrows—which we have identified with desire—further elucidates the discriminating urge of pity, suggesting that desire is the weapon with which actual pity/love maintains the integrity of individuals. For although certain forms of desire contribute to the destruction of the other's unique being—by viewing that being as susceptible to expropriation (as we noted in the previous chapter with respect to Elynittria)—desire is ultimately protective of the unique being of individuals. This is so because desire is selective, and the very act of selection presupposes difference between what is selected and what is not. Desire, then, ultimately renders the principle of homogenization impotent, as was indicated earlier "when Satan fainted beneath the arrows of Elynittria" (5:43). And as the power which directs desire (the arrows), Elynittria shows that pity actualizes itself—as a uniting with otherness—by responding to the uniqueness of the other being rather than by ignoring that uniqueness as Satan does.

[3] H. Peacham, 1577. Quoted in the *Oxford English Dictionary*.

[4] These gnomes, however—or the consciousness which utters them—are oblivious to their complicity with Leutha/cupidity: "Me," Leutha informs us, "the servants of the Harrow saw not: but as a bow / Of varying colours on the hills" (12:14-15). Those who espouse and promulgate these Satanic utterances do so under the impression that their telos (i.e., the result of their pronouncements) is the rainbow, which, as the sign of Yahweh's promise never again to annihilate "his" people, is an emblem of individual fulfillment through accord with the ultimate nature of things. The actual telos or effect of this gnomic activity is, in fact, a form of fulfillment, but what the servants fail to recognize is that it is the Leuthic, cupidous form of fulfillment: quantitative self-aggrandizement at the expense of other beings.

[5] It is significant that Leutha's plea for pity is directed toward the "Divine Vision who didst create the Female: to repose / The Sleepers of Beulah." Here cupidity is relying upon that transcendental principle which makes the ecstasis (pity) of reproduction possible: cupidity presupposes this authentic union with otherness, that fundamental unity of all individuals. But cupidity relies on this principle only in order to oppose and destroy it.

[6] This manifestation in the phenomenal world of a transcendental change is portrayed as the work of Enitharmon, the disposer of space or immediate actuality, and of the Assembly, the congregation of ultimate forms and values, which, in dispensations that can be altered by historical events, presides over the phenomenal world:

> So Leutha spoke. But when she saw that Enitharmon had
> Created a New Space to protect Satan from punishment;
> She fled to Enitharmons Tent & hid herself. Loud raging
> Thunderd the Assembly dark & clouded, and they ratify'd
> The kind decision of Enitharmon & gave a Time to the Space,
> Even Six Thousand years. . . .
>
>   (13:12-17)

As we have seen, Enitharmon is the principle of actuality—the successive actualizations produced by Los, the actualizing power. Giving Satan a new space is thus giving him a new actuality, or phenomenal manifestation, in which he is safe from punishment, which is directed against his old actuality. This new space or actuality which Enitharmon gives him is that of divinity, which makes Satan's new embodiment invulnerable. The mere fact of actuality, however, does not by itself make these new forms of Satanic destruction real. For that to happen they must have persisting actuality, and such endurance is possible only if the Assembly, that particular dispensation of eternal forms and values which constitutes an epoch, gives continuity and endurance to the phenomenal world. By giving a time to Enithramon's space—endurance to actuality—the Assembly thus gives substantiality to the new actualities of Leutha and Satan.

[7] Madeleine S. Miller and J. Lane Miller, eds., *Harper's Bible Dictionary* (New York: Harper & Row, 1973), p. 154.

[8] Ibid.

[9] Frye, *Fearful Symmetry*, p. 361.

[10] *Harper's Bible Dictionary*, p. 230.

[11] For an illuminating discussion of Rahab and Tirzah, see Sandler, pp. 36-7.

Chapter IV

[1] The vortex of a human reaches as far as the eye can see; everything that a person takes account of is drawn into that person's unique realm of being and takes on a form unique to that perspective. When one individual passes beyond the immediate influence of another, that other appears inert, isolated, and self-enclosed. Thus for an individual living in the realm of experience on earth, the heaven seems distant and without influence, "a vortex passd already," and "the earth / A vortex not yet pass'd by the traveller thro' Eternity." The heavens—the realm of transcendent realities—had an effect upon people before their being was actualized in existence, but now the influence of heaven is no longer immediate, and the earth and the realm of existence fill individuals' vortexes, stretching as far as the eye can see. From the perspective of immediate existence, the earth seems infinite, but it seems otherwise from another perspective.

[2] *Blake's Composite Art*, pp. 71-2.

[3] "Phenomenology of Reading," *New Literary History* 1,i:56.

Chapter V

[1] In another sense Milton gives death to the old Urizen by reforming him into the new Urizen, and Urizen, in being re-formed, gives life to Milton.

[2] For a psychological interpretation of this event, see Howard, p. 226.

Chapter VI

[1] Ololon appears sometimes as a single being, sometimes as a collective—hence the awkward employment, at times, of the plural verb and pronoun. It would be misleading to use either the singular or the plural exclusively when speaking of Ololon, as it would also be to refer to Ololon as a virgin throughout the entire poem, as some critics do.

Chapter VII

[1] G.W.F. Hegel, *Hegel's Logic*, trans. William Wallace (Oxford: The Clarendon Press, 1975), p. 207.

[2] Alfred North Whitehead, *Process and Reality: An Essay in Cosmology*, Corrected Edition, ed. by David Ray Griffin and Donald W. Sherburne (New York: The Free Press, 1978), pp. xiii-xiv, 29.

[3] In fact, they themselves seem to qualify their assertion in an afterthought: they assert that "Seed / Shall no more be sown upon Earth" and then immediately qualify this assertion by adding, "till all the Vintage is over...." They thus are apparently saying that although there will be other vintages, the present one is in some sense final: perhaps because it constitutes the fulfillment of the beings that are involved in it. In this sense every vintage is a "Last Vintage," for it is the fulfilling destruction of the grapes involved.

Chapter IX

[1] "Allamanda" also suggests the alimentary canal, itself an avenue of commerce between individuals, insofar as it is a fundamental means by which one individual entity interacts with (by devouring) another.

[2] I am developing this point more fully in "The Limits of Identity in *The Book of Ahania*," in preparation.

Chapter XI

[1] The two speeches are run together, and it is at first difficult to see that the statements are two rather than one. The distinction between the two accounts is further obscured by the fact that Blake introduces them with a statement that is itself ambiguous: "Then Hillel who is Lucifer replied over the Couch of Death / And thus the Seven Angels instructed him & thus they converse" (32:8-9). It is not immediately clear whether or not Hillel/Lucifer is one of the Seven Angels, and whether the seven Angels converse among themselves, or with Hillel or with someone else. Upon reading the speech, however, one can arrive at some degree of certainty regarding these questions.

[2] Blake is here speaking, of course, about the generic form of the oak tree. But he held individual human beings to be generic in and of themselves, and declared that one individual human differs as much from another as two species of animals differ from each other.

Chapter XII

[1] Blake develops this point more fully in *The Book of Ahania*.

[2] This diffusion of the self-enclosed is once more expressed through the image of a rock, this time as "the Rock of Odours." This image, like that of the rock of the fountain, expresses in oxymoronic fashion the mutuality of ecstasis and self-enclosure.

Chapter XIII

[1] Blake also develops this view in *The Song of Los*.

Chapter XIV

[1] *Complete Poetry*, p. 2.

Chapter XV

[1] For an examination of the notion of Providence in *Milton*, see Peter Alan Taylor, "Providence and the Moment in Blake's *Milton*," *Blake Studies* 4,i:43-60.

[2] *Complete Poetry*, p. 40.